Discover the real you
by uncovering
the roots of... Your
Personality
Tree

OTHER BOOKS BY FLORENCE LITTAUER

Lives on the Mend
After Every Wedding Comes a Marriage
Blow Away the Black Clouds
How to Get Along with Difficult People
It Takes So Little to Be Above Average
Out of the Cabbage Patch
Personality Plus
The Pursuit of Happiness
Say It with CLASS
Shades of Beauty (co-authored with Marita Littauer)

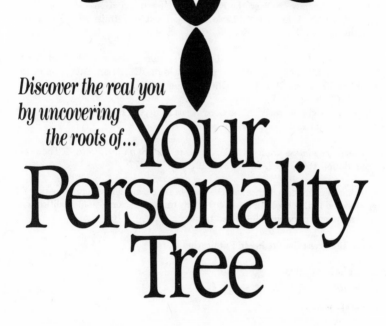

Discover the real you
by uncovering
the roots of... Your
Personality
Tree

Florence Littauer

With suggestions for individual and group activities

WORD PUBLISHING
Dallas · London · Vancouver · Melbourne

YOUR PERSONALITY TREE

Library of Congress Cataloging-in-Publication Data

Littauer, Florence, 1928–
    Your personality tree.

    Bibliography: p.
    1. Personality.   2. Typology (Psychology)
I. Title.
BF698.3.L57 1986   155.2'6   86–18972
ISBN 0–8499–0571–0
ISBN 0–8499–3169–X (paperback)

Printed in the United States of America

    5 6 7 8 9 LBM 26

This book is dedicated to Lana Bateman whose addition to our CLASS staff started my search into the different personalities on a much deeper level than I had ever done before. Her godly wisdom has challenged us all to examine ourselves, to get right with the Lord, and to take off any masks or pretenses we might have worn in the past.

I am deeply indebted to her for allowing me to develop her concept of masking in this book and to quote some of her case histories. The chapter on children's personalities is based on her material in *Personality Patterns,* a book on how to use the temperaments in counseling. Some of the parenting pointers are hers also, and I have quoted her frequently throughout this book. She is the author of *God's Crippled Children,* founder of Philippian Ministries, and a CLASS speaker.

With Gratitude,
Florence Littauer
President, CLASS Speakers

Contents

7

Foreword

When sin entered the world it brought with it a splintering or fracturing of the human personality. What was once whole and perfect is now pieced and flawed. People must now learn to live with the strengths and weaknesses of those who are totally different from themselves.

How can we understand another when we have never experienced feelings and needs so common to him or her and yet totally alien to us? How shall we then love?

Florence and I spent a week together during the summer of 1985 in Estes Park, Colorado, asking ourselves that very question. We desired to put together our thoughts and concepts on the personality temperaments in a way that would enable the body of Christ to develop a deeper understanding of themselves and of those with whom they were called to love and coexist.

We prayed that our God would take all he had taught us and fashion the information into a work capable of bringing new light to the dilemma of human relationships. We longed for tools to help the family find unity through compassionate acceptance, and we prayed for our Lord's hand to inspire our work as a healing touch for hopeless relationships and hurting hearts.

9

This book is the result of those prayers. Florence has once again written that which will change lives and bring new hope. Her style and sensitivity make the information both exciting and inspiring. Treat yourself now to the work of a master teacher, writer, and speaker and prepare for a whole new world of relationships.

Lana Bateman
Founder/Director
Philippian Ministries
Dallas, Texas

Introduction

My Dear Reader:

With lines forming outside the psychiatrist's office, Christian psychologists working into the night, and pastors adding counselors to their staffs, it is obvious there are many people who need help. This book is not meant to replace counselors or to refute their usefulness, but to give some simple insights that may arrest an irritation in its infancy before it grows into a situation that needs outside help. We'd like to take care of our own problems and live in harmony with our family and friends, but somehow we don't know where to start. We've been told Christians shouldn't have any problems and they should be prosperous, so our failure is often coupled with guilt.

Many of us have tried so hard to be all things to all people that we are not sure who we are. Is this the real me or what I've learned to be? Am I as an adult still struggling to become what mother had in mind for me? Have I blended so completely with my mate that I can't recognize an independent thought when I have one? Am I wearing a mask to hide the anger bubbling below the surface? Am I not clear as to what parts of my personality are genuine or what traits are responses to the adversities of life?

In the past twenty years of study, speaking and writing, I have attempted to discover who I really am and to share these insights with others. In addition I have set out to uncover the roots of my personality tree, to find out where my traits originated, and to observe where my own feelings were suppressed, repressed, or depressed.

In this book you will find out who you really are and begin to see why others function as they do. Those of you who have read *Personality Plus* or *How to Get Along with Difficult People* will find new, additional, and deeper information, and those of you for whom this concept is new will have an eye-opening experience which could change your self-image and your ability to get along with others.

Let's have an exciting adventure as we laugh, think, and occasionally cry together. Take my hand as I guide you along the path of personal wisdom and insight.

You will discover who you really are, uncover the roots of your Personality Tree, and recover the original spark and spirit that God intended you to have.

> With love and anticipation
> Florence Littauer

[Wisdom] is a tree of life to those who embrace her; those who lay hold of her will be blessed.

—Proverbs 3:18, NIV

PART I

DISCOVER THE REAL YOU AND AIM TO HEAL YOU

DISCOVER:

To obtain, for the first time, sight or knowledge of a thing existing already but not perceived or known.

Our aim in this book is to examine ourselves in a new way, not just on the surface, not just as we appear to be to others, not just as mother wanted us to be. By looking at our inborn desires, our underlying needs, and our repressed emotions, our eyes will be opened and we will obtain, perhaps for the first time, some insight about who we really are. There is no magic wand to transform us into angels, but as we look at ourselves as God created us to be and come before him in honesty, he will touch us with his healing power.

"The fruit of the righteous is a tree of life."
—Proverbs 11:30, NIV

❧ 1 ❧

Were You
Born Like This?

The question "Who am I?" has been around since Adam wondered what dust he'd come from and the Serpent told Eve to eat the fruit of the tree of life so her eyes would be opened and she'd know who she really was.

Throughout the centuries people have been searching for a sense of identity and a feeling of worth. As a nation we went through the pangs of new birth and the struggle to come out an independent personality. With liberty and justice for all, we attracted people from around the globe to a land where they would live happily ever after; but somehow in our dream of fairy-tale endings, we lost the sense of who we were as individuals. As we grew up and began to look at ourselves, we didn't like the confusion we saw. The sixties brought an unpopular war and the beginnings of a national sense of self-examination. Who are we and how did we get ourselves into these problems?

Sociologists named the seventies the Decade of Depression, a discouraging and defeated time when the ME generation realized that in spite of their quest to find themselves, to do their own thing, and to search for their inner consciousness on a higher plane, they still didn't know who in the world they were. Months of mystical meditation didn't seem to stir up a life-changing thought, peace marches had not produced peace, and the flower children had lost their petals. President Carter, looking down-hearted himself, declared we were in a "national malaise" and that announcement depressed the rest of us.

As the eighties crept in we began to wonder if we ever would find ourselves and so we rushed out to sign up for courses in self-help, self-improvement, and self-actualization. We bought life-long memberships in health spas, held hands in sensitivity groups, and gyrated around gypsy gurus. Surely the ME generation who had dragged through the Decade of Depression deserved a break today; but in spite of exercise and bean sprouts, we kept getting older, the sensitivity sisters showed little sensitivity beyond themselves, and the gurus were packed up and deported. What if we never got a grip on ourselves? What if we couldn't create heaven on earth? Fear gripped us, phobias replaced depression as the nation's number one mental health problem, and the decade was dubbed the Age of Anxiety.

What about you and me? We may not have drowned in depression or worried through our weeks, yet we tend to pick up the malaise and insecurities of others. We may be certain of life everlasting, but do we know who we are today? As I have taught leadership classes, I have found that education, money, prestige or a big house do not insure a feeling of worth. Even though we may have memorized Law One, "God loves you and has a wonderful plan for your life,"[1] few of us seem to believe it.

Yet it is true: God does love us and he has created us for a purpose. As David wrote to God in Psalm 139, "When I was woven together in the depths of the earth, your eyes saw my unformed body. All the days ordained for me were written in your book before one of them came to be" (vv. 15–16, NIV).

Yes, God knows us and he wants us to understand ourselves— not to be worried, confused, or depressed. He has made each one of us as a unique individual, and he uses our talents, personalities and gifts for his good purpose.

In the Bible Joseph was intelligent, charming, well-dressed, and had a gift for interpreting dreams, yet his brothers were envious of his abilities and they sold him as a slave. Because Joseph believed that God had an ultimate plan for him, he was able to stay optimistic even in difficult times and people saw that "the Lord was with him and that the Lord gave him success in everything he did" (Gen. 39:3, NIV).

Even when falsely accused and put in jail, Joseph kept his faith and behaved in such a manner that he rose to the prison's top position and cheered up those who were depressed. Later, those same personality traits that had disturbed his brothers were what found favor with Pharoah, and his gift of interpreting dreams saved the land. When his brothers came before him he wept, forgave them, and relieved their fears. He told them not to feel guilty because what they had meant for evil, God had turned into good.

God took Joseph's inborn traits, his personality and talents, and used him to save an entire nation and his own family.

Esther was an exceptionally beautiful Jewish woman who was both exiled and orphaned. King Xerxes chose her to become his queen without knowing her heritage. Because of her godly behavior she became a virtuous example to the other women and was dearly loved by her husband. When an order went out to kill all the Jews, she was used by God to persuade the king to change his mind. Her Uncle Mordecai stated wisely, "Who knows but that you have come to royal position for such a time as this" (Esther 4:14, NIV).

God used Esther, when she was willing and obedient, to save the exiled Jewish race and her own family also.

In the days of the New Testament when God was ready to evangelize the world, he needed someone who was a Jewish Christian, who spoke and wrote Greek, and who understood Roman law. He chose Paul who, while he had never taken any charm courses or self-improvement seminars, fit the job description. He was raised in a Jewish home, was educated as a Hebrew scholar, and was both a Pharisee and a member of the Sanhedrin. He spoke and wrote Greek, understood the classical intellect and had studied philosophy. Because the people of Tarsus had been cooperative with the conquering Pompey, he had granted them Roman citizenship, thus making Paul a citizen with an understanding of Latin plus a comprehension of Roman law, its government, and the military. All God had left to do was knock Paul to the ground, bring him face to face with Jesus, and convert him to Christ.

Paul might not be acceptable in the Christian pastorate today, but God saw a man for all seasons and he had a plan for his life.

When Winston Churchill was called to be Prime Minister of England as the European continent was falling prey to Hitler's greed, he proclaimed, "My entire life has been but a preparation for this very hour."[2] On his eightieth birthday Churchill summed up his contribution to his country by saying, "It was the nation and the race dwelling all round the globe that had the lion's heart; I had the luck to be called upon to give the roar."[3]

How about you? What has God called upon you to do? Do you know that God wants to use your personality, your background, your abilities, your gifts for his glory? He created you for such a time as this, but he wants you to know who you really are so that you will be a genuine and sincere person, not one hiding behind a mask of confusion.

You may ask, "Do I have to sign up for some course or move to Jerusalem?" No, just read on and enjoy discovering your true self by uncovering the roots of your family's Personality Tree.

During the Decade of Depression and Age of Anxiety I have been teaching people how to find themselves by using the strengths and weaknesses of the four basic personality patterns. Many have asked, "Were we born this way?" This question has had sociologists working feverishly to ferret out the answers. They have tried to show us that environment is more important than heredity, that we are born as little blank pages for Fate to write upon. We've been told that if you change a person's dwelling place or standard of living, or put money in his pocket, you will change him. In spite of millions of dollars spent in moving people into new buildings, the experiment has failed. We are not all the same; God created each one of us as a unique individual, a blending from our parents whether we are observing hair and eye color or analyzing personality.

In 1979 Dr. Thomas J. Bouchard, Jr., started a study in Minnesota of "Twins Reared Apart." Since then researchers have examined thirty-eight identical and sixteen fraternal sets of twins reared apart. The tests measured the physical, psychological, and intellectual abilities. The results showed amazing similarities in choices of clothing, food, and names; not to mention parallels in medical, behavioral, and intelligence traits.[4]

Dr. David Lykken, a research team member observes:

Much of what we think of as human individuality—temperament and pace and all the idiosyncrasies that make you different from your friends—may relate a lot more to your particular genetic individuality than we thought. . . . The capacity for happiness seems to be more strongly genetically wired in than I had thought. . . .

Little Mary's sunny disposition may be part of her genetic makeup, enhanced by—but not the result of her adoring parents' care.[5]

The new thinking on old truths is that we are born as unique individuals. If we come prepackaged with certain blendings of our parents' personalities, isn't it our duty to the Lord to be as true to our basic traits as we possibly can? Shouldn't it be our goal to find out who we really are and take off any masks or pretenses that we may have put on for either self-preservation or a desire to be like someone else?

Think back to your childhood, to how you felt about your parents, to how you related with your siblings, to how you reacted from the heart before you built walls of protection from the hurts of the world. Remember, you were made for such a time as this.

Were you meant to be a Sanguine? Were you a cheerful, bubbling, happy-go-lucky child? Did you avoid chores and somehow manage to find friends who were willing to bail you out? Did you have little buddies who wouldn't go anywhere without you and who thought everything you said was funny? Did you have one parent who was always trying to get you down to serious business or one who couldn't understand why you wouldn't practice the violin? Did you get good marks in everything but conduct and penmanship? Then you are a Sanguine whose chief aim in life is to have FUN.

Were you created to be a Choleric? Were you in control of the family by the time you were three years old? Did you tell your mother what you would wear and refuse to put on what she had in mind? Were you able to observe from a young age that adults were bigger but not necessarily brighter? Did you get your school work done faster than the others and then wonder what was wrong with them? Did you become captain of the teams and president of the clubs? Then you are a Choleric whose compelling desire in life is to have CONTROL.

Were you designed to be a Melancholy? Were you sensitive to your surroundings and easily moved to tears? Did you line up your toys in rows and go around shutting drawers that no one else seemed to notice were open? Did you do your homework on time and even enjoy research projects? Did you practice your piano piece until it was perfect, but not want to play in the recital? Did you feel sorry for "poor children" and want to support the underdog in any situation? Did you get discouraged when things didn't work out the way you had in mind and no one else seemed to care? Then you are a Melancholy whose hope is to someday have PERFECTION even though that may be an impossible dream.

Were you born to be a Phlegmatic? Were you passive in your playpen and understanding if your bottle was overdue? Did your mother brag that you were a good baby and never gave her any trouble? Did you like naps? Did you do your school work on time but not look for extra projects? Did you get nominated for vice-president but not really care whether you were elected? Did you try to keep everyone happy and avoid getting into trouble? Then you are a Phlegmatic whose desire is to have PEACE at any cost.

The concept of the four basic temperaments is so easy to understand and quick to grasp that even a child can learn it. Bryan Taylor from Temple, Texas, was ten years old when he heard me speak on the temperaments. He brought his friends home to listen to my *Personality Plus* tapes, and later he did a school science project based on his personal analysis of his fellow students. For his project, this Melancholy child made a chart entitled "Questions Regarding Human Behavior." Each child in his class was asked to answer the following:

Suppose a play were to be done at Meridith School. How would you want to be involved?
1. I would like to work backstage._____Why?_____
2. I would like to be student director._____Why?_____
3. I would like to be cast in a leading role._____Why?_____
4. I would not want to participate._____Why?_____

The questionnaire he showed me had been filled out by a student who wanted the leading role because "It would be fun." From Bryan's tabulations there were eight Melancholies who wanted to work backstage, fifteen Cholerics who liked the idea of directing the others, ten Sanguines who all wanted to star, and three Phlegmatics who didn't care to get involved.

When I saw how simply Bryan had taken my hours of teaching and reduced them down to four simple questions any ten-year-old could answer, I was impressed. I then asked him if he had

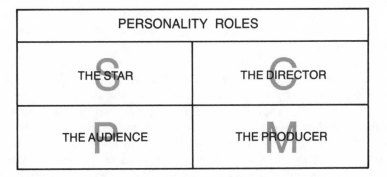

PERSONALITY ROLES	
THE STAR	THE DIRECTOR
THE AUDIENCE	THE PRODUCER

won an award for his efforts and he replied sadly, "I would have but they ran out of ribbons."

Often we can tell a child's natural temperament pattern from an early age.

My two grandsons came equipped with the same parents, Lauren and Randy, but with very different personalities. From the beginning little Randy, Jr., was Melancholy with some Choleric: neat, organized, and in-charge. When I walk in the front door Randy says, "Sit here, Grammie," and I do. He then brings me his second-grade school papers and shows me 100 percent in spelling including the word *Hanukkah*. As we sit seriously together, four-year-old Jonathan, Sanguine with some Choleric, runs over the top of the coffee table in his Superman costume and is not content until he has disrupted our conversation on spelling and has managed to get Randy depressed.

Last Christmas Aunt Marita gave them a hamster named Ginger. Each boy was constantly opening the cage to see if Ginger was still alive, and often they would lose interest in her monotonous trip round and round on the exercise wheel and forget to shut the gate. Ginger, being bright, adventurous and always hungry would run away and look for food. One day Lauren opened the trash compactor to drop in an empty cereal box and screamed when she saw little beady eyes looking up from the darkness. It was Ginger happily munching on stale crackers and missing death by a moment. Had Lauren turned the key without looking, little Ginger would have been as flat as a fur mitten.

From then on each time Ginger was missing, the boys would go to the trash compactor and there she would be, bright-eyed and bingeing.

One night I called on the phone and Randy, Jr., said, "Have you heard the bad news? Ginger is dead." I could picture her flattened out among the boxes and cans, but Randy explained, "She died in her cage. I went to play with her and she was dead." He then delivered a fitting eulogy and gave me the details. In his Melancholy way he told me how he and his father had found a little box in the garage, lined it with paper towels, wrapped poor Ginger in tissue paper, taken the box to a far corner of the back yard and buried her. "We had a funeral," he explained. "We'll always remember poor dead Ginger."

I was close to tears over his mournful musings of the memory of the hamster. When little Jonathan got on the phone, I said, sadly, "I hear Ginger died."

He replied, "Yup, she's dead all right."

"Did you have a nice funeral for her?" I asked, giving him an opportunity to share his version of the tragedy.

"No, we didn't have any funeral; we just dumped her in an old box with clowns on it, stuck her in a hole in the ground, threw some dirt over her, and that's the end of Ginger."

"Will you get a new one?" I asked.

"Well, we might get another one, but if that one dies too then it's bye-bye hamsters!"

I had to laugh over his simple Sanguine dismissal of Ginger's death as just one more event in a busy day while his Melancholy brother was in mourning.

What fun it is to understand others and have an explanation for their behavior!

Our aim in studying the temperaments is to assess our basic strengths and realize that we are people of value and worth; to become aware of our weaknesses and set out to overcome them; to learn that just because other people are different doesn't make them wrong; and to accept the fact that since we can't change them, we might as well love them as they are.

What pressure it takes off of us when we realize that we are not responsible for the behavior of those other people. How liberating it is when we realize God created us as unique individuals and we don't have to conform to someone else's image.

As Pam Phillips wrote after listening to my tapes, "I have been amazed, thrilled and set free by your teaching."

The study of the temperaments is not a theology but a tool to understanding ourselves and learning to get along with others.

"If the Son sets you free, you will be free indeed" (John 8:36, NIV).

For Further Study, Thought, and Action

We are free indeed to examine ourselves and reach for our full potential. Some of us may have the heart of a lion while some are called upon to give the roar. As a first step, check off the traits on the Quick Quiz that sound the most like you. (See page 24.)

Remembering Bryan's simple questions, what were you like as a child?

Were you the Sanguine who wanted to be a star and entertain the troops?

Were you the Choleric who innately seized control of every cast with or without having read the script?

Were you the Melancholy who would rather stay in the wings of life than stand on center stage?

Were you the Phlegmatic who fled the smell of the grease paint and the roar of the crowd but enjoyed watching?

Throughout the book, to make the concept easier to grasp, I will use charts of the four kinds of personalities. In each case, the following letters representing the temperaments will be in the background.

S = Sanguine	C = Choleric
P = Phlegmatic	M = Melancholy

Occasionally I will use a combination of these letters after a name. For example, I will refer to someone as (S/C), meaning he is a combination Sanguine/Choleric or C/M, meaning he is a combination Choleric/Melancholy.

Now fill in the box on page 25 with your total from the Quick Quiz. Is there any inconsistency between what you remember being as a child and what you seem to be now?

QUICK QUIZ OF TEMPERAMENT TRAITS

SANGUINE PERSONALITY
The Talker _____
Fun-loving _____
Optimistic _____
Animated & Excited _____
Life-of-the-party _____
Undisciplined _____
Forgetful _____
Too talkative _____
Eager for credit _____

_____
Total

CHOLERIC POWER
The Worker _____
Controlling _____
Dynamic _____
Decisive _____
Goal-oriented _____
Outspoken _____
Bossy _____
Impatient _____
Domineering _____

_____
Total

PHLEGMATIC PEACE
The Mediator _____
Easy-going _____
Calm and relaxed _____
Patient & inoffensive _____
Quiet yet witty _____
Unmotivated _____
Unenthusiastic _____
Indecisive _____
Eager to rest _____

_____
Total

MELANCHOLY PERFECTION
The Thinker _____
Deep and purposeful _____
Sensitive to others _____
Talented & creative _____
Analytical & orderly _____
Moody & negative _____
Too introspective _____
Socially insecure _____
Easily depressed _____

_____
Total

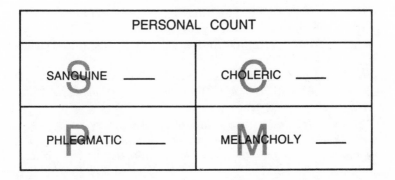

PERSONAL COUNT	
SANGUINE ____	CHOLERIC ____
PHLEGMATIC ____	MELANCHOLY ____

To benefit the most from the growth of your Personality Tree, start a notebook in which you can begin to build a pattern of your personality from birth on to your childhood, educational years, career, and marriage up to the present. As you continue to read this book you will be led to review your parents and grandparents and how they may have influenced your personality for the better or forced you to play a role that was not your real self. By keeping notes on your answers and reactions, you will conclude with a broad view of yourself and your family. You will build a family tree based on each member's personality and see how they have affected each other and especially you. This would be a fascinating study to do either with your own family or with a group of friends. You may even want to add childhood pictures as you go along or include letters and stories from relatives which shed light on who you really are.

I have gathered childhood and ancestral pictures and have put together an album of my Personality Tree plus wedding invitations, birth certificates, baptismal records, and business cards of relatives. Also I've had slides made of many old family pictures for the entertainment and edification of my children and for use in teaching the Personality Tree to others. I have framed one picture of each ancestor and have them hanging on a family tree painted on a wall in my home. I hope these ideas stimulate you into examining your roots and creating your unique Personality Tree.

Ask yourself the following questions, plus any others you create, and write down your answers. If you do this chapter by chapter, you will produce an amazing record, perhaps an autobiography, for yourself and for your children.

What is your full name and where did it originate? from a grandmother? a TV star?

What was your mother's and father's initial reaction to your looks and sex at birth? Ask them or others who were around.

What did they call you as a baby?

Were you labeled as the smart one? The pretty one? The redhead? The dummy? The black sheep? List all the labels you can remember. Have any of these labels affected your opinion of yourself?

Describe any type of participation in some memorable production of your youth. I remember trying out for the Rose and being chosen to play the Cowslip.

Do you have pictures of you in costume?

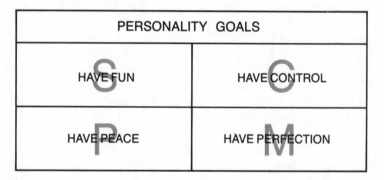

PERSONALITY GOALS	
HAVE FUN	HAVE CONTROL
HAVE PEACE	HAVE PERFECTION

From what you've read so far do you think you were born to be . . .

A Sanguine who wants to have fun?

A Choleric who wants to be in control?

A Melancholy who wants everything to be perfect?

A Phlegmatic who wants to keep out of trouble and have peace?

If you are planning *Your Personality Tree* as a group study have each person bring a baby picture, his/her baby book, and any momentos of interest for your next meeting. Discuss the previous questions and ideas and find out who you were born to be. This is the beginning of an exciting adventure.

"Memory is the diary that we all carry about with us."[6]

❧ 2 ❧

What Is
Your Personality?

"You are just like Ruth," my mother would say to me in disgust. As a child I had no idea why I was like Ruth, my mother's younger sister who had been a talented violinist, had graduated from Boston University and then eloped with a mechanic from Canada and disappeared from family view. I'd never seen Aunt Ruth, but the mere mention of her name would bring my petite Phlegmatic grandmother to tears as others would shake their heads and mumble in unison, "After all we did for her."

Somehow Aunt Ruth hadn't lived up to the family's image of her potential, and I didn't see how I was like her. I was only a child and had no feel for the violin, even though my mother had patiently taught me where to put my fingers and how to move the bow. After two years of lessons I came across more as Jack Benny than Aunt Ruth. People laughed when I played and finally Mother said to my dad, "Give her elocution lessons for she has no talent."

How could I be like Ruth if I'd failed at violin, hadn't been to college, and had surely not eloped to Canada?

One day when I was visiting at my grandmother's house in Merrimac, Massachusetts, a big semi-truck stopped out front. It was so huge it filled the entire width of Orchard Street. We ran to the window at the sound of the motor and saw a lady jump down from the cab. "It's Ruth!" Grandma cried as she ran to the door.

"*The* Aunt Ruth?" I wondered. "Now I'll find out why I'm like her."

I saw her pick up little Grandma and swing her around. She laughed as she explained how she'd met this truck driver in Canada. He'd said he was driving to Massachusetts and she'd thrown a few things in a paper bag and hopped in with him.

"Oh, you shouldn't have taken such a chance," Grandma reprimanded.

"It was the only way I could afford to get home, nothing went wrong, and we had so much fun on the drive down." Aunt Ruth turned and waved goodbye to her new "best friend" as he labored to turn his rig around at the end of Orchard Street and get on the road again.

"He was such a nice man," she said with a feeling of nostalgia while Grandma muttered, "Well, I don't know about that. Who knows what could have happened to you?"

During the next few days I watched Aunt Ruth's every move and listened to what she said and what the others said when she left the room. I found her fascinating fun, but I could see how the family found her to be a rebel. Every time she went to the bathroom, cigarette smoke came wafting through the cracks and the key hole. No one ever faced her with this "sinful behavior," but whenever she'd head for the bathroom, the sisters would whisk Grandma out on the porch to look at the birds.

Aunt Ruth always seemed to "get by with things" as my mother put it, using one of the many clichés her family lived by. I observed how Aunt Ruth charmed people into going along with her ideas and how she could take mild criticism and turn it into humor. She made the very best of a not too positive situation, and I quietly admired her skill and personality. As I listened, I realized that Ruth had always been able to "get away with murder" and that the others had often been left "holding the bag" while Ruth would be sitting on her papa's lap telling him how much she loved him. My mother refreshed Ruth's memory. "You may not recall, Ruth, but I took many spankings from Papa just to 'save your neck.' " Instead of thanking mother for her sacrifice, Ruth put her head back and laughed heartily. "I sure did know how to handle Papa." Mother sighed. Aunt Ruth was fun, and I felt sad when the truck returned to pick her up and Grandma cried, "We'll probably never see her alive again."

From then on I took note of my comparisons with Ruth and saw that my mother would comment when I had "wormed my way out of some trouble" or when someone would say I was a "bundle of laughs." I remember years later when I was teaching at Haverhill High School and my brother Ron "fixed me up" with Phil the Canada Dry salesman. As I was trying to impress him while placing an order for gingerale, I looked out the store window and saw my new friend Dick who had just "returned from the war." As he parked his restored Model T at the curb, I excused myself and turned the order over to my mother while I slipped out and led Dick across the street to Mrs. Bartlett's front steps where we sat to chat. After a few minutes I ran back to the store to get something to drink for Dick. While pouring some Canada Dry I "took up with Phil where we'd left off" and made a date for Friday. I brought the drink to Dick on the steps and was back in time to say goodbye to Phil. As I poured some gingerale for myself my mother sighed, "You're just like Ruth."

Now that I look back upon the Florence/Ruth comparison with a knowledge of the different personalities, I see that my similarities had nothing to do with the violin or smoking but with the emotional response I brought forth from my mother. She had unconsciously resented Ruth's ability to charm others while she was charmed herself into defending Ruth's actions. She had disliked Ruth's personality yet wished she were "more like Ruth." She had been judging of Ruth's behavior but had covered for her when "the chips were down."

Mother was primarily Phlegmatic like her mother—quiet, withdrawn, and unwilling to take chances. She was also Melancholy with the musical talent and ability to play and teach both violin and cello. She was always loyal to Ruth as a Melancholy is and admired her charm, while the Phlegmatic part of her was unwilling to ever confront Ruth on what she didn't like. The two of them had the typical differences of the Phlegmatic/Melancholy being unhappy but not daring to discuss it with the Sanguine/Choleric who enjoyed shocking the family and was insensitive to their inner feelings.

Without knowing what I was doing as a child, I became "like Ruth" because we happened to have the same personality.

I enjoyed "giving my mother fits" and constantly was telling her to stop worrying and to have a good time. Once I asked her why she never gave me compliments, a deep Sanguine need, and she replied, "You never know when you'll have to eat your words." How I wish now I had understood my mother's cautious clichés and realized her need to be respected as a person of value instead of my constantly seeking the praise she couldn't give me and trying to do dramatic things to make her "sit up and take notice."

People compare us with another member of our family tree not only because of our looks but because we somehow unwittingly elicit the same inner response of emotion. Our particular pattern of personality brings out in others the same feelings they have for relatives or friends who are similar.

According to Mother, my brother Ron (S/C) is just like my father. She often said, "He takes such good care of me and he's always fun, but if you cross him up, watch out."

My daughter Lauren (C) is just like Aunt Sadie. "She's talented and brilliant, but she controls the family and you'd better step to it when she says so."

My daughter Marita (S/C) is just like me and Aunt Ruth. "She's always rushing around trying to do too much but somehow it always comes out all right in the end."

My grandson Randy (M/C) is just like my husband Fred, and little Jonathan (S/C) looks like his father but is "just like Marita."

How my mother loved to sit back, quietly assess our family's aggressive behavior and sigh, "You're just like Ruth."

Although Mother came to our *Personality Plus* seminars, every time I'd try to get her to do her Personality Profile, she'd shake her head and say, "It just sounds too much like work."

How grateful I am to know that her response is not a condemnation of my teaching temperaments but a typical Phlegmatic reaction to an analysis that might suggest change and a fear of an unknown theory that might put her in a negative light. Well, Mother always said, "What you don't know won't hurt you."

One woman whose whole family was changed through an understanding of the different personalities wrote the following in a letter:

> Your *Personality Plus* revolutionized our lives, at the very least. Our family was loving but discordant until you made us realize what our different personalities meant. . . . I believe your temperament study may possibly be God's answer to the "horror-scope." When someone mentions his "sign," I explain the temperaments.

Thank you for this gentle witnessing tool. . . . In His love, Phyllis Beever, Pearsall, Texas.

In these days of soul searching what a blessing it is to understand our personality strengths and weaknesses and to trace them back to some of those other Aunt Ruths hanging on the family tree.

How about you? Are you just like your Aunt Ruth? Your Uncle Ethan? Or your grandpa?

Where can we find out who we really are? The philosophical Socrates said, "To know thyself is the beginning of wisdom." Aldous Huxley explained, "There's only one corner of the universe you can be certain of improving, and that's your ownself."

But how?

One summer when Fred and I were vacationing in Maine and chatting about nutrition while eating blueberry pancakes, a Sanguine man sitting nearby said, "My doctor diagnoses by computer."

"How does he do that?" I asked, surprised at this sudden interjection.

"He's made out a big questionnaire that took me over an hour to fill out. It asks things like, 'Are you overweight?—If yes, do you eat too much?—Do you enjoy Mars bars? chocolate malts? hot fudge sundaes?—Are you happy with how you look?—What have you done to remedy this problem?—What do you intend to do about it in the future?—' By the time I'd answered the questions, I'd solved my own problems."

As I thought about this method of medical self-analysis, I realized that many of us could solve our own problems if we had some suggested guidelines and if we'd take the time to think before we ran off to the doctor or counselor.

Aside from the administering of drugs, the doctor spends much of his time in listening to piecemeal problems and then making calculated prescriptions based on his intuition, education and experience.

If we withhold specific information, his assumption may be incorrect. One girl who has been in therapy for months told me, "I never tell the counselor how I *really* feel because I'm afraid she won't like me."

How can the counselor possibly give accurate advice when the subject gives a distorted view of her life?

How much better it would be if we who know ourselves well could search for truth in our innermost parts.

It was twenty years ago that my husband Fred and I began an informal study of the four basic temperaments. At first we looked at the concept lightly and initially used it almost as a parlor game by inviting friends into our home to "play personality." Fred made a quick chart for us all to check off, and we took his test together. We had such fun that everyone asked if we could do it again. The next week as we gathered, the conversation was high-pitched and excited. Quiet people were sharing how learning about themselves had opened up their eyes and how they were beginning to look at others in a new light. People who usually wanted to laugh and play could hardly wait to get down to business.

As we met that second time, Fred and I saw living proof that when people had some simple tool that explained their behavior, they could immediately put their new information into practice. We saw in one week's time a new understanding between husbands and wives, a release of tension and self-judgment, and a new freedom to be what God wanted each one to be.

Our parlor game turned into a time of mutual self-analysis, and as we began to find ourselves and accept those who were different, our group transformed from some people who saw each other in church on Sundays to a close Christian fellowship who loved each other and became emotionally supportive.

Since that first experience, Fred and I have taught the temperaments to thousands of people and have seen so many lives changed by a simple understanding of strengths and weaknesses brought before the Lord for his transforming power.

Although there are many other types of personality analysis, I have found that the basic theory came from Hippocrates two thousand years ago. His terms have been modified and relabeled many times, but their usefulness and validity remain the same today as they were in ancient Greece.

Temperament is a term from the Latin meaning "a mixing in due proportion." What they were mixing were fluids, or *humors,* from the Latin word for moisture. A person with a lot of red blood coursing through his veins was Sanguine: cheerful, outgoing and optimistic but not very serious or organized. The original Choleric had too much yellow bile making him "bilious," short-tempered and ill-natured, but giving him a dynamic desire for action. As his *chole,* Greek for "bile," was "mixed in due proportion," he charged into leadership positions. Too much *melas,* Greek for "black," and *chole* added up to Melancholy: deep, sad and depressive, but also a thoughtful, gifted and analytical genius. *Phlegm* was a cold, moist humor which caused people to be slow and sluggish but enabled them to stay calm, cool, and collected under pressure and heat.

According to Michael Gartner, writing about the original concept,

> If you had too much of any one humor you were considered unbalanced, a little odd or eccentric. Sometimes, normal folks would laugh at their friends with too much of a humor, and that's how the word *humor* got its present-day meaning of ludicrous, comical or absurd.[1]

When Mark Antony spoke of the murdered Julius Caesar he proclaimed his personality as a perfect blending.

> "His life was gentle, and the elements
> So mix'd in him that Nature might stand up
> And say to all the world, 'this was a man!' "[2]

How are the elements mixed in you?
Bishop Ernest A. Fitzgerald writes,

> Wise is the person who wrestles for self-understanding. Life can be wasted in anxiety over the lack of certain abilities or talents. The 'wishing well' syndrome is futile and destructive to our well-being. An intelligent analysis of self, however, and the determination to be the best we can be make for exciting and healthy living. There are really no inferior people. We all have our strengths and weaknesses. When we utilize our strengths our weaknesses are minimized.[3]

As we counsel using the temperament strengths to encourage and the weaknesses to point out areas for growth and improvement, we are still amazed at how quickly a person can see himself in the examples we use and choose to change. In Champaign,

Illinois, my husband Fred met with Terry Ridenour. Terry did not understand why he was having certain relationship problems; he was predominantly Choleric, strong and successful but typically unable to see any possible weaknesses. Terry had been seeking answers but until he saw his own problem areas, he couldn't imagine why his sincerity had not been enough.

Later Terry wrote us in gratitude for our introducing him to the basic temperaments of human nature.

I now know that many of my frustrations and searchings over the past three years were perhaps of my own doing. . . . I needed to hear the things that Fred and I discussed Saturday morning. To hear those things and to realize that I was not the only one experiencing such frustration gave me extreme encouragement. However, true to a Choleric, now that I know what the problems are, I have set a goal and will be successful. . . . I pray that I can continue to improve my temperament weaknesses and that God will use the experiences in my life the last three years to help support others, . . . Your friendship will be a constant reminder to listen to the Lord and to let my weaknesses become strengths in the Lord.

In these times of global tension and inner turmoil, I find so many Christian people who are longing for some sense of identity and self-worth, some answers to their frustrations and searchings as Terry expressed. They study the Word; they know they are created in God's image and made slightly lower than the angels; they've been crucified in Christ and have taken off the old clothes and put on the new. They've gone to church, knelt at the altar on Sunday, and taught Bible studies. In spite of all these positive spiritual steps, they still need some simple solution to who they really are as individuals.

After these twenty years of studying and teaching the temperaments, I am still amazed at how God uses this tool to open people's eyes to themselves and their relationships with others.

A young lady wrote how my putting the temperaments into "real live people situations" was what changed her life.

Thank you for being available and touchable. . . . We now have such insight in dealing with my Fred's wretched Melancholy father! Oh, what freedom for Fred at age 37 to realize he will *never* be able to reach his dad's standards—for me to now understand why my precious Phlegmatic/Melancholy dad drank himself into an early grave at 66 after living with my Choleric mom all those years. We could go on for hours and still not be able to express to you and to your Fred our thanks for your countless hours of preparation, for your willingness to be used of God in such a mighty way.

Another girl came to our CLASS (Christian Leaders and Speakers Seminars) and just gave her name as Dee. When we asked what her last name was she said, "I don't have one because I don't know who I am."

Later after hearing our explanation of the personalities, she wrote that at first she had listened intellectually but now the information had gone from her head to her heart. "The Lord really impressed these truths upon me along with Romans 8: 1–2. I now feel 'no condemnation' and the 'law of the Spirit of life has set me free.' "

Among her other comments she explained, "Remember I told you I have *no* last name. That's because I've had four marriages, and my mother was married three times. I've had a total of seven last names. Who am I anyway? You should have seen the fiasco at my daughter's wedding when 'everyone' showed up! Thank you so much for all you've given me. 'It is more blessed to give than to receive.' Dee"

As I have taught the use of the temperaments to churches, medical conventions, leaders and speakers, couples and families, businesses and other groups, I have been frequently asked how the original terms compare with other personality tests or systems. In an attempt to answer questioning minds, I have read, gathered, and sometimes "taken" different forms of analyses.

It would fill a book to report on all the theories I've examined, so I have made a chart—yes I, a Sanguine/Choleric have made a Melancholy chart comparing the different terms used. The one overwhelming conclusion I've come to is that no matter what the traits are labeled, they all seem to spring from the same rootstock of Hippocrates' theory of the humors. Few of the new theory originators make this connection and in several articles about testing, the announcement is made about an exciting "new concept." While this "new concept" has been around for over two thousand years, it can always take on a fresh face with new labels and I'm sure many of the current testers may sincerely think they thought it all up. For more detail on other forms of temperament analysis, see the chart on page 235.

For Further Study, Thought, and Action

Oswald Chambers in *My Utmost for His Highest* says, "Personality is that peculiar incalculable thing that is meant when we speak of ourselves as distinct from every one else. Our personality is always too big for us to grasp."[4]

Because it is "too big for us to grasp," we need to break our personality into chunks we can ingest with ease. We have already taken the Quick Quiz; now let's examine ourselves more deeply. At the end of this book (page 220) is a Personality Profile for you to take. Check off one word on each line of the Personality Profile that is closest to you. To help make your decisions easier there is an explanation of the words. (See Personality Test Word Definitions, page 221). After marking the best choice fcr you, transfer your checks to the Personality Scoring Sheet (page 232) where the list is in order and add up your totals. If you chose *adventurous* on the profile, check it off on the score sheet and you will see your personality fall into line. As you add up your scores, you will observe your own personal blending of the "humors" mixed in a "due proportion" that is uniquely yours. No two of us are exactly alike and yet our similarities are what provide us with a framework by which we can measure our strengths and weaknesses.

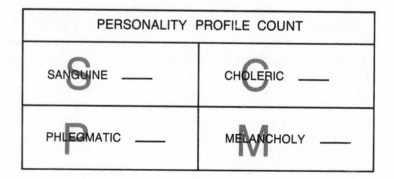

PERSONALITY PROFILE COUNT	
SANGUINE ____	CHOLERIC ____
PHLEGMATIC ____	MELANCHOLY ____

Record your scores from the Personality Profile in the chart on the previous page, and compare them with those on the Quick Quiz. For further study, read the strengths and weaknesses listed on pages 233, 234 and compare them with your scores and your feelings about yourself.

Are you beginning to get a grasp of who you are?

As you prepare to trace the roots of your own Personality Tree, you will want to have an understanding first of your own "blending of the humors." By adding this knowledge to the perception your family already has of you, you will begin to piece together the puzzle of your personality.

If you are in a group study, go around the room and have each person share what he has learned about himself so far. Don't allow others, such as mates, to correct or second guess each person's opinions or this will stifle meaningful conversation. Each person must be free to express his feelings without fear of judgment. What a great way to get acquainted with others on an emotional as well as a social level.

Think about those people in your family who are alike. In your personality notebook list those that come to mind and then beside the names jot down the personality similarities, both strengths and weaknesses. Discuss these individuals with any family member available in order to garner information. As you plant these seeds of thought in your mind, you will begin to water your seedlings with additional material as you are alert to any reference made of your "Aunt Ruths."

If you are using *Your Personality Tree* as a group study, bring your list of comparisons and be ready to share your results. There's no way we can carry on positive tradition or eliminate repeated weaknesses until we bring them to light and take an objective look at them. You will be amazed at the information there is available when you begin to seek. Older family members are flattered when you ask them to fill in your memory blanks, and even family friends may have nostalgic stories they would love to tell.

In placing these personalities of the past think about how each individual approached projects. What was their way?

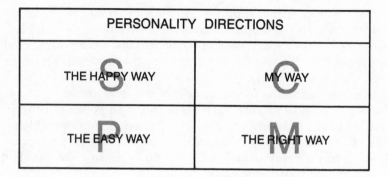

Commit your way to the Lord.
—Psalm 37:5, NIV

The Lord delights in the way of the man whose steps he has made firm.
—Psalm 37:23, NIV

❧ 3 ❧

What Are Your Desires
and Underlying Needs?

Without an understanding of the basic temperaments and the desires and needs of each, we tend to spend much of our time trying to get from other people responses that they just can't give. Many marriages, for example, come to a grinding halt because neither partner knows what the other wants or needs. With no simple tool to use, success is an accident. Once we begin to understand the basic desire of each nature, however, the veil is lifted and we have the key to getting along with others.

WHAT ARE YOUR DESIRES?

The Sanguine from the beginning wants to have FUN. Accepting this fact will keep us from false expectations that some day he or she will grow up and get down to business.

My Phlegmatic mother, after spending a week with my brother Ron, top radio personality in Dallas, Texas, and proclaimed in the *Dallas Morning News* as the one who "owns the morning,"[1] said with a sigh, "I wonder if Ron will ever grow up and get a real job." She didn't understand that a Sanguine doesn't want to grow up, that his aim is to have fun, and that he is at the top of his profession.

The Choleric wants to have CONTROL and is only comfortable when he has choreographed the cast of his world and has it completely under his inspired direction. Knowing this fact will prevent us from staging a struggle for power which we would probably lose.

The Melancholy's desire is to have PERFECTION. To know what that is, we have to enter into his perfectly organized and categorized mind and see the situation with his eyes. When we realize he cannot relax until life is in order, we can make a conscious effort to meet his standards.

The Phlegmatic's aim in life is to stay out of trouble and keep PEACE. He will not become enthusiastic about anything or take chances, so don't push him and think you can alter his personality. All that badgering him will do is increase his resistance to change.

When we see and accept that each temperament has a different desire in life, we can function out of knowledge and not ignorance. "Be ye therefore wise as serpents, and harmless as doves" (Matt. 10:16, KJV).

SANGUINES: HAVE FUN

Heaviness in the heart of man maketh it stoop:
but a good word maketh it glad (Prov. 12:25, KJV).

When we realize the Sanguine's desire for fun, we can perhaps grasp why things that would embarrass others are positive experiences for the Sanguine. As I tell my story of losing my car in the seven-story parking garage, Melancholies and Cholerics shake their heads in disbelief. Phlegmatics somewhat understand the possibility and Sanguines get so excited they can hardly wait to rush up to me with tales of their own losses. Several ladies have detailed how they lost their cars at Disneyland and had to wait until midnight when the place emptied out to find them.

One Sanguine who went to the Cotton Bowl for the New Year's game wanted to make sure she wouldn't get lost. She wrote down "Bus #104" on the back of an envelope so she would know which bus was hers when she returned. What she had not anticipated was that there were hundreds of buses all lined up and she had no idea which one was #104. "I would have been there yet," she exclaimed in typical Sanguine exaggeration, "if a friend hadn't found me gasping from the exhaust fumes and led me to Bus #104."

An adorable Sanguine girl told me that her husband brought

home a client for dinner. As she was preparing the meal she discovered she was missing a key ingredient. She didn't want her Melancholy husband to know since he constantly criticized her lack of organization, so she tiptoed to the front door. As she looked out she saw the client's car was behind hers in the driveway and she would have to go ask him to move it. But wait! There were his keys on the table so why not quietly take his car? She parked in the large lot outside the supermarket and when she came out she not only didn't know where she'd parked, she didn't have any idea what kind of a car it was. All she could remember was that there was a letter on the front seat and the only reason she recalled that was because she'd read it! She pushed her cart up and down lanes peering into each car looking for the letter which she ultimately found. She got home safely and no one ever needed to know, but in typical Sanguine fashion when there was a long pause in the business conversation, she felt led to entertain the client with her escapade of taking his car without permission and reading his letter. Much to her surprise he didn't find it humorous, and her husband was both humiliated and incensed. "Everyone else I told it to thought it was hilarious. I don't know what's the matter with them!"

A Sanguine receptionist came out after work and her '67 Gold Dodge was gone. She called the police, filled out all the forms and asked the policeman to drive her home. When they pulled into the driveway the man asked, "Do you have two '67 Gold Dodges?"

"No, why?"

"Because there's one sitting here in front of us."

She looked up in wide-eyed surprise.

"Oh, I guess I forgot. My girlfriend drove me to work this morning."

One lady told me she was hunting for her keys at the cleaners and concluded, "I must have left them at the church."

The Phlegmatic cleaner said half under his breath, "If you left them at the church how did you get the car here?"

A girl from Fairbanks, Alaska, sent me this story after I spoke there in September of '85.

I went to [the supermarket] for a few quick items, but as I walked the aisles I decided I might as well shop. By the time I wandered the aisles (with payday's bulk in my purse), I had a cart chockful of meals. I also had a 'reduced for winter' Boston fern drooping atop the edibles!

Through the checkout stand, $158 later, I pushed my laden cart into the parking lot. Adrenalin pumped as I went row by row, puzzling over *why* I couldn't remember where I'd parked. Still puzzled, I pushed the cart (topped by my Boston fern) back towards the store.

The outside of the store was being painted by a crew on a scaffolding. As I dodged their equipment with my unwieldy cart, I saw *it*—beneath their tarp sat my yellow 10-speed bike!

I had *biked* the five miles today! Now, as a newly single parent whose ex-husband was out of town . . . who was in the 'proud' stage, too proud to call on a friend . . . I began packing:

—groceries into boxes stacked on the back rack
—cord tying the Boston fern pot firmly atop the boxes
—four loaves of bread tied by their ends to the handle bars.

I rode all the way home on a bike that was ready to flip over at every little bump! My daughters saw me come up . . . looking like a gypsy caravan!

How did I feel? . . . How did they feel? Resourceful! Capable! Independent!

My very favorite episode is the lady from Newport Beach who went shopping at the vast South Coast Plaza. When she came out of Bullock's her car was gone. After hunting around by herself, she called the security guard who drove her up and down each row in the entire set of parking lots. There was no question; they both agreed; the car had been stolen. She filled out the forms and later filed an insurance claim. When she received the money, she bought a bright new car and liked it even better than the first one. Later she received a phone call from Sears, "Hey lady, when are you going to come back and pick up your car that you left here a month ago for us to rotate the tires? If you don't come soon, we're going to charge you for storage!"

Many Sanguines have sent me "car stories," but just as many Melancholies have mailed me detailed information for forgetful Sanguines on where to buy a key ring that beeps when you clap your hands or a Car Finder which costs only $99.95. These inventions were surely made for Sanguines and, if they become popular, could eliminate this Sanguine habit as surely as small pox was eradicated. One ad stated confidently:

> Spot your parked car instantly!
> Misplaced your car in a crowded parking lot? Touch the Car Finder, and your car will honk its horn and flash its lights so you can locate it at once.
> Car Finder is a miniature transmitter that attaches to any key chain. When you push the button, your car answers up to 750 feet away.

I knew the gadget was for sociable Sanguines when the ad concluded "The Car Finder is a real friend with user-friendly instructions."

So that you Sanguine men won't think these stories leave you out, here's an episode from my favorite minister of music, Jim Lacy, after his move to Columbus, Ohio.

Sanguine Jim and Melancholy Sherri went to a church Christmas party. Since they were new in town and hadn't become acquainted, Sherri was a little nervous about making a good first impression. Jim had the map to the people's home on Angela Street and Sherri was comforted when a car with some friends she recognized honked as they drove by. Since Jim had a quick errand to run at the church, he dropped Sherri off at the curb where she joined some others who were heading into the party.

Being new to the church and trying to be as outgoing as possible, Sherri greeted the hostess at the door and drifted into the room full of chatting couples. She stood by herself and observed that the new guests were all bringing wedding presents. She wondered why they were bringing these to the church Christmas party, and when she asked, the hostess replied, "This is no church Christmas party. This is a wedding reception. Are you supposed to be here?"

Sherri was so embarrassed that she got her coat and left just as Jim was driving up oblivious to the fact he'd dumped her out at the wrong party. While Jim laughed Sherri went into a depression. When they got to the right house down the street, Sherri made Jim go in and make sure first. She begged him not to tell a soul, but in true Sanguine fashion, Jim made a comedy act of the whole episode. He wrote me, "I told everyone including my *Sanguine choir!* What fun!"

Yes, "what fun" when the Sanguine tells his own story of his own error depressing his own wife. The Sanguine's aim is to HAVE FUN.

CHOLERICS: HAVE CONTROL

Sink the heathen into the pit.
Catch their feet in thy net.
Execute proper judgment. (See Ps. 9:15–16.)

The Choleric's basic desire is to be in control. A Choleric woman told me about the battle she was having with her Choleric ten-year-old son. Every day after he goes to school, she goes in and moves the furniture in his room into the position where she and the decorator want it. The first thing he does when he comes home is change it all back to the way he likes it. She maintains it's her house and she has the right to put the furniture wherever she wants it. Besides, what if her friends came to visit, and the room wasn't in order! He, being a chip off the old block, claims his room as his territory where he has the right to arrange it whatever way he wants. Here are two Cholerics fighting so hard for control that they are playing Mayflower Movers every day. I shared with her how important it is for a Choleric child to be in control of something at home, for if he is thwarted there, he will likely go out and beat up his friends. With this new thought in mind, she went home to make peace.

A Choleric man who sold medical supplies to doctors told me how he hated his job. When I asked him why he continued, he said, "I make a lot of money, and I like what I'm doing."

"How can you hate it and like it?" I asked.

He thought for a minute and concluded, "I like the job, but I hate the fact that I'll never be the boss."

Here was a Choleric in a good position but chafing because he had to play second fiddle and couldn't see any possibility of being in charge.

Another Choleric salesman told me about his "stupid" Sanguine boss. "She never gets anything done right, and she spends most of her time on the phone. I tell her each day what she's doing wrong and how to improve, but she never gets any better."

I reviewed our lesson with him. "What does the Sanguine desire in life?"

"Fun."

"What does the Sanguine need more than anything else?"

"Attention and approval."

"Now that you know this, think about your situation. Let's pretend I'm your boss and everyone tells me I'm fun to be around. Each day they all compliment me, bring me little presents, and listen to my every word. You, however, try to straighten me out each day and criticize my time on the phone. I get a memo from above that instructs me to lay off one of my salesmen. How long is it going to take me to decide which one it should be?"

He got the point.

A Choleric lady remembers when as a child she "played war" with the neighborhood boys. "They wanted me to be the nurse since I was the only girl, but I said, 'No, I'll be the general.' And I was!"

A Choleric man told his Phlegmatic wife, "I hate hard-headed people."

She dared venture, "Sometimes you are hard-headed."

He snapped back, "Only when I'm right!"

Another Choleric man told me, "I may not always be right, but I'm never wrong."

Even the Choleric disciples were scrapping for control. "There was . . . strife among them, which of them should be accounted the greatest" (Luke 22:24, KJV).

A Choleric doctor took the Personality Profile, and I observed him checking off all the strengths and none of the weaknesses. I commented on this to him and he replied, "That's because I *have* all strengths and no weaknesses, but I'll be glad to check off a few weaknesses if it will make you happy." Oh, noble man!

Later he came up to me and said, "I thought it over, and I do have one weakness. I seem to always choose weak sniveling nurses. They seem normal to start with, but they get worse. Just this morning when I walked into the office they all flattened against the wall and began to cry. I asked them what was the matter and they said they were afraid of me. I let them know right off it was their own fault. If you'd do what I told you to do when I told you to do it, you'd have no reason to be afraid!"

What compassion and understanding!

The Cholerics not only want to be in control but, as you can see, they have little ability to catch even a glimpse of their weaknesses. They have the greatest bent for leadership, but a blind spot in seeing how they affect other people.

They agree with Robert Service:

> This is the Law of the Yukon
> That only the strong shall thrive
> That surely the weak shall perish
> And only the FIT survive![2]

The Choleric's aim is to HAVE CONTROL.

MELANCHOLIES: HAVE PERFECTION

> I am weary of groaning;
> I make my bed to swim;
> I water my couch with tears.
> I cry with grief. (See Ps. 6:6–7.)

How weary the Melancholy is from trying to get life in order, watering the couch with tears and crying with grief. From the time the Melancholy can stand up and move around he is trying to make the crooked paths straight. My Melancholy son Fred was tidying up the house as soon as he could get out of his playpen, and he started collecting and sorting laundry when he was two. He's been my "housekeeper" for years, and if I leave something out on the kitchen counter, he quickly puts it in the nearest drawer. Since I can't remember where I left it, this disappearance causes me quite a search as I tear through kitchen drawers looking for a lace slip he stuck in with the dish towels.

A Melancholy pastor told me how as a child he kept all of his games in order, numbered each box and had a master list posted in his closet. He never lost so much as a puzzle piece in his whole childhood. When he had his own children and gave them his well-preserved games to play with, "They had all the parts messed up within a week. How could I have kept them perfect for all those years and see them wreck the whole system in less than a week?"

A Sanguine girl told me her Melancholy husband has rebuilt

her closet three times in hopes he'll strike the right plan which will make her keep it neat. If only he knew the temperaments, he could save his time and money. No matter what plan he has, she'll still throw the shoes in a pile on the floor.

Another girl wrote, "My Melancholy husband keeps his side of the closet in perfect order with all of his pants folded exactly the same. You can imagine what my side looks like! He even gets bothered when I don't put the shampoo and creme rinse bottles back on the rack with the labels facing forward in perfect order! It took him six months to tell me this bothered him."

One Melancholy man kept a "mileage chart" on his shoes from the time he bought them until he gave them away to the Salvation Army. He found out when he divided the cost of the shoes by the number of days he wore them that the shoes had cost him nine cents a day. Only a Melancholy would care!

Another man dates every light bulb in his house at the time of purchase. This way he is able to keep a record of each bulb and know the exact length of service.

A girl at CLASS (Christian Leaders and Speakers Seminars) took her Personality Profile and divided it into percentages proving she was 82.5 percent Melancholy. Not that we needed proof!

One father kept a file box on all his son's dates with full family background and his candid opinion of each one. The girl that married him was not pleased when she found her report that said, "Surely, he won't marry this one!"

A girl in Florida sent me this account of the man next door.

The tire on one of their trash can carriers broke. The husband replaced it. However, he noticed that it didn't match the other trash can carrier tires. To him, that was unthinkable. So he immediately ran out and bought three new tires for the trash can carrier and replaced the non-matching but perfectly good tires. A few days later he noticed that the tires on the lawn mower didn't match the new trash can carrier tires, so he replaced those tires with new ones to match. There was another vehicle on the premises with non-matching tires, which he also replaced. To top it all off, this husband realized that if one of the new tires became defective and had to be replaced, he might not locate a matching tire which would necessitate starting all over again, so he bought a second set of tires for each machine and stored them in his impeccably neat garage. His wife said one broken tire cost them $250 because of her husband's concern for matching everything! Guess which type personality he is!

All Melancholies would agree with Ludwig van Beethoven.

> Then let us all do what is right,
> Strive with all our might toward the unattainable,
> Develop as full as we can the gifts God has
>   given us,
> And never stop learning.[3]

The Melancholy's aim is to HAVE PERFECTION.

PHLEGMATICS: HAVE PEACE

> Lay me down in peace to sleep
> Make me dwell in safety. (See Ps. 4:8.)

The Phlegmatic's desire is to lie in peace and dwell in safety. While the Sanguine has a compulsion to have fun, and the Choleric has a compulsion to control everything and everyone in life, and the Melancholy has an almost fanatical compulsion to get things in perfect order, the Phlegmatic has no compulsions. They will avoid problems whenever possible and quietly face those they can't get around.

When the Melancholy says I have to think about it, he really thinks about it, but the Phlegmatic uses this expression to postpone action. It isn't that he wants to think; it's that he doesn't want to act. One lady who was taking me out to dinner asked her Phlegmatic husband for his decision on where to go. "Are we still thinking about it or are we ready to do it?"

A Phlegmatic man told me, "I'm not lazy; I'm just conservative on my energy level."

A Phlegmatic woman shared, "I married a Phlegmatic and our baby was so Phlegmatic it was like she was born in a coma."

Making decisions is difficult for the Phlegmatic. I loved the paperweight on a Phlegmatic's desk that carries the message, "Maybe—and that's final." A greeting card showed a Phlegmatic tiger draped over an easy-chair. On the inside it said, "Get up before they make a rug out of you."

Because the Phlegmatics desire peace, they are easy to manipulate and frequently find themselves pushed around by Cholerics who need someone to control. Although they usually will take whatever's handed out, once in a while, to keep peace with themselves, they will refuse to conform and they will hold their ground.

The last Christmas we had with my little Phlegmatic mother was one to remember. Her Choleric sister Jean, my favorite aunt, came out to California bringing a special present for Mother from her friends at the church "gift shop." As Mother was carefully unwrapping the present in such a way as to preserve the paper for next year, Aunt Jean spoke up. "This is a very special present. Your friends made this by hand for you and you will love it." As Mother took a look Aunt Jean continued, "That is an apron, made of unbleached muslin and edged in red bias binding." Cholerics somehow feel Phlegmatics are not bright enough to know an apron when they see one, muslin from satin, or red from green. "Written all over the apron in liquid embroidery are all your friends' names. See them right there. They all sat down and signed the apron so that every time you wear it you will think of them."

Mother quietly stated, "I won't wear this apron; it's too good to use."

"What do you mean you won't wear this apron! Do you think I'm going back to 'gift shop' and tell them that after all their time and effort you wouldn't even wear the apron!"

Lauren on the other side of Mother said firmly, "You *will* wear this apron. In fact right after Christmas dinner you will put it on to do the dishes."

As Mother folded it back up, Aunt Jean added, "I didn't drag this apron all the way out here on the plane from Massachusetts to have you refuse to wear it!"

Lauren affirmed to Aunt Jean, "She *will* wear it. I'll see to it."

Mother put the cover on the box and said softly, "I will not wear this apron." Lauren and Aunt Jean, two Cholerics having trouble with their control, said in harmony, "You *will* wear that apron."

A month later when I was conducting a *Personality Plus* Conference in Dallas, Mother was sitting right in the front row. As I was speaking I wondered if I dared tell the story about Mother and the apron. I remember thinking, "Well, she's eighty-five.

She can't hate me for too long." I took the big chance and went through the whole scene ending with, "And Mother said, 'I won't wear that apron.'"

Much to my absolute amazement, Phlegmatic Mother stood up, turned to the crowd and stated clearly, "And I didn't!" They loved her and gave her a rousing ovation.

Later when I commended her performance I told her, "You ought to be the speaker. I spoke all day and you got an ovation on one line." She gave a little Phlegmatic shrug and I could tell, in her terms, that she was "pleased as punch."

Two months later as she had desired, she died *peacefully* in her sleep to join the Prince of Peace and Lord of Lords. She never did wear the apron.

The Phlegmatic's aim is to HAVE PEACE.

WHAT ARE YOUR UNDERLYING NEEDS?

As each one of us has certain aims and desires, so also do we have underlying needs that we don't always communicate clearly to others. We think if they really loved us, they would know what we needed, but unfortunately we tend to give what we want to receive and then wonder why we don't get it back.

Fred loves colognes so he is constantly buying me perfume to make me happy. I don't have as keen a sense of smell, I have more bottles than I could ever empty, and I keep forgetting to put the perfume on; therefore, when he gives me another new spray I don't get too excited. He takes that to mean I don't appreciate his thoughtfulness. Because he has such a collection of colognes, I never think of buying him more, but in his mind he could never have too many. In his romantic heart I am neither caring nor grateful, but I see my attitude as practical. I had no idea that fragrance was an issue until one night after I had ignored a new bottle, Fred stated clearly, "I will never buy you any perfume ever again. You don't even notice what I give you."

That caught my attention. As we discussed the situation and I apologized for my callousness, we agreed that he was attempting to meet a need I didn't have in hopes it would spur me into meeting his for him. He needed sentimental signs that I loved him, and I had figured there was no point in buying more of what he already had in abundance. We were at a perfume stalemate and didn't recognize our opposite needs.

To prevent this type of problem in your life or to heal some underlying wounds of which you may not be aware, sit down with your mate and ask, "What needs do you have that I'm not meeting?" Listen, take notes, and don't be defensive. Thank him, and if he shows interest, share one or two things that you would appreciate from him.

The Sanguine Needs Attention and Approval

By learning the underlying needs of each temperament you will have an advantage in your human relationships. While the Sanguines want to have fun in life and appear to have no serious requirements for happiness, underneath they have a craving for approval. They need to know they are acceptable in your sight. They feed on compliments and criticism wounds them deeply. Usually they are married to Melancholies who see no reason to give praise to something that's not done properly in the first place and who feel constant criticism will provide positive motivation. How pitiful it is to realize how many couples are sitting in this stalemate, neither one meeting the other's need.

The Sanguine needs approval and will wilt into uselessness under negative comments. Given praise and encouragement the Sanguine will go to extremes to please you, for they want to be loved.

When Marita and I come home from a trip, Fred asks, "How did it go?" We reply in unison, "They loved us." Only Sanguines would be this presumptuous even in humor. Once Fred questioned us, "Did the people say they loved you in so many words?"

"Well, no, we just know they did."

The Melancholy often won't believe compliments when they are verbalized, but the Sanguine will make positive assumptions even when no one said a word.

My little Sanguine grandson Jonathan stood on the edge of the pool and stated loudly, "My Mommy loves me! My Daddy loves me! Grammie loves me! Poppa loves me!" He added a few extra names, stretched out his arms and looked to the heavens proclaiming, "The whole world loves me!" Another type personality might take this statement as juvenile conceit, but at four years old he is expressing how he actually feels and demonstrating that Sanguine need for love.

In the *TIME* cover story on the Statue of Liberty Celebration, the question was headlined, "What Makes Reagan So Remarkably Popular As a President?" They then listed many Sanguine strengths: he has found the American sweet spot, he grins his boyish grin and bobs his head; he has a genius for American occasions; he is a magician, a master illusionist; he will hand out the sparklers; he has a genial, crinkly face that prompts a sense of wonder; he has the luck that comes to the optimist. His life is a sort of fairy tale of American power.

They then ask, "How does he do it? How does he always come out on top? Why is he called the 'Teflon President'?"

The answer they give is, "He enjoys an easy and sometimes mysterious communion with the American people. He has become a ceremonial presence."

As the interviewers listened to his humorous anecdotes, they asked why he was so successful and he answered simply, "I love people."⁴ When you love people, they love you back, and oh how the Sanguine loves love.

Everyone likes attention and approval, but for the Sanguine it is an emotional need.

The Choleric Needs Achievement and Appreciation

Because the Choleric is a born leader, he has the need to see things accomplished and has a mental progress list stored in his brain. Where the Melancholy writes his agendas on paper, the Choleric plots his life out quickly in his head and gives instant commands to everyone in sight. He assumes others both need and want instruction and feels those who aren't marching to his drumbeat are lazy. A Choleric man wants to know what his wife did all day. One man told me if he didn't post a list of what needed to be done each day his wife wouldn't get out of the chair.

Choleric women keep the children moving, use all available manpower, and get frustrated when their husbands don't respond to their call to arms. Since they are usually married to Phlegmatics who look forward to the weekend's rest, their insatiable need for getting things done now is often thwarted. Once they've tried suggestions, lists, demands, and threats, they storm off in anger and the husband says, "I wonder what's wrong with her?" He may not care enough to get up and find out, but he does think about it during commercials.

Because the Choleric wife is now on the roof nailing down loose shingles, she is expecting some moderate praise for her noble efforts; however, the husband will choose not to mention the subject at all in hopes she won't remember he didn't do it. She waits for the appreciation she feels she deserves, and the more she hints for it the more determined he is not to give it. Unfortunately this cold war exists in many marriages and even in business situations where the Choleric will do extra work and then expect credit for his efforts. Since the others didn't want to do the job and he jumped into it on his own, no one sees a reason to praise him. What a cycle of misreading one another's needs.

The Choleric workaholic nature appears self-satisfied, but much of what he does is inwardly a cry for recognition. If he has not received praises as a child, he will work himself to death trying to stimulate his parents to enthusiastic comments. He wants to hear those words, "I don't know how you've ever accomplished this much!" When Cholerics don't receive credit or others don't thank them, they often say, "After all I've done for them."

Because of her need for achievement, a Choleric woman can't watch TV without something moving in her hands. She must knit, paint, or iron—anything rather than waste precious time. I even consider brushing my teeth a time-waster, and I often polish the mirror with my other hand while shutting a drawer with my foot. Sometimes I walk through the house picking things up while brushing, get a phone call, lay the brush down, and that night I have no idea where my toothbrush could be. Yes, Cholerics have a compulsion for constant achievement.

We all like to accomplish what we set out to do and we enjoy being appreciated, but for the Cholerics, these become emotional needs.

The Melancholy Needs Order and Sensitivity

The Melancholy is a perfectionist who must have his life in order and hopefully everyone else's as well. For some, this desire is restricted to the area of artistic expression while others need perfection in physical surroundings. A Melancholy with a Sanguine wife who is a poor housekeeper either takes over the duties, criticizes her mistakes, or gets depressed.

If the Melancholy leans toward the Choleric he will be much harder on himself than if he is part Phlegmatic, in which case he will occasionally give up and say in disgust, "Oh what's the use." The Melancholy also has a deep need to be understood and longs for others to respond with sensitivity to his inner struggles and to commiserate with him over flip comments made by shallow people attempting to be funny.

Because the Melancholy mind is a series of charts, you can be sure he knows when you have sent a gift and when you forgot. He will say, "It doesn't matter," but it does. Fred's grandfather, who always insisted that we not buy him any presents, was able each Christmas to keep a mental record of what each family member gave him. Even though there would be droves of great-grandchildren, he was able to check off each one without benefit of paper or pencil and announce at the end of the day, "I guess little Tommy doesn't love me any more. He didn't give me a thing."

Because the Melancholy is so unwilling to express his needs, he throws others into a constant guessing game. Each year I tell Fred everything I see that I would possibly want for Christmas—which is of course almost everything I see. Although I ask him often what he'd like, he never tells me. This year I asked him why he wouldn't give me gift suggestions when I am so helpful to him. He replied, "If you really loved me, you would be sensitive enough to my needs to figure it out. If I tell you, there's no joy of response." He then proceeded to gently reprimand me for my constant suggestions that I had considered a virtue. "When you point out everything you like, it leaves nothing to my imagination and there are no surprises."

Isn't it amazing how different we are? How what seems right to one is wrong for the other?

I now bite my tongue when I see a soft aqua robe that I would love to have, and I try to read Fred's mind before Christmas.

This intense need of the Melancholy for others to delve deeply into his subconscious and come up with his innermost thoughts puts a tremendous amount of pressure on any relationship, and because the Melancholy keeps score, this combination can terminate friendships.

One young couple with a Sanguine wife and a Melancholy husband rented a large cabin sailboat for a weekend. Another couple had expressed interest in going out with them sometime, so they invited them. The rental was several hundred dollars, and at the end of the three days, the other couple thanked them for the good time and left. The husband kept waiting for them to send him a check for their part of the bill.

When I asked, "Had you made this clear to them ahead of time?" He responded, "If they had any sense they would have known how much it cost and that they should pay half."

"They should have known" is a frequent statement of the Melancholy. Probably they should know, but what a shame that the hurt Melancholy refused to ever see this couple again.

We all appreciate order and hope for sensitivity, but for the Melancholy these traits become emotional needs.

The Phlegmatic Needs Respect and a Feeling of Worth

The Phlegmatic's goal in life is to keep the peace, and when this is not possible, the Phlegmatic sometimes withdraws and emotionally shuts down, often refusing any communication until some facsimile of peace is restored. Rather than face the enemy, the Phlegmatics retreat until one side wins the war, and then they join the victorious team.

Because the Phlegmatic's desire is to have peace, we might assume that a quiet room with a recliner chair would meet his needs, but underneath, like Rodney Dangerfield, he is longing for respect.

Because I am not Phlegmatic, it took an inspiration from the Lord for me to see this need for worth in my Phlegmatic mother. It is so easy for the other temperaments to ignore the Phlegmatics since they are not crying out for attention and after a while the Phlegmatic feels useless and of no value. Others seem to want to change the Phlegmatic to be what they are.

Sanguines assume no one could be happy if they are not jumping up and down with enthusiasm, so they feel called upon to elicit some cheer from the Phlegmatic. I would try to excite my mother with tales of grandeur, and she'd only respond, "That's nice." I felt I'd failed and so I'd get more dramatic. The harder I tried, the less she responded. I didn't realize that my adventures made her feel as if she didn't "amount to a row of pins." She needed me to settle down and give her credit for her peaceful accepting attitude about living in the retirement home.

Because Sanguines want approval, they try to make the Phlegmatics excited and fail to realize their need for respect.

The Choleric tries to make the Phlegmatic get moving. For the Choleric what they perceive as laziness is a sin unto death. How could anyone not want to produce? I asked a Phlegmatic friend to pass out some outlines at the beginning of a seminar. She dutifully agreed. Next to the morning pile of outlines was a stack clearly labeled "Afternoon Outlines." When the program started after lunch I noticed no one had outlines. As I went to get them and hand them to her, she said, "I didn't know I had to do it twice."

A Choleric cannot understand this passive thinking, or lack thereof, and the Choleric's innate reaction is one of disgust which signals to the Phlegmatic, who truly did not understand, that he is stupid and worthless.

The Melancholy tries to get the Phlegmatic interested in details and seeking perfection. The harder he pushes, the more the Phlegmatic pulls back and softly comments, "It doesn't make that much difference to me and who cares anyhow." The Melancholy cares and can't imagine how anyone with intelligence could possibly be indifferent to the complexities of life. The Melancholy ponders awhile and assumes he didn't make the point clear enough, so he tries an explanation of greater detail which so turns the Phlegmatic off that he just shrugs. This lack of zeal is taken by the Melancholy as rejection, and he becomes depressed. Isn't it amazing how we so badly misread others unless we understand their basic personalities and their underlying needs? The Phlegmatic does not want to be goaded on by the others to become something he really isn't; he just wants to be accepted as he is and be considered a person of value and worth. Where would we all be if we didn't have the peace-loving Phlegmatic to give us much needed balance and to tone down our compulsions? Thank your Phlegmatic mate, friend, or child for their easy-going nature. If they didn't have it, how would they put up with the rest of us?

We all want to feel that we are people of worth, but for the Phlegmatic, respect is an emotional need.

While I often get letters with fun examples I could use from Sanguines and straight suggestions from Cholerics and additional facts and details from Melancholies, I seldom hear from Phlegmatics. I assume their feeling of not being worthy prevents their writing me a letter, but when I do receive one like this I get excited.

Your seminar helped me so very much to understand who *I* am. . . . One of the things that has been so difficult for me to grasp is the fact that God accepts me just the way I am. My question has always been, "But who *am* I?" I am . . . always trying to figure out why I am so blaaaa. . . . Something must be wrong because I can't organize a good outline like another Sunday School teacher, or always have boundless bursts of energy, planning lots of things and staying up late, and making fun out of cleaning my house. You described me well, when you said if you gave a Phlegmatic two hours to do the job, they would take all of two hours, (with me it is usually more!) When I finally got ahold of the truth that it is OKAY for me to not have all those qualities that everyone else has, and that there was nothing wrong with *my own* character, I began to see myself for the person I really am. How freeing, and what hope! I am excited about me. I'm not dumb and stupid and non-interesting. My blankness that I sometimes feel is not because the Lord left something out of my brain. Just because I can't follow directions as well as I am expected to, doesn't mean that I "don't listen."

How refreshing it was to sit for three hours after I drove home from the retreat and to share with my husband these simple, and yet vital truths about our personalities. And he listened!

We hear so much about accepting . . . other[s] "just the way they are," but we really don't know who they are so that we can accept them.

May God bless you and your ministry in bringing people to a position of knowing themselves so that Christ can balance their lives to be a glory to Him!—Loretta McClure

One lady came to a *Personality Plus* seminar and later wrote, "Since I've started to grow up emotionally, I've stopped playing *What's My Line?* and I'm into *To Tell The Truth.*"

In the Shakespearian play *Hamlet,* the aging Polonius gives his young son some advice.

This above all; to thine own self be true,
And it must follow, as the night the day,
Thou canst not then be false to any man.[5]

For Further Study, Thought, and Action

It's hard to be true to yourself until you know who you are.
Is it possible to understand others when you are confused over
your own identity?

According to what you've already learned—

What is your primary personality? _____
What is your basic temperament desire? _____
What are your general underlying needs? _____

If you are married, answer the following about your mate:

What is his/her primary personality? _____
What is his/her basic desire temperamentwise? _____
What are his/her general underlying needs? _____

Now that we have looked at the general underlying needs of
each temperament, let's get more specific. One day I sat down
and made a list of the three personal emotional needs I had as
a child.

1. Because I lived in three tiny rooms behind my father's store
and ate in front of the customers, I longed for a normal house
with a dining room. Everyone else had at least a front door,
and to go from *their* bedroom to *their* bathroom they didn't have
to pass a cash register. I felt abnormal and deprived, and a simple
house became an emotional need.

2. Each night when my father counted up the day's receipts
there was anxiety over whether we could pay our bills. We always
did manage to eat, but there was never anything left over and
the total allowance for us three children was one cent's worth
of candy a day. I can remember longing for enough money to
have a banana split, and I went to work at fourteen, selling chocolates in Mitchell's Department Store so I could have some sense
of security. For me, money became an emotional need.

3. Because there were no cosmetics or permanents when I was
young, a girl was either a natural beauty or plain. I fell into
the latter category. I envied Peggy who had thick blond braids,
long eyelashes, and a turned up nose with freckles on it. Her

mother bought her dresses while mine were homemade, and Peggy was pretty. A longing for looks and clothes became an emotional need.

Before showing my list to Fred I asked him to think about his three emotional needs.

1. He immediately remembered how he never felt loved. Although he lived in a big house with a maid and nursemaid, he never felt his parents really cared. They both worked daily and while he was well provided for, he felt ignored. The lack of personal and physical love created a vacuum in his life and became an emotional need.

2. Because no one seemed to pay attention to what he was doing, Fred excelled in sports in the hopes of winning his parents' approval. The only time his father came to an event was at a track meet where his dad arrived after Fred had won the race. Even though he won letters and trophies, he never felt his parents took note of his achievements, and his desire for approval became an emotional need.

3. Fred remembers being lonely even when there were people around. Activities seemed to be planned by adults for adults, and in his Melancholy memory, homelife was not much fun. Although large parties took place on weekends, Fred felt he was on the fringes of the family fun. This lack of participation and excitement became depressing, and his desire for family fulfillment became an emotional need.

As Fred and I compared our childhood needs we saw that they were not at all alike. We then added a Sufficiencies column and were even more surprised.

FLORENCE		FRED	
NEEDS	SUFFICIENCIES	NEEDS	SUFFICIENCIES
House	Love	Love	House
Money	Approval	Approval	Money
Looks & Clothes	Family Fun	Family fun	Looks & Clothes

My needs were his sufficiencies and his sufficiencies were my needs. No wonder we had failed to communicate our opposite needs to each other. He had the big house, plenty of money, and was voted most handsome boy at Camp Agawan.

I was surrounded by love, people were applauding me as I recited my elocution pieces to an ever-changing audience in the store, and life was one comical Sanguine experience after another.

As you pause to analyze your needs and write them down in your personality notebook, first look at those that are general for your temperament pattern, and then list your personal childhood needs and sufficiencies as Fred and I have done. Are they opposite or similar? Have you ever discussed your needs before? Can you accept that even if yours aren't anything alike or even if your mate's seem foolish to you, if that's how they feel, it is a genuine emotional need for them?

For a group study compare your needs and sufficiencies list with that of others noting similarities and differences. Be careful not to put down another person's feelings if you have a different point of view. Group fellowship takes place only in an accepting atmosphere.

If you have time, project the understanding of your needs into your relationships at business, in church, or in your family. Have each person share a marriage, business, or social problem that could have been avoided "if you'd only understood."

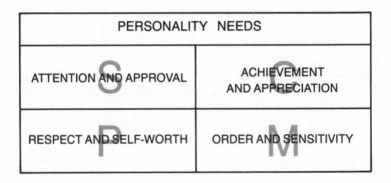

PERSONALITY NEEDS	
ATTENTION AND APPROVAL	ACHIEVEMENT AND APPRECIATION
RESPECT AND SELF-WORTH	ORDER AND SENSITIVITY

How much more appreciation we have for the game of life when we hold the scorecard and understand the personalities, aims, and needs of the players. One morning on the "Today" show Norman Vincent Peale explained why he and his wife Ruth have had such a successful marriage.

We each do what we do best, and we respect the other's differences. [6]

❧ 4 ❧

What Leads You into Temptation?

From the time we were children, many of us have been able to recite the Lord's Prayer at least in a group situation, and we know the line, "Lead us not into temptation, but deliver us from evil." However, few of us ever thought the verse applied to us, as we are "good people" not given to plucking forbidden fruit. We were brought up on Bible stories and know that if we ever ran into Evil in an alley he would be properly dressed in a red costume, would carry a pitchfork and would look like the Devil. In my childhood church we worshiped the god of good works and were taught the Five Commandments essential for eternal security: Don't drink, don't smoke, don't fool around, don't play cards, and don't sew on Sunday. I knew how to not smoke or drink, but I wasn't too clear on what it meant to not fool around although I didn't think I was doing it. In college I went through a rebellious period where I learned to play bridge, and once when visiting my virtuous grandmother, I sewed on Sunday and stitched my thumb into the seam. Grandmother looked first to the heavens and then down at me as she intoned, "God is punishing you for your sin," a condemnation I would still hear today if I should sew on a quick button before leaving for church.

When I wrote *After Every Wedding Comes a Marriage* in 1981, I inserted the chapter on "The Other Woman" with some apprehension. Was I bringing up a subject the Christian world didn't want to handle? Was I answering a question no one was asking? Was I five years ahead of my time? In retrospect the topic of infidelity in the church was brought up none too soon and the

"Other Woman" chapter has been the most popular. The list of *dos* and *don'ts* for those women who find themselves with an unfaithful husband has brought forth repeated comments such as: "I wish I'd read this a year ago. I did all the *don'ts* and none of the *dos*."

As I speak on this subject I take the assumption that no one in the audience has an adulterous mate, but "If your husband was looking for another woman, what would she be like?" We then go over a chart where each woman fills in what her husband would want. Perhaps the most provocative question is, "If your husband were looking for a place to have an affair this afternoon would he choose your bedroom the way you left it this morning?"

This thought produces gasps, screams, and occasional laughter from the ladies as the image of their bedroom flashes before their eyes in living color. Many have whispered to me on the way out, "I'm going home to clean the bedroom," and some have written later to tell of redecorating in the hopes of restoring romance to a boring relationship.

We ought to spend some creative time in analyzing our partner's obvious desires and underlying needs. While a messy bedroom and a dead philodendron on the windowsill probably won't send a man off to search out a new mate, these conditions do indicate a lack of concern for the other person. A man who says he'll be home for dinner each night at six and repeatedly returns hours later with no call of explanation may not be "fooling around" but he surely communicates to his wife that her time is of no value and that she is not worth much more.

As Christians we should be examples to our children and our community of what a loving marriage is like and of how it is still possible to have a positive relationship in an increasingly negative world. Yet as I listen to stories of rejection and rebellion among Christian couples, I know we all need help.

If I had a magic formula for a happy marriage, I could make a fortune, but I can at least share that when we start understanding and then meeting our partner's needs, we do reduce the risk of their looking somewhere else for fulfillment. Isn't it worth a try?

We often read in magazines and self-help journals about "meeting needs," but seldom are we told how to do it. We don't know what other peoples' needs are, we don't think to ask, and if we do, they give us the wrong answers. It's difficult to put your finger on an emotional need. We can look around our home and notice we need new carpeting; we can look in our closet and see we need new clothes; we can look in our refrigerator and see we need new supplies; but we don't know how to look into our hearts, or harder yet into the hearts of others, and see what's needed.

Now that we understand the four basic temperaments, we have a most practical tool for sensing inner hurts and needs. We are no longer grappling in the dark. We have just seen in the last chapter that each personality has its own needs. The Sanguine needs approval, the Choleric appreciation, the Melancholy sensitivity, and the Phlegmatic self-worth.

THE SANGUINE LONGS FOR ATTENTION AND APPROVAL

The Sanguine who appears on the surface to be happy in any situation is, underneath, longing for attention, acceptance, and approval. Sanguines need to know they are loved and that you accept them just as they are. They want an audience who applauds and they wilt under criticism and poor reviews. Now that we know these needs, let's carry this information one step further.

What happens when the Sanguine does not get his needs met? As a child, he will do whatever it takes to get attention, often becoming too loud, too annoying, and too much of a show-off. The worst punishment for a Sanguine child is being put in a room alone with no phone or TV. In school the Sanguine child will usurp the teacher's attention and chatter constantly with others. This child is craving attention, and he will get it in either positive or, if necessary, negative ways.

When the Sanguine grows up, he marries with the idea that he will finally have someone who will have to pay attention to him. He buys himself an approving audience.

Since we tend to marry opposites whose needs are totally different from ours, the mate doesn't have the same point of view. While the Melancholy may have applauded the Sanguine's humor before marriage, it soon wears thin and after a while the Melancholy won't even sit in the audience, let alone clap enthusiastically.

Because the Sanguine can always charm someone into being his friend, he begins to wonder why the only person who doesn't think he's cute is his mate. The combination of an outgoing personality and the need for attention makes the Sanguine the most vulnerable for temptation from the opposite sex.

A Sanguine flight attendant named Tricia told me her story. I had noticed her friendly, bubbly personality and started to talk with her. When she found I was a speaker and often spoke on marriage she sighed, "Well, maybe you can help me with mine."

Tricia had married a Melancholy businessman who had been attracted by her zest for life. In typical fashion, he wanted her joy, and she was impressed by his stability and success. On their honeymoon, he got upset over her dropping her clothes wherever she stepped out of them and hanging her wet bathing suit on a doorknob instead of rolling it up in a towel and twisting it dry as he did. He picked up after her and pointed out the error of her ways. Tricia assumed he'd stop all this correction when they got home and he was busy, but she didn't understand the Melancholy nature.

She was stunned when he made her place a large towel on the floor each time she sprayed her hair so that the "residual chemicals would not ruin the carpet" and when he gave her a polishing cloth to use in shining the bathroom mirrors immediately following her hair sprayings or tooth brushings. Because she resisted his best-laid plans, he continued to criticize her casual behavior.

He hoped his withdrawal of approval would encourage her to change, but he didn't understand the Sanguine. He stopped complimenting her on her looks and personality that he had worshiped before marriage, and he shook his head when she told him exaggerated stories from her latest trip—the kind of stories that had formerly amused him.

Soon they were both discouraged with each other and they didn't know why. They each felt they had somehow made a terrible mistake in selecting their mates.

Tricia didn't set out to be unfaithful, but because of her need for approval and acceptance which was not being met or even understood by her husband who was trying to make her "toe the line," she was vulnerable. By the time she told me this story she had already been out for dinner a few times with a handsome pilot "Who thinks I'm just adorable." You don't have to be a marriage counselor to see what will happen to this couple as each one heads off in opposite directions seeking someone who will say, "I understand."

So many feel that sex is the initial attraction between those who ultimately become unfaithful, and while that may often be the case, I find that the underlying cause is that they are seeking fulfillment of unmet and unexpressed needs.

While just knowing this principle may not change a marriage, if both partners are aware of the other's needs and try to meet them, the understanding alone will make a difference. As one lady said, "Just knowing he knows gives me hope."

THE MELANCHOLY SEEKS A SENSITIVE SPIRIT

The Melancholy above all others craves a mate who will be sensitive to his deepest inner needs, and yet he tends to marry a Sanguine who doesn't even think of digging below the surface. As the Melancholy gets depressed, the Sanguine turns to happy people plunging the Melancholy deeper into the pit where he awaits someone with sensitivity to rescue him.

The Melancholy doesn't set out to be unfaithful, but some are led into temptation because their own marriages are not filling their needs. Many years ago Fred and I were in a church where the Melancholy pastor felt unloved and misunderstood. While he was telling Fred his part of the story in the church office, his Sanguine wife was crying to me in the foyer. The "other woman" had walked through the hall, and the wife had fallen apart at the sight of her. The "other woman" was plain at best, while the wife was stylish and attractive. Surely he had not been drawn to this woman by her looks, but somehow she had been meeting his needs to have someone who was sensitive, thoughtful, and caring—attributes that were not natural in his wife.

This woman had been "volunteering" to help in the church office and had a knack for anticipating the pastor's needs. She came in each day, straightened up his office and served him coffee.

When he finished a long day of counseling, she'd drop by and listen attentively to the depressing problems which he couldn't share with his chatty wife who didn't like to listen, who would have spread the case histories as gossip, and who didn't like sad stories anyway.

Here was a man who hadn't meant to stray and who knew better, but who was vulnerable. Gratefully, the eruption took place when Fred and I were there, and when he saw what he was heading into, the pastor was willing to keep the woman out of his office and cease the relationship; his wife became willing to discuss his needs, which she had never even noticed before, and to curb her tongue which had gotten them both into trouble in the past. What a difference it can make when we start meeting each other's needs at home.

THE CHOLERIC WANTS TO BE APPRECIATED

Because the Choleric appears to have life under control, his mate, usually Phlegmatic, doesn't sense he's craving appreciation for "all he's done."

One lady said of her husband, "I just thought he loved to work— it never occurred to me to make a big deal of each project." A man stated, "She knows she can run circles around everyone else. If I tell her she's great, she'll get a swelled head." In today's world where any man can find someone to smile at him, or any woman can find a listening ear, how important it is for all of us to understand each other's needs, talk about them, and try to fill them before it's too late.

A doctor's wife told me, "He thinks he's God. The nurses bow when he enters and the patients' very lives depend upon him. When he comes home, I bring him down to size." That's exactly what this Phlegmatic lady was doing, and he didn't appreciate her deflating and sarcastic comments.

Since Cholerics only want to play games they can win, they will avoid any place where they are looked at as losers. This Choleric doctor had ceased coming home until late at night when his wife was already asleep. In the morning for punishment she'd not talk to him, and she'd purposely neglect to pick up his shirts at the cleaners until he ran out, at which point he'd yell at her. She then blamed his terrible temper and unreasonable nature for their marriage problems.

Neither one was meeting the other's needs, and they had declared war. He was already spending his evenings with an assortment of nurses, and she was taking a course at church on raising her self-image. Once she understood that he needed to come home to a positive personality and be praised for how hard he worked and how well he provided for the family, she was willing to make these changes. Once she saw that his apparent conceit was increased by her lack of affirmation and that he wasn't out to get her, she stopped her quiet war to scuttle his ship of state.

THE PHLEGMATIC JUST WANTS RESPECT

Because the Phlegmatic is a low-key person, the mate often takes him or her for granted. As one wife said of her Phlegmatic husband, "I hardly notice he's there, for he and the couch have become one." A busy Choleric wife tends to pass the Phlegmatic husband by in a hurry and think, because he's quiet and undemanding, he has no needs. It is true that the Phlegmatic can become content in whatsoever state he's in, but after a while he wonders if he matters at all. One Phlegmatic man stated about his wife and family, "It's like they are on some great team and I'm in the last row of the grandstand."

A Phlegmatic wife said, "Our family is an army battalion. He's the general and I'm on K.P."

While the Phlegmatic with his cool relaxed nature doesn't set out to have an affair, it is easy to see that when someone makes him feel important, he perks up. A Phlegmatic lady came to me at a conference after I'd spoken on adultery to tell me of her relationship with the church choir director. "My husband hasn't even noticed me for years. No matter what I wear or do, he doesn't see it. He hasn't given me any presents, and he just takes me for granted."

In contrast, the choir director complimented her on everything she wore and gave her solo parts because he loved her voice. He had sent roses to the hotel that day and had called her three times while her husband hadn't phoned once. As she stated, "I haven't done anything wrong yet, but it's the first time I've felt worth anything in years."

If only her husband knew that inside that quiet, unassuming woman was a heart crying out for some feeling of significance, some sign that he cared.

If only each married person could meet the other's needs, we could cut down the rising number of divorces in the church. Without any "how-to's" we tend to bumble along, but from here on as we function with knowledge, we can redeem our marriages before it's too late. Remember:

Sanguines need attention and approval; they wilt under criticism.

Melancholies need order and sensitivity; they become depressed in chaos.

Cholerics need appreciation for all they've done; they stay away from ungrateful people.

Phlegmatics need respect and a feeling of worth; they withdraw when they are ignored.

Don't let your partner be led into temptation.

For Further Study, Thought, and Action

Remembering what I wrote about "The Other Woman" or could have written about "The Other Man," state your partner's desires and underlying needs as you now understand them.

Ask yourself:

If my partner were vulnerable to temptation, what would the other person look like?

What needs would he/she fill that I don't fill?

In what kind of a setting would they choose to meet?

What would they talk about?

What can I do to prevent another person from coming on the scene?

Am I willing to do that?

Write down your answers.

Sit down with your mate when the two of you are alone and ask these same questions. Do you both agree?

In a group, draw up a profile of a typical person of each temperament and what each would be most easily tempted by. Then personalize this list with group members. Discuss one underlying need that each person has that is not being met and what can be done about this.

For those who are single, divorced or widowed, review past relationships, see where mistakes were made, and prepare for prevention of these problems in the future.

Study Philippians 4:8 and apply it to mates or friends.

> What about this person is . . .
> True and honest?
>
> Noble and worthy?
>
> Right and orderly?
>
> Pure and blameless?
>
> Lovely and attractive?
>
> Admirable and appealing?
>
> If anything is excellent or virtuous or praiseworthy, think on these things!

PERSONALITIES LED INTO TEMPTATION	
When mate doesn't give compliments or laugh at his humor.	When mate doesn't get things done and doesn't appreciate his achievements.
When mate takes him for granted and he feels worthless.	When mate lacks sensitivity to his needs and life is no longer in order.

Now that you know this truth how happy you will be if you put it into practice.
　　　　　　　　　　　　　　　　　　—John 13:17, TEV

❧ 5 ❧

What Gets You
Depressed?

Life's but a walking shadow, a poor player that struts and frets his hour upon the stage and then is heard no more.[1]

There is a national depression today similar to this statement by Macbeth. We're all playing our parts, doing what's expected, but for what? Where are we going anyway? What's the use? Soon we'll be gone, heard from no more.

In the past twenty years I have observed increasingly more depressed people than I ever thought possible. Every one who has a problem is depressed to some degree. People with marriage conflicts are depressed; parents with rebellious teens are depressed; patients with incurable diseases are depressed.

The word *depressed* literally means "pressed down" or as my mother would say, "just not up to snuff." Picture a foam rubber pillow and then push your fist into the center. The pillow is depressed; it's not up to its usual bounce. Pull your hand out and the pillow pops up. This is a simple example of a mild depression, that pervasive feeling that we're somehow not functioning at our usual capacity.

There's not one of us that's not pressed down occasionally as we strut and fret our hour upon the stage, and some of us may sense that someone is standing on our pillow and trampling us underfoot. As depression overtakes us, we begin to have feelings of helplessness followed by hopelessness. If I can't help myself, then there's no hope.

In my book *Blow Away the Black Clouds* I give the symptoms

of depression and some solutions both self-directed and spiritual. This has been my best selling book and I have just revised it to add an analysis of teen depression and suicide, some suggestions for the healing of pains of the past, and a chapter on Christmas depression. The one area I have not covered is the different causes of depression according to a person's temperament pattern.

Since we now understand the desires and underlying needs of each personality, we can see how these traits relate to depression, that feeling of inner loss. As we view the Sanguines' desire for fun and need for attention and approval, we can easily guess at what depresses them. Even though they are optimistic people with an above average ability to bounce back from adverse circumstances, if they find themselves in a position where life is no longer fun and where no one is giving them attention or approval, they will become depressed.

As the Cholerics innately seek control and need appreciation for their achievements, they drop into depression when they find life out of control with no one applauding their good deeds.

The Phlegmatics just want peace and need to feel that someone considers them worthwhile, so when they are dropped into a cauldron of constant contention and controversy and can't face the conflict, they drown in depression.

Because the Melancholies have the deepest natures to begin with and want the most out of life, they are the most easily disappointed. Because they are aiming for perfection in both themselves and others and because they expect those others to be sensitive to their inner feelings, they are laid open for frequent bouts of depression. When perfection is the goal, disappointment is often the result.

Since the Sanguine and Melancholy usually marry each other, they are doomed for depression if they don't understand each other's personalities. The Sanguine needs praise, and the Melancholy won't give it until the Sanguine is perfect. The Sanguine isn't ever going to get perfect so he doesn't get the compliments he desires and he quits trying. When the Sanguine performs more poorly than usual, the Melancholy gets depressed and the Sanguine goes out to find someone who will appreciate him.

When these two can see each other's weaknesses as part of their opposite natures and accept them, this frees the offending person to put his strength into improvement and not use it all up on defense and depression.

SANGUINE DEPRESSION

A Sanguine deprived of fun and attention may become depressed. After speaking at a luncheon and explaining the underlying needs of each personality, I was surrounded by people who suddenly realized why they were depressed. One Sanguine lady told me of her husband, the leader of a large Christian organization. She explained he had married her for her bright personality and sense of humor and then had worked to eliminate all her creativity and zest for life. He told her she was trivial, superficial, and self-centered while he was deep, intellectual, and concerned for others. With his superior abilities, he had worked his way up Jacob's ladder to the top of his denomination, priding himself on his spirituality while totally ignoring her personal needs.

As she told me her story, I could see before me a typical depressed Sanguine, one whose greatest abilities were considered as faults, whose joy of life had been stamped out, who received no praise from her husband. She was pretty but overweight, another sign of Sanguine depression; when life is no longer fun, cheer yourself up with hot fudge sundaes.

She realized as she poured out her heart to me that the reason she worked full-time was twofold: (1) She had to get out and find people who would praise her, (2) She had to earn money to be able to buy the things that would pull her up from her Sanguine depression.

If only I could have talked with her husband and explained her innate needs—so simple to fill—shown him she was normal to crave praise and dislike constant criticism, and taught him that the root of her depression was not a spiritual problem, but the fact that he, a well-known Christian leader, wasn't willing to meet his wife's emotional needs or even consider she had any.

Another Sanguine lady sought relief from her headaches and after much questioning by different doctors was shown that these pains appeared only on days when her husband took her car to work and she was left without easy transportation. She was wide-eyed as she told me that her pains were produced by the depressing realization that she couldn't go anywhere for the whole day and by the unacknowledged anger she had for her husband's leaving her wheelless. Once she found the source of her problem, she was able to laugh about it and share her recovery with me. She explained, "It wasn't that I needed to go anywhere every day, but just the thought that I couldn't get out if I wanted to had me close to sick." When she stopped complaining about headaches, her husband became willing to carpool and leave her the car.

Anyone that's not Sanguine would find this case to be ridiculous, but those who are can relate to that need for the easy accessibility of fun and for the constancy of an applauding audience.

As I talk with Sanguine women, I find that their most consistent cure for depression is to go shopping. The basic negative to this program is that the Sanguine is usually married to a Melancholy who can count and when the bills come in, *he* gets depressed.

Marita and I both love to take an hour here and there across the country and go shopping. Even when we need absolutely nothing, we love to look. Cholerics consider this shopping without goals to be a waste of time, Melancholies feel these forays are without purpose, and Phlegmatics find these wanderings to be too much like work. But for the typical Sanguine woman, "just looking, thank you" can be the upper in a down day.

One rationalized it this way, "Even if I do buy something to cheer me up, it's cheaper than a psychiatrist."

In *USA Today* an article, "The Lure of the Store," examined the attitudes of different celebrities about shopping.

Singer Jennifer Holliday said, "I love shopping for shoes with a passion. I feel that shopping has numerous psychological benefits in that it can provide consolation in times of depression, and on the other hand it can provide ultimate reward in time of success. Everyone should go shopping!"[2]

Well, maybe not everyone, but for Sanguines just knowing they can get to a sale provides "consolation in time of depression."

When Sanguine men get depressed because work is no fun, or the wife doesn't laugh at their jokes, or a check just bounced, contrary to logic, they go out and treat everyone in sight. They must be accepted by their friends and buying their way to popularity is one method of cheering themselves up while denying there is any problem.

Melancholy wives find it hard to imagine that their Sanguine husbands can so easily transfer negatives into "out of sight out of mind," that they can sign up for a lifetime membership in Jack LaLanne when the Cadillac is about to be repossessed, that they can go off on an important business trip when they have no business.

One frustrated wife told me of her Sanguine/Phlegmatic husband who was a builder. The new homes hadn't sold and the bank kept calling and insisting he get down there immediately. She was deeply depressed over the embarrassing situation, for as a Melancholy she could see that nothing was going right. As she went into his office to beg him to go to the bank she found him happily typing. When she asked, "What are you doing typing at a time like this?" he replied, "I'm writing a novel."

In just telling me the story she burst into tears. She had been in a long-range depression of humiliation as the bank foreclosed on the houses, and he had been discouraged for a while but had abandoned his literary career for a new venture manufacturing air-conditioned dog houses. The thought of another financial risk had her distraught, but he was happy because he'd managed to get financing from a rich man he'd met while playing golf.

Besides buying things, treating everyone in sight, and starting new ventures, another way the Sanguine handles depression is to overeat. Somehow the pleasure of pasta and petits fours picks up their spirits. Unfortunately this momentary lift doesn't last, for the Sanguine loves clothes and gets additionally depressed when nothing seems to fit right any more. To solve this a new wardrobe is needed giving reason for more shopping. One Sanguine I met has three separate wardrobes hanging in her closet: one in size 8, one in 10–12, and one in 14. As she ate chocolate donuts while telling me this story, she laughed and said, "The size 8 is pure history."

Sanguines are very circumstantial people and while they may drop into a depression when the fun slows down and they are no longer the center of attention, a change of scene or outlook will help them bounce back again. While growing up and becoming responsible would be a better choice, it is unlikely without a clear revelation from the Lord.

Remember, a Sanguine without a spotlight may become lonely and depressed.

CHOLERIC DEPRESSION

A Choleric without control becomes depressed. This concept has opened the eyes of many women as to why their out-going optimistic, goal-oriented husbands have totally changed their personalities. A fifty-year-old woman came up after a seminar to tell me about her husband, a Choleric with some Melancholy, the director of an engineering unit. He had always been a healthy, dynamic man until he went for a routine physical and found he had a degenerative eye problem. Even though his vision had not bothered him to that point, he instantly changed and began saying things such as: "What good will I be with no sight? An engineer who can't see might as well be dead. They'll fire me any day now. I might as well quit and die."

His wife was so stunned by this "crybaby" attitude that she didn't know what to do. "He sits around at home and drinks and he's started to smoke. These are two habits that the doctor told him would make his eyesight worse, and yet when I tell him that, he gets mad at me." She explained how angry she was at him and how she'd pulled away from him emotionally. These moves have obviously affirmed to him that she doesn't love him in his time of need.

When she heard me say a Choleric who is physically disabled often gets depressed, she brightened up and exclaimed, "Now I see the problem. He's got both of the Choleric causes for depression, a disease that will destroy his eyesight and the fear that he will lose his job. He sees a future where he will have no control. Now that I understand what's wrong with him I can be more compassionate and encouraging."

Another lady who was standing in line waiting to see me spoke up and said, "I can't believe this coincidence; my husband has got eye problems also, and he's in a depression. He got fired from his executive position while he was in the hospital having eye surgery. He was so upset that his blood pressure went up complicating his recovery. Since he's come home he's become addicted to Pepsi Cola and he eats Oreos by the bag. If I hide them, he goes to the store and buys more. He's gained weight and looks awful; he's developed a speech impediment, and he's no longer even polite to waitresses."

Here was a typical description of a depressed Choleric man, both physically disabled and unemployed.

Many healthy men also get discouraged at the mere thought that they might not be eternally invincible. They see no realistic challenges, and they're afraid they're going downhill. I feel that many mid-life crises are caused by men who sense they may be losing their grip, their hair, their shape, their macho image, or their sex appeal. To overcome this fear they tighten the reins at home, start rubbing Miracle-Gro into their scalps, join a health spa and buy jogging suits, lease a Mercedes and take the secretary out to lunch. What they're saying is, "I've got to do everything I can to make sure life doesn't slip out of my control. I've got to prove to myself that I'm a man."

How many Christian homes I've seen destroyed by a Choleric man who feels no one at home appreciates all he has done for them and who reaches out for something to restore his slipping self-confidence. In strutting his stuff, he finds a friend who makes him feel like a man again, and he walks away from his family.

An understanding of the personalities is so important in a marriage, for without it both partners may be depressed and not understand why they tend to think the marriage is failing and a new mate might make a difference. Without any new concept of their temperaments, changing partners just moves the actors to a new stage but the plot remains the same. A California marriage therapist warns, "Remarrying on the rebound is self-defeating. Unless one takes the time to learn something from the collapse of the first marriage that will make the second stronger, he or she is likely to repeat the destructive behavior, or pick another unsuitable partner."[3]

Choleric women tend to marry Phlegmatic men and unconsciously take control of them and the children. As long as everyone has an obedient attitude, the mother stays happy; but when anyone of the group rebels, she may become depressed. Without a knowledge of her temperament, she won't understand what's wrong. One lady handed me a note ripped out of a spiral binder, "Today you gave me the answer I have searched for, for years! I am terribly depressed. I can't remember when I haven't been. It's been so long. I now see it's my eighteen-year-old son that I have held down for years and tried to make into a different personality from what he was meant to be. He hasn't turned out right and now I see why. I didn't know about these personalities, and I've been pushing him in the wrong direction. I couldn't understand why he was so different, and he's had me depressed for years. Now I see that it's because I couldn't get him under control. I didn't think I needed this seminar, but I was wrong. I pray I can use this information correctly. Thank you so much!"

Dale and Sherry came to me with their problems after one of our CLASSes. They had each done their Personality Profiles; he came out Phlegmatic with some Sanguine and she, Choleric with some Melancholy. Dale was handsome, charming, and laid back as he sprawled in the most comfortable chair. Sherry was sitting straight, almost rigid, and she looked angry. Even if they had not shown me their scores I would have known what their personalities were. The question they came to ask was whether or not he should give up his job and go into full-time Christian service.

I started with him by asking an appropriate question for a Phlegmatic/Sanguine man. "Do you have any problems with handling money?" Before he could take a breath, she answered his question, "He's impossible with money, and I can make more money in a day than he can make in a week!" Just this one outburst gave me a quick view of their marriage: an easy-going friendly man who was viewed as incompetent by his Choleric wife.

When she finished her statement Dale asked me, "Why did you start with a money question? How'd you know?"

"Because Phlegmatic/Sanguine men frequently have money problems."

As I heard their story, I heard nothing new. Dale had shifted jobs at least twice a year in the eight years they'd been married. He got bored easily and several of the jobs were just "too much like work." Because of his cool charm, he could always get a new one and he lived on dreams of what might be.

Sherry jumped in, "He had one decent job and while he had

that we got out of debt for the one and only time in our marriage!"

"But it was so boring. It was a government job where you just did the same thing day after day. It was no fun."

"Does everything have to be fun to you? Don't you ever think of us? Don't you feel any obligation to support your family?"

With this outburst Sherry banged her fist on the table and Dale turned to me, "Do you see what it's like to live with her? It's impossible."

"I might not be so impossible if I could pay the bills. Tell her what you're doing now." The "her" was me and I then listened while he explained that he was in sales, but he didn't realize before he took the job that there was no draw and he wouldn't receive any money until he sold a whole roomful of office furniture. Since he hadn't sold so much as a desk in three months, there had been no income. Sherry jumped in, "Didn't you even ask them before you took the job?"

"I just assumed."

"You always just assume."

So far I had done nothing but ask the opening question on money and they had produced a soap opera.

"The worst thing is he thought he was going to make a lot of money and we bought a new house on his anticipated income. Now we have high payments and no money."

"If you didn't charge so much we might be able to make it."

"I only charge to show you what a mess you've put us in. If it weren't for the three kids, I'd go to work and show you up— and I wouldn't just *assume* I'd get paid."

At this point I decided to step in for a commercial.

Here were two Christian people who were both depressed and who couldn't carry on a civil conversation in front of an audience of one.

Sherry, the Choleric, was desperate because life was out of control and Dale, the Phlegmatic/Sanguine, was sick of constant conflict. Sherry had come from an affluent family, and she wanted Dale to be like her successful father. She had goaded him on and was partly responsible for his changing jobs so often. She had also been the one who wanted the new house and had encouraged him to buy at a point when he had no fixed income. She constantly berated him and reminded him of how much she could make if he hadn't stuck her with these three children. Can you imagine how the children felt?

Dale was tired of being badgered and admitted he only came home to see the children. He had a poor grasp of money and didn't care if he ever "got rich." There was no chance of his getting rich with his low income and her high style.

As I showed them what typical problems they had and did a little arithmetic with them, they began to see their mutual responsibilities for the depression they were in and the destruction they were bringing to their home. I learned that she was an excellent typist, but she had refused to do any work "because I didn't want to make it easy for him." And she hadn't.

He agreed to get a job with a steady income, at least until they caught up, even if it was boring. She then became willing to do some typing in her home office to help make the payments on the big house she felt she needed. They saw that they had been on opposing teams, and they determined to stop undermining each other and get on the same side. Sherry understood that in her mind her depression came from his lack of achievement and his inability to give her what she wanted, but that underneath she was angry because she couldn't control him and his jobs. Because her underlying need to be appreciated for all she'd done for him had not been met, she had quit helping him at all.

With no help or encouragement he had been unable to achieve and was facing daily conflict that he didn't know how to handle. His underlying need, to be considered a person of worth, had not even been considered, and she took pleasure in putting him down.

After laying out a realistic plan for them, I complimented them both on their acceptance of this new solution and then prayed with them before leaving. On the way out I said to Sherry, "Dale's so adorable if you don't watch out he'll find some woman who will be glad to support him."

He replied, "If I weren't a Christian, I'd have already left."

Too many have already left, often because they don't understand either themselves or their partners; they're depressed and don't know why, and they've grown up in a society that's said, "If it doesn't work, throw it away."

A few months later I received a letter from Sherry telling me how they'd pulled their marriage together through mutual understanding and support. At the end she said, "I realized later that you never answered our original question about whether we should go into full-time Christian service. In looking back I can see why. We didn't have our own life in order; how did we think we could shape up others? I see now that Dale wanted an escape into ministry and I wanted a Christian excuse for why we were losing our house. I hope God has a sense of humor."

Remember, a Choleric out of control, unappreciated, or sick may become depressed.

PHLEGMATIC DEPRESSION

As we have seen with Sherry and Dale, Cholerics get depressed when they don't have control or don't receive appreciation for the good works they've done. The Phlegmatic sinks into despair when he faces daily conflict or contention and concludes he is not worth, as my Phlegmatic mother often said, "a pinch of snuff, a row of pins, a tinker's dam, or the powder to blow him to thunder."

Because the Phlegmatic is a low-key person who is not pushy or pretentious, others often overlook him and don't bother to pull him into the conversation. Although the Phlegmatic doesn't appear to mind being ignored, there comes that day when he asks himself, "What am I doing here? If no one seems to need me, why don't I find someone who will really care?"

Where the Choleric male in mid-life goes into a crisis when he feels he may be losing his grip, the Phlegmatic is groping for some significance. By mid-life, he looks around at his children who only speak to him when they want money and his wife who is busy running whatever she can get a hold of, including him, and he suddenly wants out. He wants out of crises into coasting, out of insignificance into somebody, out of subordination into some kind of control.

The Phlegmatic control is a different breed from the Choleric's in that he doesn't want to climb mountains or join a wrestling team, he just wants to feel that he could do something his way once in a while. This mid-life shift of attitude, or display of a suppressed attitude, may take the Phlegmatic's wife by surprise, as he's never appeared to even care before; however, if she does not see these symptoms of depression as significant and help him to feel he's a substantial member of the family, he may find someone who will.

Do you remember the Peter Principle that says we all tend to rise to our own level of incompetence? For the Phlegmatic this applies when he rises from a peaceful position where he performed well to a place of perpetual problems. Although a Phlegmatic stays content in almost any state, when put in a spot where he has to face controversy each day and has to fire an occasional orphan, he may sink into a depression which even he doesn't admit or understand.

Strangely, the Phlegmatic can handle conflict if he is not personally threatened, and he makes the best mediator or arbiter between factious Cholerics. He is an excellent counselor giving objective views to other people's problems, but he doesn't want to be the center of the controversy or be told by someone else to change his ways.

A Phlegmatic mother is the very best at adaptability and in keeping her head when all about are losing theirs; however, she is easily threatened by a Choleric child who finds sport in controlling mother. Usually the husband is a Choleric whose very word causes the child to shape up and the mother to feel helpless. She wonders, "What is wrong with me? Why can't I handle this child? Why is he out to get me? Oh, woe is me!"

If the Choleric partner understands the Phlegmatic's problem with control and conflict and wishes to be of help, he will provide his discipline in cooperation with the mother and not in contrast, but left to his own, the Choleric will take charge of the child, exclude the mate, and make both her and her offspring see her as incompetent. Piecing this puzzle together, it's easy to see why the Phlegmatic parent often feels betrayed by the Choleric mate and overwhelmed by the children. This combination of conflict and insignificance leads the Phlegmatic into depression.

One couple that came to Fred and me following a marriage seminar were both depressed. She was Choleric and he was Phlegmatic/Melancholy and the understanding of their differences started them on the road to a healed and happy marriage. Ginny started the action and Wally responded. She wrote:

I guess I so desperately want this marriage to be great because it's my first and only marriage and it is Wally's third. Both his other wives left him, and although I can see why, those things would *never* prompt me to divorce. (Murder maybe.)

You really opened my eyes in your seminar. I had always deep inside wanted to know why his other marriages failed (hoping to prevent the same tragedy in ours).

I've tried to chart out his two other wives and they were both Choleric and could not take the slow moving pace of a Phlegmatic who seemed to never get ahead. They both left for other good-looking men and more money. (Wally's so kind and Phlegmatic he never would tell me really why.) He used to always say he never understood why they left. During each marriage he gained up to nearly 300 pounds.

Well, here he's married another Choleric, me. I don't see his past as the tragedy he does. I say, move on, forget it. The Lord put me in your life. His income has doubled in four years and we've started an additional business, and he's seemed happier than ever in his life.

But these old destructive traits keep cropping up on him. He's just recently become vice-president of a huge management company, but has put on seventy-one pounds since we married. Of course the obesity affects every area of our life.

Sometimes I feel I need some kind of a chart to have Wally live by. He's a little Melancholy but he's too Phlegmatic to fill in the chart!!

I see that I won't always be able to have my way, but at least I'll still have Wally. He's so good to me, so patient, all those wonderful things Phlegmatics are, but because he does not see results from his efforts, he feels a failure. I know he doesn't need another Choleric wife to drive him into the ground and then walk off in disgust. We love each other so much and with the knowledge of our different personalities I know we'll make it!

Even though Fred and I put our marriage back together through the understanding of the different personalities, we are still amazed and thrilled when others let us know what has happened to them. One woman who had been to our *Personality Plus* several years ago came again and heard what I had added about depression. She then wrote:

As outstanding as the material was for me before, it is even more beneficial now.

Three weeks ago my husband was dismissed unexpectedly from his job of 24 years. With my Choleric personality I want to get right in with investigating all possible careers and franchises and then move into a decision. But my Phlegmatic husband, so afraid of change and the unknown, keeps dragging his heels.

Understanding temperaments is helping me to sit on myself and choose to trust God with my husband and our future, rather than pushing on him to do things "my way." I know that once he makes a decision it will be a good one, and he will do well in it. But it is hard watching him move at his pace rather than in mine. He's a wonderful balance for me with my eager, let's-get-it-moving attitude, and understanding this has kept me from getting depressed.

Remember, a Phlegmatic facing conflict and feeling insignificant may become depressed.

MELANCHOLY DEPRESSION

The reason I have left the Melancholy depression to the last is because it is the classic case of what we all think of as depression. It's not so circumstantial as the Sanguine's or Phlegmatic's and it's opposite from the Choleric's. The Choleric hates sickness and will work to his dying day while the Melancholy is apt to gather up ailments during depression and in extreme cases simply takes to the bed in a bid for sympathy and sensitivity.

A lady came up to me recently and explained, "My mother is Melancholy and depressed. She doesn't work anymore and she seems to go from one ailment to another. She has had blood tests, liver tests, and x-rays of all her parts. Is she really sick?" What a question for me who has never seen the sick lady and who is not a doctor! However, a calculated guess would be that she is depressed and has focused her attention on her health, hoping someone will care enough about her to listen to her symptoms and be sensitive to her needs.

The Melancholies are depressed more frequently than other types because their deep desire is to get everything and everybody in perfect order. Since this nirvana never comes, the Melancholy either has to lower his expectations and accept life as it is or sink into despair. How many of us have ever had our house perfectly decorated, our tulips in bloom and all our buttons sewed on at the same time?

The Melancholy depression is harder to pinpoint because it is a generalized feeling not caused ostensibly by any particular event or deprivation. Things just aren't right—and don't look as if they ever will be. Because the Melancholy is innately sensitive and is easily hurt, he has no trouble remembering the negatives which when filed in the mind become heavy and depressing.

A Choleric woman wrote to tell me about administering our Personality Profile to her family.

> What a time we had with your test! My Choleric father loved it and told my mother that she was Phlegmatic. She believed him because it was easier than doing the test and what does it matter anyway? My Melancholy sister-in-law opened up to us for the first time in seven years. She said it was the only time she'd ever felt we cared about her feelings or thought we'd listen. We apologized, which is not easy for Cholerics. Two weeks later my husband's family came and we had to break up fights over the test. The Cholerics started telling the Melancholies what was wrong with them and they took it all to heart and got upset with each other. My husband's mother and aunt got depressed and went to bed crying, but the next day they all made up and could see how the different personalities had all behaved in typical fashion. Amazing, isn't it!

The Melancholies are so sensitive and have such a need for order that it is easy to see how they get so quickly depressed. A Melancholy pastor's wife received my *Personality Plus* tapes from a friend who in turn sent me a copy of the thank-you note.

> Dear Suzie, You will never know how much the tapes by Florence Littauer meant to us. They came at a very crucial time when I as a Melancholy had given up on ever understanding my Sanguine husband. I was sick of doing all his behind the scenes work and having everyone tell me how lucky I was to have a husband with such personality. The whole situation was depressing.
>
> He seemed to be sensitive to everyone but me, and I was left to be the disciplinarian of the family. As I listened to the tapes, I found why I was so easily slighted and realized that my husband wasn't out to ignore me, he just went where the audience applauded him. I analyzed the family and found I have one child of each kind. No wonder I'm depressed. I've been trying to make them all perfect

and alike. What a lot of wasted effort I've spent trying to turn Sanguines, Cholerics, and Phlegmatics into Melancholies.

Your gift may have saved our home! The tapes have meant so much to us that we are circulating them in our church. Everyone is excited as they find out who they are. It's really been life-changing!

Remember, a Melancholy facing an imperfect life with insensitive people may become depressed.

For Further Study, Thought, and Action

We know it is not God's will that we be depressed. "A merry heart doeth good like a medicine" (Prov. 17:22, KJV).

Do you have a "merry heart" today? If not can you pinpoint the reason?

Are you a Sanguine who is in a situation that's no longer fun? Where no one pays any attention to you? Where you're not getting any compliments? Are there people who don't think you're funny any more?

Are you a Choleric who is somehow out of control? Not full of your usual energy? Unemployed? Sick? Are there people who don't appreciate *all* you've done for them?

Are you a Phlegmatic who is facing conflict? Who is sick of trying to mediate everyone's problems? Who's tired of being ignored or made fun of? Are there some people who make you feel you're not worth a nickel?

Are you a Melancholy who knows nothing is ever going to get straightened out right? Who hasn't asked for more than perfection? Who doesn't feel anyone loves you? Who can't find a doctor who can help you?

Are there some insensitive people who just don't seem to understand your needs?

After thinking on these questions about yourself, project them onto your mate and other members of your family. Are there times when you can see you didn't understand each other's needs and you both became depressed?

If doing this as a group study, you may want to read *Blow Away the Black Clouds* for a more thorough study of depression. In your discussion time let each one share what really gets him depressed and what others could do to help him. Most people would be understanding if they were only told the situation and what they could do to be of service. Hiding your problems and then being depressed when no one seems to care only isolates you from any solution.

PERSONALITY DEPRESSION	
When life's no fun and there's too much criticism.	When life's out of control and there's no appreciation.
When life's full of problems and there's no peace.	When life's a mess and there's no hope.

Review some basic steps in overcoming depression.
Analyze your temperament needs.
Admit you have a problem.
Consider what you can do about it personally.
Discuss your differences with your mate, children or friend.
Devise an appropriate plan of action.
Write down your true feelings as David did in the Psalms.
Pray to forgive those that you perceive have hurt you.
Commit to changing what you do that bothers others.
Ask the Lord for Joy.

Hitherto have ye asked nothing in my name: ask, and ye shall receive, that your joy may be full.
—John 16:24, KJV

❧ 6 ❧

Are You
Wearing a Mask?

When I first started CLASS (Christian Leaders and Speakers Seminars) in the fall of 1980, I intended to teach Christian speakers how to "Say it with CLASS," but as I worked closely with the men and women who attended, I became increasingly aware of their emotional needs. As I began a study of the four personalities on a deeper level than I had ever done before, I looked beyond the obvious behavior characteristics of each temperament type and into the hurts of the hearts. I found Sanguines who were depressed, Cholerics who were out of control, Melancholies who had given up on life and Phlegmatics who were overwhelmed by adverse circumstances. I saw women who were repeating their mother's mistakes and men who refused to be introspective or enlightened any more than their fathers had been.

Marriages of Christian leaders were falling apart and no one seemed to be doing much about it. Currently, we find that anywhere from one-third to one-half of those attending CLASS are already divorced. As I teach about the personalities, the different desires and underlying emotional needs, lights go on and people begin to find themselves and understand why they are in their present dilemma.

As Lana Bateman came on our CLASS staff, she began an indepth study of what she perceived to be the masks people wear to cover up their birth personality. In both our CLASS counseling and her own Philippian Ministries, Lana took note of the different types of masks, when and why people wore them, and how they could be removed. Eventually we both started teaching Lana's concept and recording the reactions and results.

As I researched the personalities of both my family and Fred's, I saw repeated patterns of behavior and areas where some of us had unconsciously stifled our natural traits in a vain effort to please a parent or partner. Some had played a part foreign to their own inborn personality and in the process had lost any sense of who they really were and any sight of who they might become. Some had put on the mask of comedy or tragedy to get applause from the crowd and some had changed costumes so many times that they had forgotten their original identity.

One day I traced our family's personality tree on the board at CLASS and showed how many of us strong Cholerics had put on Phlegmatic masks when repressed by other Cholerics. Immediately people came up to confess that they had been wearing masks and hadn't realized what they were doing.

NATURAL PERSONALITY TRAITS

Some people couldn't "find themselves" because their true God-given nature had been trampled under, had died for lack of attention, or had been masked by rejection or guilt. I began to see how childhood abuses of any kind from emotional neglect to physical mistreatment could warp a little one's feelings about himself and make him unable as an adult to know who in the world he really was.

Some women I talk with don't have any grasp of which traits are real and which are learned. What I'm now observing in the above-average men and women we train at CLASS is that a totally subconscious manipulation has changed them from what they were meant to be to the insecure questioning people they are today. These are adults who have dedicated their lives to the Lord and thought they had taken off the old clothes and put on the new. Somehow new clothes haven't been enough, but as we help them examine their personalities by looking back to what they were meant to be, the blinders fall away and they begin to see with a new light.

The Bible tells us that Jesus is the vine and we are the

branches, yet some of us are not connected with what we were originally intended to be. Because of adverse circumstances, lack of love, sibling rivalry, or the desire to please demanding parents, we unconsciously changed our birth personality to fit our situation. Fun-loving children were forced to get serious and keep quiet, while introverts were told to put on a happy face to be popular. Born leaders were disciplined into an unnatural submission and those who would rather watch were pushed into leadership.

Some who stayed true to their birth personalities through childhood put on accommodating masks after marriage in order to please a mate.

Let's look first at the natural traits of each temperament and how uncomfortable we feel when we try to be like someone else.

Personality

When we think of someone who has "personality" we are usually referring to a Sanguine even though we may not know the term. If we enroll in image improvement lessons, we want to learn how to lose our self-consciousness, be confident before groups, be the life-of-the-party, and ingest an instant sense of humor. There is nothing wrong with these goals, but we must realize that unless we are Sanguine to start with, these traits may come across as unnatural. A Melancholy may try to repeat a story he heard a Sanguine tell and wonder why no one seems to respond. A Choleric may try to make jest over a person's pratfalls and appear critical. The Phlegmatic, even with his natural dry wit, may twist his tongue and easily become sarcastic.

Enjoy the Sanguine personality, but don't be envious, for with their charm comes a lack of discipline and they seldom reach their full potential even after receiving the ribbon "Most Likely to Succeed!"

I once took a charm course from a teacher who was naturally charming. She sat with her hands delicately posed and her legs crossed neatly at the ankles. While this looked fine for her, it didn't do the same for the rest of us. As I glanced around the room it was laughable to see all of us sitting in identical positions trying to be clones of our teacher. We should look, sit, and walk

our best, but it should be "our best" not a replica of someone else.

Be yourself; for a phony personality is never attractive.

Power

In an age where we are all stimulated to become supermen
and superwomen, we are often jealous of those who seem to have
it all together. Why can't we be in charge? Why don't we seem
to have the power of persuasion?

As a member of the National Speakers Association I have the
opportunity to spend time with some of the top motivational
speakers, and I have learned that most seminars are conceived
by Cholerics, written by Cholerics, taught by Cholerics, and only
the Cholerics can catch the vision. The Cholerics in the audience
can relate to the speaker, charge forth, follow the grail, and meet
the challenge. The Sanguine girl who attends means well and
wants to get her act together, but she can't even lift the syllabus.
If she doesn't lose it on the way home, she'll put it away to
look at another day and when she can't remember where she's
put it, she'll take this as a sign from the Lord that she's good
enough as she is and doesn't need the book anyway. The Melancholy at a seminar comes prepared with his own notebook, as-
sorted pens and 3 x 5 cards. He can follow the details and sense
the direction of the speaker's "Seven Steps to Success," but he
becomes overwhelmed with the vitality of the visionary waving
his arms wildly as he yells "terrific" and "tremendous." *No one
is really that terrific or tremendous,* he muses. Once the Melancholy senses the speaker is insincere and shallow, he loses interest
in the program.

The Phlegmatic didn't want to go to the seminar in the first
place, and he has no intention of changing his way of life. He
measures all activity by how much energy it will take to succeed,
and this all looks too much like work. People who are flambouyant
and frequently shout "fabulous" strike fear in the heart of the
Phlegmatic. He can't believe they are for real and he plans to
leave at the next coffee break.

Enjoy the dynamic delivery and powerful confidence that is
natural in the Choleric and learn what you can from his presenta-

tion, but don't get depressed if you don't desire to go out jogging at 5:30 each morning or meet Zig Ziglar at the top. Cholerics are sensational at seminars, but they aren't always a big hit at home.

While speaking to a group of motivational speakers I inserted a line that I had no intention of saying. "You may be terrific and tremendous and fabulous and fantastic on stage, but you may have a sad wife at home who, if she hears one of those words again, is going to throw up."

I bit my tongue as I heard those words slip out, but when I finished, a nationally known motivator came up with an uncharacteristically humble expression. "Just this week my wife said, 'You may be a hot shot on the stage but you're a zero at home, and if you say "fantastic" one more time, I'm going to throw up.' "

The Choleric has power in his presentation but he needs to get off his pedestal and look into the hearts of the people.

Be yourself; and don't envy those leaders who seem to have it all together.

Perfection

"Can't you ever do anything right?" How many of us heard that as we were growing up? For the Melancholy there is no other way. As a man said to me, "Why would anyone want to do less than his best?" And he is right. Certainly we would not aim to fail or want to do a shoddy job, but only the Melancholy has the innate drive for perfection. The Melancholy male must have his shoes polished, his mirror spotless, and his toothpaste tube without wrinkle. He can't possibly understand how his Sanguine wife could lose her shoes, keep open jars of make-up all over the counter and twist the tacky toothpaste tube beyond recognition. He is constantly picking up behind her, shutting doors she's left open, and putting the cap on the catsup.

Fred is so neat that he has been known to fold up his clothes before putting them in the hamper. One day I took his pile of laundry to the foyer and placed it on the table while I went into the kitchen to collect the dish towels. Within a minute I came out and the laundry was gone. I assumed he had taken it to the washer, but there was no pile there. When I found him and asked what he'd done with the laundry, he replied, "I thought it was clean and I've put it away."

The Melancholy mind is constantly tying up the loose ends of life and they wonder, since they are right, why the rest of us don't see it their way. The Choleric is more interested in getting things done quickly than perfectly. The Sanguines don't realize they haven't done it right and the Phlegmatics just don't care that much. The world needs the Melancholy to keep the rest of us on track, but sometimes the standards are set so high that no one can achieve them and then we all get depressed.

Be yourself; life is never going to be perfect.

Peace

While the Sanguine is running around spreading joy unto the maximum, and the Choleric is trying to get things under control, and the Melancholy is dusting off the details, the Phlegmatic is trying to keep peace among us all. Lana says her husband calls her a natural tranquilizer. When his Choleric energy bursts in the door at night, he takes one look at her calm, cool, and collected expression and begins to come down to earth. The heart of the Phlegmatic is peaceful and he will do anything, including compromising his principles, if he can avoid a potential problem.

From the time the Phlegmatics were children, they had a calming influence on others, and while they may enjoy some sports, especially those on television, they do not have the competitive spirit of the Choleric.

Other temperaments admire the Phlegmatics' ability to keep their heads when all around are losing theirs.

Be yourself; and don't obliterate your personality to keep peace.

As you begin to understand the truth of your personality, the Lord will show you who you were born to be and remove any mask you might be wearing. He wants you to be yourself for he has created you for such a time as this.

CLUES TO MASKING

One of the first clues that you might not be functioning in total honesty with what you were born to be is when your Personality Profile comes out with relatively even splits between Sanguine (outgoing-optimistic) and Melancholy (introverted-pessimistic) or when you are half Choleric (aggressive-active) with half Phlegmatic (passive-peaceful). Since these are diametrically opposed sets of traits, these combinations indicate there may be a masking. God didn't create us with antagonistic personalities in one body. "A double-minded man is unstable in all his ways" (James 1:8, KJV).

As Lana began a study of all those she counseled who had these splits, she found that the individuals with opposite scores were somehow masking their true identity. They weren't phonies in that they had determined to be something artificial, but they had unconsciously adjusted to some set of circumstances where a change was necessary for acceptance or survival. Based on Lana's discovery, our staff began to counsel with a new set of tools and we immediately saw results. Take, for example, the following letter I received from a woman who spent a day in counseling and prayer with George Ann Dennis, our CLASS principal.

> So much has happened to me since I last saw you at CLASS. I kept my appointment with George Ann Dennis on October 31. That was seven weeks ago, and I think I've started another life at a different level. I talked fast enough in those eight hours with George Ann to find forty-one areas to pray about. I finally found out I am a Sanguine/Choleric. What a shock to me as I had always seemed to be so Melancholy. George Ann laughed when I asked her what she saw. It seems my whole foundation is Choleric. God has been showing me glimpses of my childhood as this Choleric kid. I never knew I was. I'm so excited, I'm having fun getting to know the real me. She said I never really had a childhood and I was dealt double whammies ever since I was born. Now Jesus is between me and all those negative memories. Praise God. I'm not out looking for someone to like me like the lost little child I was before, as I know I'm loved!

Because of the difficult and repressive circumstances of this woman's childhood, she had grown up thinking she was Melancholy and yet not comfortable about it. When she saw herself as she was meant to be, a Sanguine/Choleric, she was free to be herself and get out from under the pressures of the past.

The person who functions as a Sanguine/Melancholy split has

happy highs alternating with deep periods of depression. The Choleric/Phlegmatic, on the other hand, swings in and out of controlling and submissive responses. Although many studies of the four basic temperaments, no matter what labels are used, show the Sanguine/Melancholy and Choleric/Phlegmatic combinations to be normal blends of people who have fluctuating extremes in their natures, we have found these conflicting traits to represent an adaptation to adverse circumstances of the past.

We feel that a God who created man to live in peace of mind would not have built opposite traits into one person causing him lifelong inner turmoil. As we sought answers to this apparent contradiction, we asked individuals with conflicting traits to review their childhood and their parents' personalities. And we soon found that one of the opposite temperaments is a mask, an unnatural veiling of the original personality.

A Greek sage once said, "I take the world to be but as a stage whence net-masked men do play their personage."[1]

I've found that many honest Christian people are playing roles they never auditioned for, on stages they didn't design, while glued to masks they don't know how to remove.

How many bewildered individuals we see who say, "I just don't know who I am." We are never truly content when our inner feelings and our outer personality don't match up.

When do these masks first appear? Usually we find that a child who lives in a stressful environment where his natural personality is not acceptable for one of many reasons will try to adapt to what is expected of him. He may have pain he cannot express, trauma that shocks him out of his true nature, molestation that floods him with guilt, an oppressive parent that grinds down his personality, a well-meaning but dictatorial parent who plans out his life, a favored sibling he is encouraged to emulate, unrealistic goals not suited to his abilities, or crisis situations where he has to adapt to survive.

At the time he is faced with odds he can't hope to beat, he may put on an appropriate mask and play a role for which God was not the casting director.

Nathaniel Hawthorne said in *The Scarlet Letter,* "No man, for any considerable period can wear one face to himself and another to the multitude without finally getting bewildered as to which may be the true."

Maxine Bynum grew up wearing a mask of Phlegmatic submission and wondered why she never felt right about herself. After coming to both *Personality Plus* and *Lives on the Mend* conferences and spending some counseling time with me she wrote:

> I was very interested in your "family tree" concept with the temperaments. I've been looking back and thinking about how my grandmother influenced my temperament and actions as I was growing up, and even after my marriage when I was nineteen. My mother died three days after I was born and my father couldn't deal with her death or with me, so he gave me to my mother's mother when I was three weeks old, rejecting me, and was never a part of my life when I was growing up.
>
> My grandmother was a strong Choleric and I became Phlegmatic to make sure I did just what she wanted, so as to win her approval and love. I couldn't stand another rejection. My grandfather died when I was six years old, so I really don't remember much about him, but he was probably Phlegmatic. The only times I could really be in control were the two summers while a college student at S.M.U., when I was a camp counselor and away from home for three months each summer. It was then that the Choleric part of my temperament surfaced and I could be in charge of a girls' cabin and tell them what to do. And I did! Except for these two summers, I've worn a Phlegmatic mask.

I'm so grateful that God has used me to help Maxine remove a Phlegmatic mask that was hiding a repressed Choleric nature. Now she is free to be herself without feeling she must apologize for her actions.

Another lady who has been wearing the Phlegmatic mask of peace wrote, "I feel like a chameleon, taking on the color of each situation, trying to be all things to all people, never saying how I really feel about anything. Now I'm so mixed up I have no idea who I really am."

A man stated, "I had to play one part to please my mother and a different one to humor my father. I don't know which one—if either—is the real me."

Lana tells of a woman who came to her for counsel:

> Joy showed me her temperament test revealing her personality to be Melancholy/Sanguine. She was convinced that this was a true

evaluation so we did not pursue any other possibility until after she had spent a day with me in a time of emotional healing and prayer.

During our counseling time together, we found that she had experienced a very painful childhood under the oppressive hand of a powerfully manipulating and controlling Melancholy/Choleric mother and a sadly passive Phlegmatic father. The mental abuse was agonizing and left that little one totally incapable of expressing her true self. A well of pain and repression filled her heart, and a broken spirit rather than a broken will resulted.

After that pain was released in tears and prayer, a whole new flower blossomed. Joy's friends found a Choleric/Sanguine with a heavy emphasis on the Choleric, a major change from what she had originally seemed to be.

What an amazing thing it is to see the real creature after the environmentally imposed facades have been stripped away. Joy is but one of many examples of those who thought they had two incompatible temperaments as the major components of their personality. Words cannot properly express the peace that comes from discovering one's true identity.

Yes, what a freeing experience it is to finally know who you really are. One day after a seminar where I had put the Littauer Family Personality Tree on the board and had explained how the Cholerics in Fred's family had been forced by the preceding generation to play Phlegmatic, a lady wrote me this letter.

> Thank you so very, very much. I feel so free. . . . [What] you shared about parental influence masking traits that show up later was such a key for me. I have yet to take the personality inventory over again with this new information in mind, but know when I do it will be much more accurate. . . .

How free the butterfly feels when it first flies out of the cocoon!

Dr. James Carr, a management consultant, writes, "We cultivate illusions of competency—masks—which help us to camouflage our anxieties. And the precious drive we have within us . . . becomes obscured in compromise, complacency and concern for immediate, rather than long-range goals. . . . What are the masks behind which so many hide?"[2] What are masks that a person puts on "because he doubts his ability to handle some area of human relationships?"[3]

THE SANGUINE/MELANCHOLY SPLIT

So many of us don a false front when we meet up with circumstances we can't control or relationships we can't handle. We wear masks that so gradually become a part of us that we no longer know where the mask ends and we begin. If your Personality Profile shows an unusual split, if you feel uncomfortable about your identity or if you sense your offspring are confused, begin to question these conflicting patterns.

"Why is my teen-age son Melancholy at home and Sanguine outside?" a mother asked me after I spoke on the personalities. "His friends say he's the life-of-the-party, but he has nothing very bright to say to me." As we conversed I quickly learned that the father was Melancholy/Choleric and the mother Melancholy/Phlegmatic. Neither one put much value on humor and without realizing what they were doing, they had let the boy know his light-hearted Sanguine nature was trivial and without any serious purpose.

When we review the Sanguine desire to have fun and his underlying need to feel approval and want attention, we can see that this boy received neither. Brought up in a wealthy home with achieving parents and goal-oriented siblings, he just didn't fit the mold. When he found his funny stories received no applause at home, he gave up trying. Why not save your good lines for those who are appreciative of wit? Don't waste your best stuff on an empty house.

This boy is not a Melancholy/Sanguine split but a Sanguine who feels depressed at home. He wears a Melancholy mask caused by parents who didn't accept him as he was. He becomes his true self when in the presence of his friends who find him funny.

To remedy this situation both the mother and father would have to understand what they had done to show this boy he wasn't acceptable and begin a conscious course of affirmation and approval.

THE CHOLERIC/PHLEGMATIC SPLIT

A pastor's wife told me of her daughter-in-law who seemed to be a Choleric/Phlegmatic split. Before marriage she had seemed good-natured and willing to go along with any family plans. After marriage she took over strongly and now does not want her in-laws to even visit or see their grandson. In tracing the girl's family background, we found a Choleric mother with a Phlegmatic father. The mother had disliked her in-laws and wouldn't allow them to be part of the family. The daughter had played Phlegmatic at home, but upon marriage she took over her Phlegmatic husband and reenacted her mother's role even though she didn't personally approve of her mother's domineering personality. She was subconsciously perpetuating her mother's sin and was excluding her in-laws without a valid reason.

Since it was the outcast mother-in-law who came to me, a solution was not easy. She had already sat down with her daughter-in-law and asked if she had in any way offended her. The answer had been, "No, but this is just the way it's going to be." The daughter-in-law herself didn't even understand why she was laying down these rules or see that she was patterning her marriage after the poor one her mother had produced.

Her Phlegmatic husband doesn't dare to cross her, and so he secretly brings the little boy to visit his mother while lying to his wife about the trip.

Here is a repressed Choleric who wore a Phlegmatic mask at home to keep peace with her mother, married a Phlegmatic, took over with a vengeance and is now taking out her hostilities on her in-laws. This girl has to be unhappy and confused, but she doesn't see what she's doing and is not looking for any answers.

She is not only destroying the in-law relationships which she doesn't seem to care about, but she is emotionally destroying her husband and turning him into an unwilling liar. Ultimately, her child will suffer as he lives under the overbearing dominance of his mother and the frightened submission of his father.

Possible Homosexuality

Unfortunately, this parental combination is one which fits the pattern of potential homosexuality: a strong mother who emasculates a weak father who in turn provides no "normal" role model for the boy. Other combinations are a weak possessive mother who binds the boy to her weeping side while the father has either left completely or is the workaholic who has no time for the family. In either case, the boy is in an emotional search for a loving father figure and is therefore vulnerable for the inordinate affections of an older male who presents himself as a genuinely caring friend.

The gays I have talked to, including seven young men in one seminary who were all training to be youth pastors, were all led into their current "life-style" by Christian leaders—scout masters, choir directors, youth pastors—who originally filled the void of a missing or emotionally bankrupt father.

A well-meaning Christian father told me he had been so concerned about the possibility of his ten-year-old son becoming gay that he had stopped hugging or kissing him and had pulled away from any physical contact with him. After hearing me speak on the pattern of potential homosexuality, he realized his withdrawal of affection was exactly the opposite of what he should be doing, for when a boy gets no healthy love from his father, he is open to receive it from someone whose motives may be unhealthy for the normal growth of the child.

Because this subject is so seldom dealt with in the Christian community, we don't understand the enormity of this pervasive problem. As the divorce rate has risen, removing the "real father" from the home, so has the increase of homosexuality followed closely behind.

A nurse told me of her conversation with a handsome young man in the hospital awaiting a sex-change operation. She asked him openly how he got to this point. He explained that his father had left when he was a baby and all he knew for a role model was his mother. He played with her clothes and make-up and loved feminine things. When he was in his pre-teens, a scout master took an interest in him, and he now sees how he attached himself to this man as a father image. The man told him, "You're too pretty to be a boy. You should be a girl." Later this affectionate man led him into a homosexual experience. "Once you've done that you know you're not normal and you don't feel right about yourself. I'm having this operation so I'll be on the outside what I feel on the inside." This was his way of trying to become real.

As I talked with one divorced lady, raising two boys alone after her husband had left her for another woman, I asked her what the church could do to help her. She immediately answered, "What my boys need is for some normal Christian man to take them out occasionally to a ball game or some activity where they can see a positive male role model to make up for the rejection they feel from their father."

What a service that could be for the men of your church and how many potentially distorted lives might be spared.

We first put on masks as some form of protection, and the young person who turns to homosexuality is often trying to put on a happy face over the rejection he feels from the same sex parent or the absence of any emotional attachment to that parent. He tries to hide his hurt and find a live substitute for the father God intended him to have. As he gets involved, he then tries to hide his activity from his mother, leading him into guilt-producing deceptions.

As we have seen, there are all kinds of masks put on initially for some kind of protection or self-preservation, masks to hide guilt, abuse, rejection, perversion, and poor parenting. In order that we can most easily examine what masks we are wearing or, equally important, what masks we have forced our children to wear, let's use our tool of the temperaments and divide the possibilities into four types.

SANGUINE MASK

This fellow's wise enough to play the fool,
And to do that well craves a kind of wit.[4]

The person who puts on the Sanguine *mask of personality* is usually one who learned early in life that his parents valued a happy face beyond any other attribute and that being "on stage" brought approval and applause. A child does not need to know his own name before he can sense what brings affirmation from his parents. When parents, one or both, need an adorable child to bolster their own self-worth, they communicate this to the little one. I often see Sanguine masks worn by Melancholy musicians who are part of a performing family of gospel singers. Usually one of the parents is Sanguine and is the crowd pleaser while the other Melancholy partner arranges the music and is the pianist. As the children come along they must all duplicate the Osmonds and sparkle out front. The Sanguines fall into this easily and are the favorites of the "stage-mother," but the others have to put on Sanguine masks or be considered rebels or at least poor sports. I counseled one Choleric girl who had refused to sing along and had been left home with grandparents. By refusing to wear the Sanguine happy face and bang a tambourine, she had been, in effect, dismissed from the troupe who went bubbling on without her. By the time I talked with her she was so angry at what she perceived as rejection that she had developed stomach ulcers in her teens. One of the Melancholy sisters who had been a forced Sanguine for years had gone on drugs, but the parents refused to see her problem and kept marching onward as Christian soldiers.

What a shame it is to see Christian entertainers who are more interested in what's up front than what's inside.

Not all Sanguine masks are on performers. Many are put on unconsciously to keep someone happy. One girl with a many-times married mother told me that she learned to be cute to keep her mother's varied spouses from "getting mad" at her. She was Choleric underneath but learned how to be coy and adorable. By the time she was a teen, this appeal she had developed led her into being molested by one of the "fathers" and telling me, "I'll never be charming again. Who needs it?"

The difference between a born Sanguine and one masquerading is how natural the personality is. Anyone can learn to say cute lines and memorize jokes, but any astute person can tell when it's strained. The real Sanguine has a sense of humor that bubbles out easily, and he can take any ordinary event of life and turn it into a hilarious story. The one wearing a Sanguine mask, on the other hand, doesn't have the innate sense of timing and can fail to be funny when repeating a story exactly as he heard it.

When Fred first came to visit me in our store, he saw what a comedy routine my brothers and I kept alive and tried to fit in and be like us. I'll never forget the long joke he told that seemed to go on forever. As my brothers were looking at me sideways, Fred stopped and said, "I've forgotten the punch line." And indeed he had if there had ever been one.

Now as we have learned to accept each other as we are, he is happy for me to be funny and for him to provide the depth and stability so natural for the Melancholy.

In taking the Personality Profile, the person with the Sanguine mask checks off the strengths that he has worked so hard to possess, not realizing they are acquired. If you suspect you have been forcing your fun, ask yourself how you really feel about these traits versus how you think you ought to feel. Many a mask has been thrown away by the mere asking of this question.

A young journalism major listened to my tapes and realized she was wearing a Sanguine mask. Her mother wrote to tell me of the relief Lynn felt when she found she could relax and be herself.

> Lynn has had her life changed from your insights. She now realizes that her Melancholy traits are part of her natural makeup . . . like her dad. But, she can now see her weaknesses and strengths and better understand how to make changes. Prior to this, she said that she thought there must be something wrong with her because she didn't feel comfortable being the cheerleader-type, and was more content to listen to others in a quieter way. Now, she feels free to just be herself.

Lana Bateman puts it this way:

> The Sanguine mask is a clown's mask demanding that its possessor be cute, funny, and constantly striving for center stage. It doesn't matter that he may not be innately humorous or sociable. This mask may take a normally quiet, sensitive person and thrust him into a very uncomfortable role of constant chatter and force him to try to become the life-of-the-party when in truth, he may have been terrified to even appear at the door.
>
> I first saw the Sanguine mask in a young woman who was thirty-two years old. Leann had grown up in a home with a sister who was almost entirely Sanguine. It was obvious that Leann's older sister Suzanne was her father's delight. Leann, however, was a more sensitive and quiet child. She felt deeply and therefore seemed to have more struggles as a little girl.
>
> Every time Leann had a problem or hurt, she would run to her dad, as most girls long to do. Her father would listen to her and answer, "Oh, Leann, why can't you be like your sister? Why do you let things bother you? Just watch Suzanne. She knows how to handle these situations. You need to learn to laugh and be fun like her. That will take care of all of these problems, and you'll find you have more friends than you know what to do with!"
>
> Leann lived on a steady diet of this response from her well-meaning father. This little one was soon engulfed by a Sanguine mask. She tried to be cute and funny. She memorized things her sister

said, jokes she heard and any attention-getters she noticed. In spite of the fact that she tried as hard as she could to be another Suzanne for her father, she never found his words to be true.

The friends he had promised never came and while she was laughing and joking on the outside, she never stopped crying on the inside. As a Melancholy child she was never encouraged toward the strong points of her true temperament. She was covered by her Sanguine mask and by her late twenties she began to cry out, "Who am I?"

After I led her through some emotional healing, she found out who the real Leann was. It was not until then that she could accept herself and begin to function as the person God made her to be.

The Sanguine mask is indeed a tragedy for it produces not joy and laughter but pretense and loneliness. The people responding to such a mask are repelled. They hear the funny clever words, but somehow sense the inconsistency between what is said and the person saying it. It is not surprising that the wearer of this mask experiences a great deal of rejection. Perhaps we need to look a little more closely at our Sanguine friends for some are not truly Sanguines at all. Not all talkers are Sanguine; some are masquerading under a torrent of nervous chatter. Understanding this mask will better equip us to minister to that hurting heart and will keep us from pulling away when our friend genuinely needs love and wise counsel.

The mask of the clown never quite seems true even though a casual observer will not understand why he senses this person to be phony. It takes an effort to play a role God never intended us to fill.

Jane came to CLASS elegantly dressed and meticulously groomed. When any funny line was given she would respond loudly and clap her hands. As I observed her I sensed her enthusiasm was forced and there was probably some masking of her real personality. During a break time I asked to see her Personality Profile which was scored half Melancholy and half Sanguine. I said nothing about the totals but asked her about her childhood relationships. She explained that her mother was Melancholy and frequently depressed. The continual gloom weighed heavily upon Jane and when her mother cried she would cry also. She was so frightened that her mother might get upset again that she made a pledge, "I will never do anything that will make my mother cry."

Her Sanguine father would often send her to her mother's

room to cheer her up. "See if you can say anything that will make your mother smile. If you succeed, I'll give you a dollar." Jane, in trying to please her father and cheer up her mother, developed funny things to do and say. She tried to do only what would make her mother happy, and she never dared express how she really felt.

As Jane told this story, I could see that she was innately Melancholy like her mother and felt deeply for her mother's moods even though as a child she was frightened by the crying. Because of her circumstances, Jane put on a Sanguine mask and tried her best to make her mother smile, encouraged by dollar bills from her father.

As an adult her personality shifted in different situations. She was ill at ease with people and frequently depressed when alone. Whenever anyone was sick or discouraged she would don the mask of the clown and endeavor to cheer them up. She was married to a Sanguine like her father who fled when she was depressed and told her to "cut it out" when she tried to be funny and failed. Her daughter was the one bright light of her erratic life, and she suddenly saw she was producing a confused replica of herself in her child, calling her in when she needed a lift out of her own depression as her mother had done to her.

Because Jane was intelligent and wanted God's will for her life, she was able to work on her personality without further counsel. She began to emphasize her Melancholy strengths and stopped her unnatural bursts of phony entertainment. Even more important was the freedom she gave her daughter to be herself and stop having to be her mother's dose of "happiness pills" as she had been for her mother.

What a blessing it is when we are able to see ourselves as we were meant to be and are willing to break the cycle of artificial habits. As with any problem in life, we have to see what we're doing that's unnatural before we can make constructive changes.

William Thackeray tells of the depressed patient whose theatrical profession made him wear the mask of the clown covering his true feelings.

Harlequin without his mask is known to present a very sober countenance, and was himself, the story goes, the melancholy patient whom the Doctor advised to go and see Harlequin.[5]

MELANCHOLY MASK

The world's "a stage, where every man must play a part; and mine a sad one."[6]

The Melancholy mask is one of *attempted perfection and frequent pain.* When I was first married and Fred announced he was going to put me on a training program, I was stunned. The Sanguine part of me saw this would be no fun and the Choleric part didn't want to be made over; however, for self-preservation I put on a Melancholy mask of attempted perfection and tried to act out the role Fred wanted me to pursue. I played a part and it was a sad one.

I knew nothing of the four temperaments in those days, and I accepted this unnatural role as the price of being a wife, part of growing up. What a relief it was when I found my first description of a Sanguine and realized my basic personality was acceptable. I didn't have to be serious and sober to be an adult.

Now as I look back on it, I functioned for those first fifteen years of marriage as a split personality. At home I alternated the Melancholy mask with the Phlegmatic pseudosubmission of "Yes, Fred dear," while in public I was myself: directing plays, teaching speech, and being president of women's groups. As soon as I'd walk in the door, the mask would go back on and I'd hide my frivolity until I ventured out again. I was afraid if I looked too happy, Fred might think I was "up to something." I love this little verse that sums me up in my early years of marriage.

> I'll make my Joy a secret thing,
> My face shall wear a mask of care;
> And those who hurt a joy to death,
> Shall never know what sport is there![7]

Those who put the Melancholy mask on as children were often ones with parents who demanded perfection either because they were Melancholy and knew no other way or because their status couldn't accommodate a frisky child. I find this latter masking frequently among pastors' children whose fathers feel their whole ministry depends upon the proper behavior of their children.

One Choleric man told me how his pastor father had insisted

he be a model child, but set the Choleric mother on the task of enforcing the rules. He said, "I always felt like a whipped dog with my tail between my legs. My spirit was broken early, but my repressed anger was boiling beneath the surface. I played the perfect role, and my mother praised me in public but disciplined me harshly at home. I grew up feeling I had no personality, but now I see it was because I was playing a role foreign to my nature. I did things to scuttle my mother's plans, and as an adult, I've had to work at even liking her. When she died suddenly, I was left with a terrible guilt because I never made peace with her."

This dear man is now in therapy trying to resolve the pains of his past and the guilt of his present, neither of which was necessary had his parents had any realization of what changing his nature was going to do to his life.

The Personality Profile of one pastor who came to CLASS came out Melancholy/Phlegmatic. But the twinkle in his eye and the bounce in his step told me he was a Sanguine. As I sat down to talk with him, he asked me about his score and I began to question his childhood behavior. His father was the pastor and his mother the organist. They made him sit in the front row and not wiggle and they both kept a watchful eye during what he remembers as endless church services. The one statement he heard over and over again was, "Don't you dare cause any trouble." Once his father had pinned him up against a flimsy wall in the church men's room and said, "Here's what I'll do to you if you ever cause any trouble." He then smashed his fist into the wall going right through to the ladies' room. "I knew right then I had better not cause trouble."

As he told me this story his eyes got big, his voice gained volume, and he literally bounced up and down in the church pew where we were sitting. Here was a Sanguine man who had been scared out of his wits as a child by a Choleric father who had to appear in perfect control to his parishioners. He had played Melancholy, tried to be perfect, and wondered why he'd never felt comfortable with himself. When I asked him to think of Sanguine-type actions of his childhood, he answered, "I used to go out in the fields and preach to the trees. Would that be Sanguine?"

As we reviewed his life together and saw repeated Sanguine

incidents, he began to cry. "Why did it take me this long to find out who I really am?" Before he left CLASS two days later he thanked me and said, "This freedom I feel is worth a thousand dollars."

Later he told me how his sermons had changed since he found out it was "okay to be funny" and how his people had noticed a big improvement in his preaching.

We will never reach the potential that is within us until we pull off the mask and become the real person God intended us to be.

A Sanguine tour guide from England told me a familiar story. She had married a Melancholy professor who had made her over until she was wearing a Melancholy mask every minute that she wasn't describing the architecture of St. Paul's Cathedral to an appreciative audience. One day he came home and out of the blue stated that she wasn't the fun she used to be. Ultimately he divorced her and even had the nerve to tell her that the new woman had a great sense of humor "like you used to have when I married you."

How often I've heard the pitiful story of a person who puts on an obliging mask for his or her mate only to be cast aside for a copy of the original model.

Divorce frequently changes a person's apparent temperament. If a woman has been held under in marriage, having to wear a false front for survival, divorce often frees her to become herself. If she has been her normal self in marriage and has been cast aside for another woman, she often puts on a Sanguine mask to hide the pain and tries to become a new person who hopefully will be more successful than the last one.

Besides the Melancholy *mask of perfection,* there is the very common Melancholy *mask of pain.* When the Personality Profile comes out with Sanguine strengths and Melancholy weaknesses this is a clue that the person is either a Melancholy wearing a Sanguine mask or a Sanguine that has somewhere along the line put on a mask of pain and become depressed. Phlegmatics and Cholerics may also wear this mask of pain if they have met with severely traumatic situations or have lived in homes where very little love was ever expressed. When a child does not experience love by being held or touched during the formative years of birth to eight, there can be an inner unexplained feeling of rejection even though both parents may be in the home, and this can damage his natural personality for life.

When a child is abused or molested, the victim usually puts on the mask of pain unless he is Choleric enough to push away the pain, deny reality, and forge ahead to become an achiever. The victim usually loses his own feelings and drowns in depression and guilt.

As adults, victims assume they have put these problems behind them and can't understand why the black cloud is always with them.

They are often negative, resentful, and complaining. No matter what people do for them, it is somehow not enough. They frequently have unexplainable physical symptoms such as headaches, body pain, asthma, and allergies. Sometimes in extreme sexual abuse cases they have blocked out the original attack and can't understand why they always feel guilty for something.

Whether the cause was trauma or lack of love, the person wearing the mask of pain needs help in releasing these past problems. For some, sitting down with a patient and compassionate friend who will listen may be enough to peel away the mask. Some may need a pastor or counselor who will work with them over many months. We have seen miraculous results when Lana, or any of her Philippian Ministries counselors, spends a day in searching the memories, praying intensively over the past pains, and healing the hurts through God's almighty power.

Lana tells her own story:

My life is an excellent example of the Melancholy mask. I grew up in a home where well-meaning parents did not know how to express physical affection and were not able to effectively communicate with children. While there was no abuse of any kind, I was left with a deep longing for love, and that need, eventually distorted, drove me to emotional bankruptcy. It turned me into a totally negative child and adult. Those who knew me would have declared me 100 percent Melancholy, at least where all of the weaknesses were concerned. That is a key for discerning the Melancholy mask which expresses itself through the Melancholy weaknesses rather than strengths.

The longing for love which produces the Melancholy facade cannot be overstated for it crushes many of our children and leaves them "licking their wounds" rather than leading productive lives. One who unknowingly wears the Melancholy mask will often show an expression of deep pain, hurt, or deadness in the eyes.

When I was speaking in California, I met a young man who responded to my description of a Melancholy mask. He came to me after I had spoken that evening and described the feeling he had experienced while I was speaking.

He said, "I've had everything a man could ever want in life. I graduated from a large university as an All-American football player. I was the athlete of the decade in that university. I married a Miss Universe. I own my own bank and trust company and am a prosperous man, but I have never been happy.

"When you were sharing your childhood and the Melancholy mask you wore, I found myself five years old again. My dad had lost his temper with me and told me to go out into the woods. He said, 'Don't you ever come back!'

"I was terrified out there alone. I cried and cried. The sun went down and it got very dark, and still no one came. I can't tell you the terror I felt as such a little boy. I knew I'd never see home again.

"At last, late into the night, someone came to rescue me. I guess I'll never forget that night. When you started talking about your childhood, I found myself wandering in those woods again, lost and afraid. I think I've been there all of my life and I wonder if I'll ever come out."

This was a gentleman who wore the Melancholy mask. His life was permeated by the pain of his childhood and the pain was produced by far more than one frightening incident in the woods. Until this man could work through that deep hurt and fear, releasing the accompanying emotion—the world would see him as a Melancholy rather than the Choleric/Sanguine he truly was. And not until then would he be able to leave the prison of his mind and rest in the productive and humorous person God created him to be. What a glorious transformation comes when one can cease striving and find freedom in God's original design for life.

CHOLERIC MASK

"Boldness is a mask for fear however great."[8]

In our modern American society power denotes success. We see magazine articles giving us the secrets to happiness and health, prosperity and wealth. Everybody wants to be somebody and the somebodies all seem to be Choleric. These powerful people are earning their livings by showing people with no power how to get it. The diploma from success courses could well be a Choleric *mask of power.* Unfortunately for many who get caught up in the "Ten Easy Steps from Wimp to Wonderful," a mask is all they have. They don't suddenly acquire a longing for the eighteen-hour work day, and the simple stairway to the stars seems to have no end.

I often talk to Phlegmatic men who have had Choleric masks of power put on them by eager mothers or aggressive wives whose own self-worth will rise proportionately with their husband's income. The man feels he's on a treadmill to nowhere and when he adds up the Personality Profile he is half Choleric and half Phlegmatic and frequently depressed. A Phlegmatic with a Choleric mask and a lack of understanding of the temperaments is a very discouraged person. He's trying to be dynamic without the drive, he's trying to be aggressive when his nature is passive, and he doesn't have a clue as to why he's killing himself and not becoming president. What relief comes over the Phlegmatic when he finds out he doesn't have to be a Choleric. He can drop the phony back-slapping personality that has turned people off and become the pleasant, agreeable, and witty peacemaker he was designed to be.

Bill came to CLASS as an aggressive Choleric who was depressed. In counseling we found he was a Sanguine who had been told by his father that real men were serious and high achievers. He tried to become what he thought he ought to be, and even though he was popular in the family business, he knew he wasn't what his father wanted. After listening to our teaching on the temperaments, he suddenly saw he was a depressed Sanguine struggling to keep on a Choleric *mask of power.*

Alicia came thinking she was Choleric but not showing any of the true signs of overt leadership. In talking with her we found a Melancholy girl whose Phlegmatic mother had been sickly and whose Sanguine father had taken off with a healthier model. Alicia called him her "runaway" father and branded him irresponsible. Because there was no one in charge at home, she had to take control and hold things together for her mother and younger sister. By practicing the actions of a nature not her own, she became an obsessively controlling adult and had a constant fear of losing the control she'd worked to develop.

Alicia married a Sanguine/Choleric man, the opposite of her true temperament and they battled for control. She was not about to give up until she got her first glimpse of the four personalities at CLASS and began to see the Choleric mask she had been wearing. Once she realized where her unnatural Choleric had come from and why she didn't need to fight for control any more, she was able to relax and slowly become the easy-going person God had intended her to be.

Besides the *mask of power* that makes any temperament appear to be an ill-at-ease Choleric, there is the related *mask of anger.* Any person who represses anger over a long period of time can appear to be Choleric when the cork blows and a temper tantrum surprises those in view. Often a Phlegmatic who keeps all his feelings under wraps will put on a Choleric *mask of anger* when he sits behind the wheel of a car. He can vent his anger on other drivers and shake his fist at traffic lights. When he gets to work, he often puts the mask away with his coat and doesn't put it on again until he hits the freeway at night.

Often we spot a Choleric mask when a person has Choleric weaknesses and strengths of another type, indicating valid strengths paired with controlled anger. This person may be working under extreme stress where he is helpless to do anything about it or he may have had a repressive childhood causing him to fight for survival. As he grew up the anger produced impatience, bossiness, and an argumentative nature that so overshadowed his strengths that he appeared to be Choleric. Extreme cases like this would be the person who handles his emotions at work and then one day murders his wife. Everyone is in shock as he seemed like such a nice man. Rapists and molesters are often low-key people who are carrying inside them the residue of an abusive childhood that comes out in violent acts.

Lana tells of a charming performer who came to CLASS.

Brian had taken the Personality Profile and scored about 80 percent Choleric and 20 percent Sanguine. We found he did not know his real father but his mother had remarried when he was five years old. His stepfather was mentally ill and would sometimes threaten to kill the boy's mother, occasionally even getting a gun and aiming it at her.

The little boy's response was to pick up a stick or rock or gun in order to protect his mother. He was drawn into the adult world of emotions and responsibilities through the sick relationship of his parents, yet he derived none of the benefits of that world, for when he would try to protect his mother, the stepfather would beat him unmercifully.

The product of such a distorted childhood is not hard to imagine. As Brian became a teenager, he had to find a place to express this terrible churning inside of him, this repressed rage and sense of injustice. He found release on the athletic field where his aggressiveness knew no limit, causing him to get his letter in virtually every sport the school offered.

It was not until this man faced himself honestly and released this inner rage through counseling and prayer, that he was able to rest in his real and God-given personality. Once the pain was poured off, a new temperament was discovered. This man was 80 percent Sanguine and only 20 percent Choleric. What freedom came when he understood what God had created him to be! His response? "I can't tell you how many questions this answers for me. I feel a peace I can't begin to describe."

Because Brian is now a friend of our CLASS family, I can joyfully attest to the changes in him which have also produced a restoration of a shaky marriage. Now, both his career and his ministry for the Lord are on the rise.

Many times we have found pastors who had repressed anger because they had been pushed into being pastors by their families and had not known how to say no. They were all godly men, but were in the wrong calling. One explained to me, "My mother told me from the time I was little, 'We've had six generations of preachers in this family and you are it.'" She nicknamed him "Rev" as a child, and he seemed to have no options in life.

Two of the pastors, when they realized why they had physical manifestations of their controlled anger, decided to leave the clergy for more appropriate careers. Another, after freeing himself from having to be a pastor, decided, now that he had a choice, that's really what he wanted to be. In all three cases the pent-up anger has been relieved, and the men feel at ease with themselves and are in better health.

PHLEGMATIC MASK

The words of his mouth were smoother than butter, but war was in his heart: his words were softer than oil, yet were they drawn swords (Ps. 55:21, KJV).

The Phlegmatic mask is often the result of someone who gives up on life and becomes apathetic, deciding it's easier to mouth agreeable words than to fight for what's right. Cholerics who can't win in a given situation may put on a Phlegmatic *mask of peace* and pretend they don't care. Sanguines who marry mates who no longer think they're cute may turn Phlegmatic at home and save their humor for social occasions. Melancholies who sense no one cares just won't bother to even communicate any more.

A Choleric girl told me she had two Choleric parents who so overwhelmed her as she was growing up that she realizes now she played Phlegmatic "just to stay alive." She remembers "There were no additional opinions needed, and I was raised by the saying children are to be seen and not heard. I didn't know I had anything to say until I went away to college." Even though she had no understanding of the temperaments, she married a Phlegmatic, the opposite of her natural Choleric, and soon found herself having to make decisions for both of them. After hearing me speak, she suddenly saw her personality pattern and later wrote me, "Now that I'm working on removing my mask I shift back and forth. When my Phlegmatic husband wants to stay home my Choleric says 'I'll go anyway,' but then I sink back to Phlegmatic and mutter 'What's the use and who cares anyway.'"

A teenager whose mother told me he was Phlegmatic, asked if I'd do the Personality Profile with him when I was visiting in his home. The more we conversed the more Sanguine he became. I asked him why his mother felt he was Phlegmatic, and he replied, "My whole family is Sanguine/Choleric, and they are all talking at the same time and bossing each other around. It's a lot easier to keep quiet, play Phlegmatic, and stay out of trouble."

A Melancholy doctor explained, "By the time I get home at night I have no heart to buck my Sanguine wife's ideas, ridiculous though most of them are, so I keep my mouth shut, nod often, and say 'yes dear' once an hour whether I agree or not. I guess you'd call that playing Phlegmatic."

One evening I went out to dinner with a family who seated me next to their twenty-five-year-old son who had moved home after a divorce. "We can't get a thing out of him. Maybe he'll talk to you." Once they'd given me my assignment, they all started talking at their end of the table. I asked the young man how he felt about himself. For over an hour he told me his life story. His parents were both professionals, one Choleric/Sanguine, one Choleric/Melancholy, and as long as he could remember they'd always worked. "They always gave me everything I needed, but they never had time to listen. Now that they're trying to pump me for information, I'm not going to tell them anything."

Later his mother asked, "What did you ever do to make him talk so much? We can't get a thing out of him?" As I opened my mouth to answer her question, she changed the subject, and I could see why this sensitive Melancholy boy had not bothered to share his feelings.

Who really cared?

Often when children grow up with scrapping parents, they take on the role of peacemaker or mediator no matter what their own personality was meant to be.

Lana tells of a girl she counseled with this type of background.

Sherry came to me several months after taking the Personality Profile and she was very confused. The only temperament she thought might adequately describe her was the Phlegmatic, and yet she had many checks in the other columns as well.

I couldn't come up with a logical answer until a year later when she had thought her life over and she realized that she had indeed taken on the false responsibility for not only her parents' happiness but also for keeping peace in the home. This need had permeated every area of her life and had masked her true temperament which was Sanguine/Choleric. Once she was able to reject that unnatural sense of false responsibility and stop being all things to all people, Sherry's real personality began to clearly emerge. The fun-loving Sanguine part of her expressed itself more freely and the Choleric became obvious as she began to verbalize her need for order and for quick responsiveness to her leadership.

Once more we see the results of finding one's true self and removing undesired pretenses. Free to be what God created her to be,

Sherry is now a joy and delight. Her spiritual and emotional growth is marked by a new reality of her true strengths and weaknesses as the distortions have been properly put away.

There is a fine line between the Phlegmatic *mask of peace* and the one of *apathy* when the person gives up on life and just doesn't care any more. Carried to an extreme this person could become catatonic, unable to express himself at all.

One young girl who had developed severe emotional problems told me that she was two different personalities. Because her home life with an abusive stepfather and weeping mother was so traumatic, she had learned to literally tune out and shut down any feelings or emotion. This repression had caused her headaches, and she only felt good when she was away from home. In going over her Personality Profile with her, I found she was a Choleric who had put on the Phlegmatic *mask of apathy* and was out of touch with reality.

Her comment on our meeting was, "As you talked I realized all these years I had been covering my true God-given personality with a Phlegmatic mask. That's the reason I was struggling with two people. Now that I know this, I have taken home the real me, I'm claiming my true personality and celebrating the freedom. My family won't know how to deal with me, they haven't seen me for so long, but as I explain the change, I hope they'll learn to love and accept me."

Since Lana first started teaching the masking concept at CLASS, we have had hundreds of people who have found out why they didn't know who they were. What a joy it is to take off the mask and find the real you underneath. How exciting it is to me when I receive a letter like this one that says, "You've just saved a life—mine."

Two months have passed since you presented CLASS here in the Seattle area. Little did I realize how transforming that experience would be. My parting comment to you that snowy day was "You've just saved a life. Mine." And those words are a living testimony daily. How desperate I was—in need of unlocking the prison of myself hidden behind a concrete mask that covered me from head to toe. Your material on temperaments revealed gaping discrepancies. Once shattered by truth, the REAL ME GOD CREATED is slowly emerg-

ing. . . . A miracle continues to unfold bringing healing and whole-
ness. . . .   God Bless, MarVel Berglund

For Further Study, Thought, and Action

In Psalm 51:6 David states, "You desire truth in the inner
parts" (NIV), and in Psalm 19:12 he asks, "Who can discern his
errors? Cleanse thou me from secret faults" (KJV).

As we meditate over these verses, let's realize that God does
want us to know who we really are. He wants us to discern that
original child within us and get rid of any masks or pretenses
we may have been hiding behind.

In reading this chapter, has the Lord shown you any masks
you've been wearing? What are they? When did you first adopt
a behavior pattern that was not how you really felt inside? Can
you see how this mask warped your original personality? Do
you or any family members wear the

Sanguine mask of Personality?
Sanguine mask of the Clown?
Melancholy mask of Perfection?
Melancholy mask of Pain?
Choleric mask of Power?
Choleric mask of Anger?
Phlegmatic mask of Peace?
Phlegmatic mask of Apathy?

If you are doing a group study, review these different masks
noting that the second of each type is the more serious. The
Sanguine mask of personality—a phony charm—is insincere but
carried to an extreme the individual trying to play the fool becomes ludicrous. The Melancholy mask of perfection may start
as the only way to get along with a demanding parent or mate,
but eventually the person is so full of pain and rejection that
he no longer can see himself objectively at all. The Choleric power
may be a learned response to situations that demanded decisions,
but the mask of anger is like a cork pushed down into a bottle:
under heat it may explode. The Phlegmatic mask of peace never
seems to bother others, but if it becomes a lifelong cover up, it
will lead to feelings of apathy where real emotion is totally suppressed. An example of this anesthesia over feelings comes from
a girl who had a nervous breakdown, was put in a mental hospital,

and played the game she called "I'm ok" just to get out. She wrote, "When I started coming apart at the seams, I put on a mask. In counseling I couldn't open up, share, or be honest. I've done this so long I pretend with everybody. I've developed the attitude, 'I don't care whether you understand me any more.' I have no feelings at all."

How about you? Do you have feelings you can't express? Start sharing with someone today. Pull off your mask and find out who you really are.

PERSONALITY MASKS	
Personality Clown	Power Anger
Peace Apathy	Perfection Pain

Oh what a tangled web we weave,
When first we practice to deceive. [9]

PART II

UNCOVER YOUR ROOT AND PROTECT YOUR FRUIT

UNCOVER:

To expose to view by removing some form of covering.

As you look at your family history to see what personality traits you have inherited, you will uncover your roots and expose to view some of the positive qualities that have been passed down to you and some of the manipulations and controls that have shaped your Personality Tree. By taking off the masks that you may have developed for self-preservation throughout the years, you will see yourself as God originally intended you to be, you can lay down the burdens of the past, you can throw off the covers that have hindered your progress, and you can be free to spread out your roots.

. . . be as a tree planted by the waters . . . that spreadeth out her roots by the river.
—Jeremiah 17:8, KJV

❧ 7 ❧

What Is a
Personality Tree?

*The trees in the street are old trees
used to living with people,
Family-trees that remember
your grandfather's name.* [1]

Throughout the Bible the Hebrew people show a continuing interest in genealogy, family ancestry and history. The pattern of their past played an important part in their present. They referred to themselves as from the tribe of Judah or Reuben or one of the other twelve tribes of Israel. The apostle Paul often mentioned his rootstock from Benjamin. The New Testament opens with the genealogy of Christ, and in the back of study Bibles, we find family trees of some of the greats of the faith.

When I got married in 1953, my generation, having come out of the Depression, worked hard at forgetting our past. We were sick of old furniture, and we wanted to put the pangs of poverty behind us. The word *ethnic* had not come into vogue, and people with obviously "foreign" names were changing them to Smith and Johnson. We wanted to send our European stock away and become affluent Americans. My mother and I threw out several sets of washbowls and pitchers that reminded us of pre-plumbing days and I'll never forget the look of unbelief that came over her as we saw a similar set on sale in an antique shop for over one hundred dollars.

In the last few years there has been a renewed interest in discovering our roots. The ME generation decided *me* wasn't

121

enough and turned to *them*. *Roots* became a bestseller and served as a catalyst for research of relatives. Genealogists sprouted up and family trees began to flourish.

Ethnic neighborhoods dared to label themselves. And dressing as if you had the lead in a Russian folk opera became chic. Continental cuisine was chopped up in chunks, and one buffet could easily include Turkish melon, Swedish meatballs, Armenian crackers, French bread, Belgian endive, Mexican frijoles, Irish potatoes, Spanish paella, and Hungarian goulash followed by Italian *gelati*, English trifle, Danish pastries, and oriental fortune cookies whose hidden message might well say, "Eating this dinner may prove to be a big mistake."

Cajun food is the current rage, giving casual cooks a new line of excuses for errors. The next time you forget the poor poultry until the oven is in flames, serve it proudly as Blackened Chicken, and you'll have a hit on your hands.

With all this interest in our roots, you may have already done a family tree for yourself or perhaps you hired some certified genealogist to do "tomb rubbings" of your royal ancestors. For the last twenty years I have had a family tree painted on a wall of my home. I gathered pictures of each family member and hung them on the branches framed in gold. An ancestor fitly framed is like an apple of gold.

I remember at first that Fred's mother didn't have time to hunt up pictures of any of the dead relatives, so I proceeded with the artwork and created a heavily lopsided tree in the foyer full of Chapmans and MacDougalls. At the first sight of this tree with bare branches on Fred's side, Mother Littauer gasped, "You didn't tell me what you were doing was going to amount to something!"

Within days she had collected up a veritable heritage including Ludwig and Louisa *von Littauer*, meaning "from Lithuania." These new ancestors balanced out the tree which I still have in my current home. My children have grown up knowing where they came from and what each ancestor looked like.

What is the difference between a family tree and a personality tree? The first has pictures and biographical research while the latter adds the temperament traits to the best of your ability and assumptions.

I first thought up this idea when Fred's Choleric mother took the Personality Profile and came out Phlegmatic. How could a dynamic, controlling woman who was constantly seeking affirmation of how much she had done for you, possibly see herself as Phlegmatic? I was confused. How could a competent Choleric, a superachiever who graduated from Cornell University at nineteen, a businesswoman whose walk and talk exhibit confidence and strength possibly come out Phlegmatic?

Several times she has come to hear Fred and me teach *Personality Plus* and each time she scores Phlegmatic. Once when we divided the audience in four sections, she chose the Phlegmatic group. Fred went over and said, "Mother, you are Choleric. You don't belong in this group." She slammed her fist on the back of the pew in front of her and vehemently replied, "I'm here because I'm Phlegmatic, and this is where I'm going to stay, and you aren't going to move me!" Does that sound like a Phlegmatic?

I remember saying to Fred, "Your mother has less idea of who she really is than anyone I've ever met."

Once she left my home to go to a grandchild's graduation where the parents were divorced. The two parents had predetermined there would be no controversy, but they were concerned that Mother would "stir something up." She attended with the conviction that she was needed as a peacemaker "in case there's any trouble."

How could a Choleric, who would by her mere entry into a room of relaxed people bring them to their feet, possibly think she was a peacemaker?

This contrast in her behavior and her perception of herself led me to think back to when I first met her. I remember standing in the Littauer library wearing my purple knit dress with matching shoes, purple paper violets behind one ear, and a gray kidskin cape I had bought in Filene's basement for ninety-nine dollars. By Haverhill's standards I was put together, but I faded back a step when Mrs. Littauer came sweeping in the front door wearing a full-length mink coat. Do you know what happens to a gray kidskin cape when it stands next to a full-length mink? It turns into what it really is: dead goats. I stood there trying to look chic and realizing I had, as my mother would say, "more than met my match."

From this moment on, I could see this elegant lady was firmly in control of every situation. Fred's Phlegmatic father had died a few years before, and she ran the household with authority and style. Her sons stood up when she entered the room, held her chair as she was seated, and ate only after she had lifted her fork. She kept everyone motivated to good deeds. She plumped pillows the moment your seat left the sofa, and she gave instructions to everyone as if we were all in first grade.

On one of my visits I was to spend the day alone at Orienta Beach Club while everyone else went to work. I had been there several times before and knew the way. "To make sure"—one of her Choleric expressions—Mrs. Littauer drew me a map and explained in detail what color building was on the corner at each turn and taught me the difference between North and South. I listened patiently while wondering how dumb she thought I was. As I was leaving, she called out, "Remember to turn left on the Post Road, not right or you'll overshoot the club." Then she added, as I soon learned she always did, "I've put my phone number on the bottom of the map for when you get lost."

When any one of her sons would be driving to New York City, she would tell them how to go, over and over again, even though they had been doing it since they were sixteen. One day Fred and I were taking Grandpa to the city and Mother Littauer made it very clear we should "take the Cross County, not Hutchison River." Since Fred is also part Choleric, he decided to go down the Hutchison River Parkway in spite of what she'd said. As we drove defiantly along, a patrolman pulled us over for speeding, and we were taken to the police station where Grandpa paid for the ticket. When we returned that night, Grandpa told Fred's mother about our troubles on the Hutchison River Parkway. She immediately looked at Fred and said, "What were you doing on the Hutchison River? I told you to take the Cross Country. If you'd gone where I told you to go, this wouldn't have happened."

Even though I didn't know about the different personalities then, I learned that if Fred's mother said, "turn left," I turned left. Cholerics constantly give instructions to "the dummies," and they are usually right.

After Fred and I were married and Mother Littauer would come to visit, I was shocked and hurt that she would dive into cleaning my house with a vengeance. Once she spent a full day on the stove, scrubbing each rod on the oven racks with Brillo. One February when she had cleaned everything imaginable, I came home to find she had brought in all the deflated pool rafts that had been folded up on the patio for the winter and laid them out on the kitchen counters where she was hard at work scrubbing them.

I used to get so crushed at her cleaning campaigns that I would polish for weeks ahead of her arrival so there would be nothing she could find to do. She didn't seem to notice and as she repolished shining shower doors, I would withdraw insulted. Once I began to understand the different personalities after fifteen years of marriage, I saw Mother Littauer in a new light: a Choleric person whose self-worth was wrapped up in accomplishing tasks and who couldn't relax. As I realized that, for her, work was fun and that doing nothing was a horrible waste of available manpower, I could accept her constant cleaning as her way of being a positive house guest and not as a criticism of my housekeeping. I stopped dreading her arrival and left the kitchen floor in need of a powerful waxing.

The last time she cleaned the stove I rewarded her by opening the top oven doors which automatically put on the light showing up the gleaming oven racks and I placed a potted philodendron on the top shelf to draw attention to the cleanest stove in town.

What a difference it makes in our attitude when we understand the other person's personality and know why they behave as they do.

Now I can see how Mother could go into Howard Johnson's on a rainy day and bring the whole restaurant to attention. My shy, Phlegmatic/Melancholy sister-in-law Nancy recalls how they entered the restaurant together. Mother saw there were two empty seats at the counter, one at one end and one at the other. Without a moment's hesitation, she picked up a knife from a man who was already eating and clicked loudly on his glass. As all eyes turned in astonishment, Mother Littauer announced, "My daughter-in-law is a little weak and she needs me to stay beside her. Would all of you please stand up and move yourselves down one seat so we can sit together at this end of the counter?"

Nancy watched in humiliation as each patron dutifully arose; shifted plates, silver, and glasses down one spot; gathered rain coats and umbrellas; and relocated without objection.

As Nancy collapsed in the newly vacated seat, Mother clapped her on the back and said proudly, "I did it for you, dearie."

As I thought over this Choleric woman, I truly wondered what ever gave her the idea that she was a peacemaker!

This question led me to a new study of the four personalities taking our ancestors into consideration. What are we really like? Are some of us playing a role written early in life by other authors?

Have some of us been wearing a mask for so long we think that's who we really are? What about you?

Do you have an underlying doubt as to who you are? Does your mother have a confused self-concept? Is your mate in an identity crisis? Start answering these questions by tracing your family back and seeing at what point your natural personality was turned in a different direction.

THE LITTAUER PERSONALITY TREE

As I reflected on Fred's grandparents and gathered information on them, I came up with a fascinating profile. Richard Oelkers was a self-made Melancholy/Choleric. His parents immigrated from Germany to New York, and his tailor father died when young Dick was fourteen. As the oldest of the family, he went to work to support the others. By long hours and extreme diligence, he fulfilled the American dream of rags to riches and never ceased to preach the work ethic. He married Maria Louisa Schissel and together they built a successful chain of millinery stores in New York. Maria Louisa was Sanguine/Choleric—she wanted everything done her way, but she wanted to have fun doing it. Grandpa wanted everything done his way, but it should be serious, purposeful, and not taken lightly.

I have learned that when two Cholerics are married, they do one of two things: either one puts on a Phlegmatic mask and plays a submissive role or they choose to fight. Grandpa and Grandma chose to fight. They scrapped for control constantly but seemed to thrive on controversy as is so typical of Cholerics.

Grandpa would today be called a workaholic and Grandma was a forerunner of women's lib. She "went to business" each day and had little interest in domesticity. A family joke was that Grandma's most complicated culinary achievement was three-layered Jello. Grandma's flair for glamor led her to change her name to fit the Hollywood image of the time. She went from German Maria Louisa to a French version, Marie Louise and later hyphenated it to Mari-Luise.

Fred's mother was born into this feisty family and was called Pearl Louise, a compromise name that neither one of the parents really liked. Shortly thereafter Grandpa won some money on a horse named Marita and he had the birth certificate changed to reflect his good fortune. Grandma liked the name better, but couldn't let anyone think she had given in to Grandpa so she always claimed she had found "Marita" in a romantic novel she had been reading.

Later when Fred's mother Marita gave birth to her first son, she named him Frederick Jerome Littauer, Jr., after her husband. The grandparents went into a Choleric tear and insisted the name be changed to Richard Oelkers Littauer after Grandpa. Threatened by disinheritance the new parents hastily made the change, and it wasn't until the second son, my husband, that the Phlegmatic father was allowed to name one after himself.

From the time Fred's mother was eleven, she ran the household. Her innate Choleric nature gave her the ability to take charge and raise her young brother, but when she was in her parents' presence, she played a submissive role. It was either fight or switch. Their word was law and they became as close to royalty as I've ever seen.

When I first met the Littauer-Oelkers family, I was amazed at the regal control which the grandparents had over everyone. We would all be sitting in the parlor and Mother would look up to see Grandma making a dramatic appearance down the circular staircase. Mother would rise to her feet, gesture toward the stairs, and sing out, "The Queen is here!" We would all stand and applaud as she made her entrance. Even her daytime dresses were dotted with sequins or beads, her neckline pulled low by a heavy diamond brooch and her fingers so bejeweled she could hardly lift them for her grand gestures.

What made Grandma's theatrics acceptable was her Sanguine wit and an occasional wink that let us see even *she* knew she was an act—but wasn't it fun! As Grandma stood centerstage, Grandpa lined up the grandchildren and with a brief clear message on the value of money, he would hand out quarters to each child who would kiss him. No kissey—no money. When my Lauren was little she refused to kiss Grandpa because "his face is prickly." He not only refused to give her a quarter, but he went into a sulking depression for the rest of the day.

I thought back over what Mother Littauer's childhood must have been like. Grandma saying, "You will do it my way and you will enjoy it." Grandpa saying, "You will do it my way and you will not laugh about it."

She had to work hard and be quietly obedient, she had to be the buffer between their Choleric tempers, she had to be serious and deep for Grandpa and yet imitate the Sanguine humor to keep her mother happy.

I can remember a visit to the Oelkers' apartment when they were both over ninety. Grandma sat at the head of the table waving hands heaped with diamonds at Mother who quickly responded in a servant's attitude. Grandma, just a touch senile, kept sending for the mythical chauffeur to take her to the ball. Grandpa, disgusted with her histrionics, tried to quiet her down, an effort which only made her more anxious to leave for the ball.

My husband, assuming a French accent, started charming Grandma by pretending to be the chauffeur. He kissed Grandma's hand and on up her arm while saying sweet nothings in pseudo French. Grandma giggled like a school girl and quickly fell in love with the "French chauffeur."

Grandma's memory at that point in her nineties lasted about two minutes, and she constantly asked us who we were. Because of this inability to know her own children, Grandma surprised us all when Fred walked in the next morning for breakfast and Grandma looked up with a radiant smile of recognition and exclaimed, "The French chauffeur is back!"

While Grandma was ever dramatic and the queen in her self-constructed castle to the very end, Grandpa was the hard pragmatist constantly commanding the real people around him. One day when Fred's mother was seventy-two she asked Grandpa if it would be all right if she went to the bank. He said, "No, you stay right here."

She replied, "Certainly, Daddy dear," and did not leave.

Now let's analyze this family situa
daughter born of two Choleric parents.
more Cholerics have? Fight or submit.
fought; their daughter gave in and play
came all things to both people: Grandma's
pa's serious business partner and a buff
them as they fluctuated between romance

No wonder when she analyzed herself she
She was the peacemaker, the mediator, the
had to be patient, keep her true feelings hi
purpose person. When she took the Personal
ceived herself as she was trained to be as a
at the words and resumed the daughter role
parents' lives until they died at ninety-seven a

What happens to a Choleric child who has
true feelings? What type of a mate does she cl
Phlegmatic role make her marry a Choleric?

As Lana Bateman and I have observed, we ha
people usually seek out the opposite of their true
even if it has been successfully masked for years. If t
is a "closet Choleric" he will probably marry a gentl
and then take over with a vengeance. The weddin
is like taking the cork out of a bottle. Out shoots
personality which takes over in the extreme to make
those unnatural years under pressure.

Fred's mother married a quiet, easy-going Phlegmati
of a wealthy silk-merchant. Before long he was brought
Oelkers' business, Bargain Bazaar, where he served duti
der the three Cholerics. Fred remembers little of his fathe
that he hardly ever spoke up and didn't attend the athletic
in which Fred participated.

Fred's natural temperament is Melancholy/Choleric li
grandfather and the sensitive part of him was frequently
because as the middle child of five, he was too young to get
privileges and too old to get the attention. Childhood movies sl
him crying frequently, and he was called "Lala" for his ma
tears.

Every time his Choleric part would try to win, he would eith
be ignored and thus become depressed, or thwarted and becom

Since his family was deeply involved in a cult that wor-
ppiness, both depression and anger were totally unaccept-
otions in his childhood.

uently he and his mother disagreed and she always won.
rents had always been victorious over her. Wasn't it her
ow?

once told me Fred was her worst child. "He always bucked
thing I told him to do."

d tried to be himself but that didn't work, so he put on a
uine mask as a teenager. He became the loudest boy in
y group and tried on dirty jokes for size, an effort rewarded
he nickname of Filthy Fred. He practiced fancy dives so that
time he went out on the board everyone would look up
watch him plunge into the pool.

What happens when someone tries to be something he isn't?
hen a serious Melancholy tries to be the life-of-the-party, people
k up and say, "Who does he think he is?" The answer is,
He has no idea!" How many confused teens I talk to today who
ave no idea who they are, who have tried to be what their
arents wanted when even their parents couldn't agree on a mu-
ual goal.

How helpful it is to understand these basic personalities and
know who we are. Only then is there any hope we can help
our children in their insecurities.

Because Fred felt emotionally neglected at home, although he
was physically well-provided for, he was constantly seeking attention and reading any rebuff as a rejection. He tried tears, athletic
prowess, and a Sanguine mask, but none brought him the love
and sense of approval he longed for. When I asked why he put
his Sanguine mask away, he thought back for a moment and
then replied, "When I realized it wasn't going over well."

In his relations with his mother, nothing went over well but
dutiful obedience. Since he loved her dearly and wanted to please
her, he learned in his late teens to agree with her and keep
his opinions to himself. He put away his Choleric desire for control and played Phlegmatic with his mother who responded well
to his new submissive spirit.

While Fred was attending the University of Miami, his father
died and Fred was the son available to return and take over
the male responsibilities of the home.

In order to show compassion for his mother and avoid conflict, he continued in a peace-keeping role through college and a brief stint in the army. When I appeared on the scene just before Fred was discharged, I saw him as the strong, silent type. He was extremely respectful to his mother, always calling her "Mother-dear," and I was impressed with how he put her needs before his own.

I remember the weekend I went down to visit and we had planned to go into New York City. At breakfast Mother announced, "Fred, today you will cane two chairs." I had no idea what caning a chair meant, but I learned as I sat all day watching Fred pull cords through chair seats. Fred's mother's wish seemed to be his command.

I expected this dutiful spirit would carry over into marriage. Had I understood the four basic temperaments then I would have assumed Fred to be Phlegmatic (agreeable peacemaker) and Melancholy (deep, thoughtful, and introspective) and myself to be Sanguine (life-of-the-party) and Choleric (let's get this show on the road.)

Surely a marriage made in heaven!

For Further Study, Thought, and Action

On the next page is the Littauer half of our family tree. As you record the husband's half of your tree, first write their names under each leaf and then insert the personality combination in each leaf. If you don't know what each ancestor was, ask questions.

Was he optimistic or pessimistic?

Was he controlling or passive?

Was he fun-loving or serious?

When looking at any given project did he want to talk about it? get to work on it? think about it? observe others doing it?

By asking questions such as these, you will be able to at least guess at what each person's personality was meant to be. Copy this tree into the notebook you've been keeping.

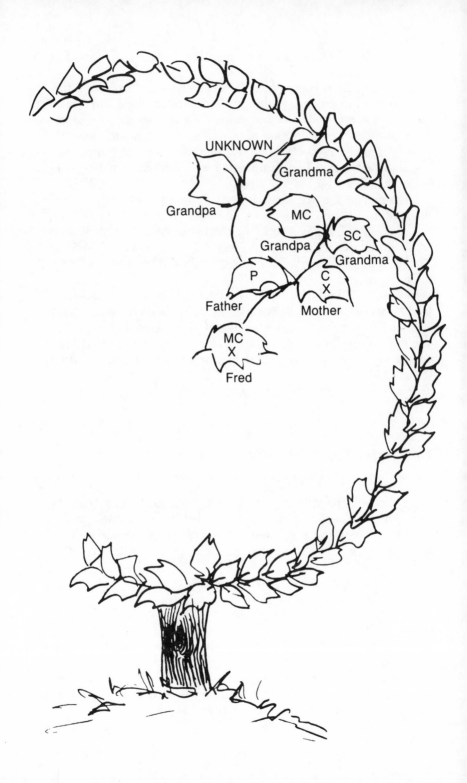

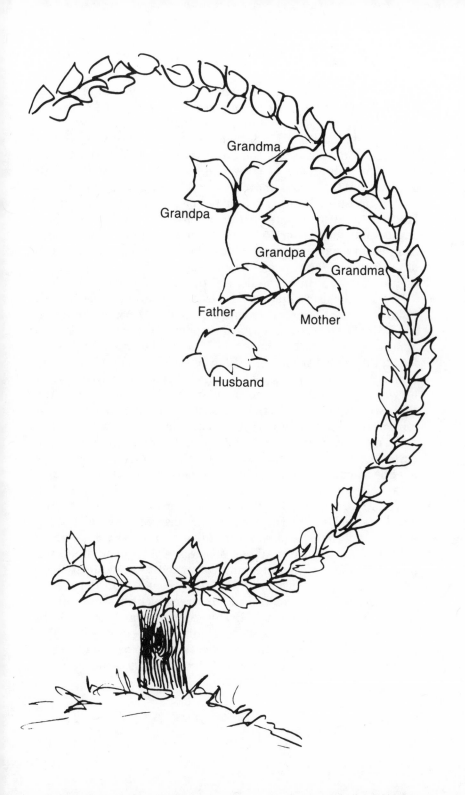

THE CHAPMAN FAMILY TREE

Today we often hear the expression "Here's where I'm coming from." Taken literally, we will all be able to understand ourselves better if we take the time to go back and find out where we're actually coming from. My father Walter Chapman was born in England, son of Thomas, the harness-maker, and Mariah, who died when Walter was fourteen and his brother Arthur was still a small child. Thomas moved the remaining family to Exter, New Hampshire, and my father became mother to his brother. His Sanguine/Choleric temperament gave him the ability to take charge and the humor to make the best of difficult situations. His formal education stopped when he was sixteen, but his love of the English language and history and his keen sense of politics and oratory kept him a student of the mind forever.

I remember as a child sitting next to the arch-shaped Zenith radio with my father as we both listened to Winston Churchill, Franklin Delano Roosevelt, Alf Landon, Wendell Wilkie and James Michael Curley (mayor of Boston who was convicted of fraud, ran for governor from jail, won the election and pardoned himself). Although Curley's honesty was frequently in question, he was a master orator who freely quoted Shakespeare and the Bible with equal ease. At the conclusion of each Curley broadcast Father would say, "Always listen to him, but never vote for him."

On my maternal side I remember my grandmother Florence Ann Conrad, a Phlegmatic/Melancholy milliner who sighed a lot. She had married James Ellis MacDougall, a Choleric carriage-maker.

Katie Florence MacDougall, my mother and their third child was born in Dartmouth, Nova Scotia, prematurely, with teeth and no fingernails, and was kept alive on the oven door which served as an incubator. When she was a few months old, the family moved to the States and continued to grow until there was Annie, Sadie, Katie, Willie, Ruthie, Jeanie, and Donnie.

While Grandma baked bread, preserved pickles, sewed all the clothes by hand, and made Easter bonnets, Papa kept a tight control on his brood of children, similar to the lead in the play *Life with Father*. When the five o'clock whistle blew on the roof of Judson's Carriage Factory in Merrimac, Massachusetts, the

MacDougall children ran from all over town to get home before Papa did or get a licking.

Music was the central core of family interest. Annie wrote poetry which Sadie, the pianist and organist, set to music. Katie played both violin and cello, Willie the cornet, Ruthie and Jeanie violin, and Donnie sang "Asleep in the Deep" and "The Lost Chord." They had their own chamber music ensemble. Sadie and Katie took advanced studies in Boston and later opened a studio together where they taught music. Their recitals included an orchestra of pupils with my mother, Katie, as the conductor.

Annie, Sadie, and Katie all married men about twenty years older than they were—father images, men who were about the same age as the girls' diminutive mother.

Katie was often sickly and was so frail and consumptive at the time of her wedding that the honeymoon was scheduled for the White Mountains where she could breathe cool, clear air. Walter, who had been a controlling adult since he was fourteen, became her new father and enjoyed protecting his delicate Phlegmatic/Melancholy bride.

By the time I was four and my brother James was a baby, the Depression had set in and money was scarce. Four years later when Ron arrived, I overheard Mother ask, "Will there be enough money to feed him?"

Each night when my father counted up the cash from the day's sales in our little Riverside Variety Store, my mother would sigh and worry.

Each morning at breakfast she would start with "Another day, another dollar." There was always another dollar when it was needed, but I grew up with the underlying fear that there might not be any money next week.

Another concern I had was my mother's health. When she had to go to the doctor's, I would accompany her on the bus. My father's last words would be, "You take care of your mother. Do you hear?" I heard what he said and what the doctor said as he gave me the instructions. "She needs to drink a half pint of heavy cream each day to put some meat on her bones. See that she takes three of these pills a day for her nerves. You make sure that she does it. Do you hear?"

Mother gagged on the heavy cream so I whipped it up and

put it on top of everything imaginable. I kept a mental record of when she took her pills and how often she ate as I felt responsible for her health.

I doted on my little brothers, protected them, helped with their homework, and represented my mother at P.T.A. In high school, I got on the high honor roll and desperately wanted to go to college, but there was no money, and my father felt what little might be found should be used for my brother James. "Boys need education more than girls." I persuaded him I had to go; I would get a scholarship, I would work to support myself, and I would put James through afterwards. The Choleric part of me loved goals and challenges and the Sanguine bounce kept me from seeing this project of putting myself and my brother through college as overwhelming. I would make it. I would have fun doing it. And I did!

I carried enough credits to graduate with three full majors and a minor. Not only that, but I stayed on the dean's list and received honors in speech. At the same time I performed in or directed many plays and musicals, was on the debate team, and orated myself into becoming the "Best Female Speaker in New England Colleges" in 1948.

My British father who had sent me to fifty-cent-an-hour elocution lessons from fourth grade on and who had taught me to recite poetry for minstrel shows was thrilled that I excelled in the one area where he had the greatest interest. Months before I got my degree, Dad dropped dead of a heart attack and my cheering section was gone. This encouraging, uplifting man with his English sense of humor, this store keeper whose personal charisma had caused customers to continue buying throughout the Depression, this father who would pat me on the back and say, "You can make it," was gone. Suddenly there was no one to play to; my grandstand was empty.

I had planned to teach as far away from Haverhill as possible, but now my mother needed me at home. If my father was light to me, he was life to her. For months she languished while a family friend ran the store, and in June, I moved back to those three little rooms behind the store. At twenty-one I took on a mantle of responsibility for my mother and two brothers. On thirty-three dollars a week I helped James through college and became mother-sister-friend-guardian-mentor-teacher to Ron.

With my mother's permission, I took control of the family and because my brothers are both Sanguine, I had fun doing it.

Mother slowly recovered, in spite of the harsh realities of her life. She continued to run the little store while Ron and I went off to Haverhill High School together each day.

When I met Fred I was attracted to his all-American good looks and to his deep and sensitive nature. He saw me as a ray of sunshine adding sparkle to his serious style. Although we knew nothing about personalities at that time, we were attracted to our opposite strengths; we innately looked for those positive qualities we lacked in ourselves.

Fred described us to his mother as "two irregular gears which, when turning towards each other, mesh perfectly." It sounded almost poetic.

Had we understood the four basic temperaments at that point, this is what we would have seen on the Chapman Personality Tree. (See p. 138.)

For Further Study, Thought, and Action

Following the instructions from the Littauer half, fill in the female half of your Personality Tree. Copy this into your notebook and add pictures.

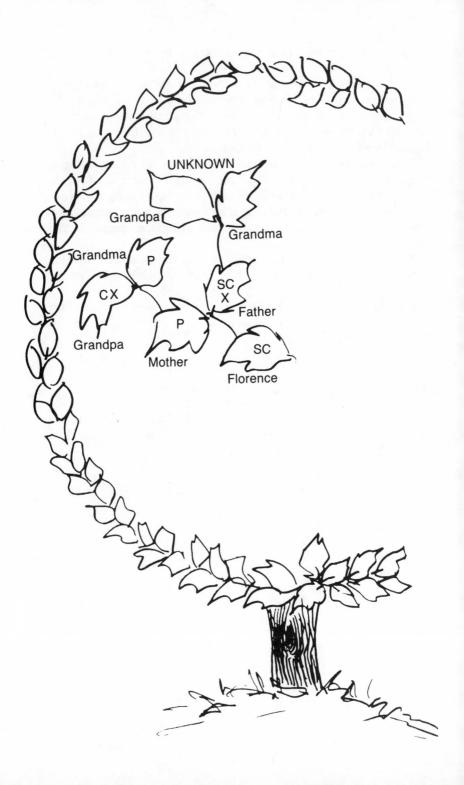

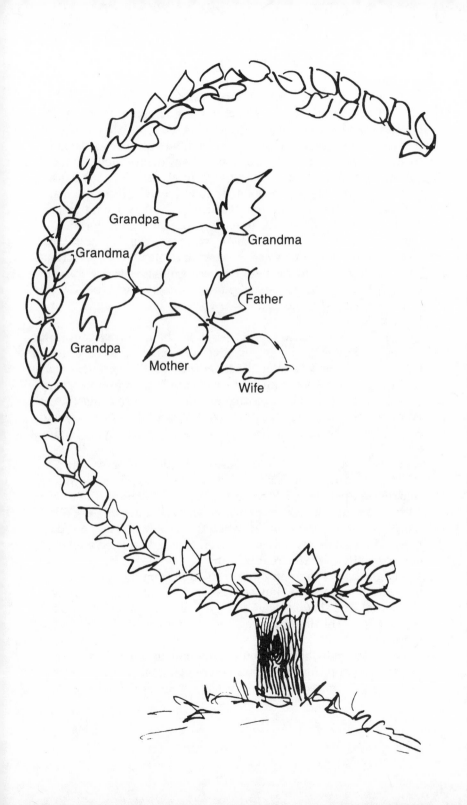

OUR PERSONALITY TREE

On the Oelkers branch we trace back to two Choleric grandparents who were attracted by each other's Sanguine/Melancholy opposites and who enjoyed scrapping throughout their seventy-five married years. Since each one ran into resistance in attempts to remake the other, they unconsciously threw their Choleric control and power onto their Choleric child. With such overwhelming pressure, she was forced to put on a Phlegmatic mask and become, against her own nature, a low-key mediator and the household manager at an early age. She sought permission for each step of life when in their presence, always nodded with "Yes, Daddy dear," and was still seeking to please her perfectionist father up until the moment he died at ninety-seven. For social occasions her mother insisted she be a charming hostess, and so she developed a Sanguine mask to put on for company and to satisfy her mother.

This Sanguine mask was an asset in their church, the Cult of the Perpetual Smile, as everyone was expected to be universally happy. They all smiled the same and talked cheerfully about the weather. It never rained on their parades. On Sundays they would put on a happy face, turn on their "infinite minds," and eliminate sin and mortal error from the earth. Their theme song was "Pack up your troubles in an old kit bag and smile, smile, smile."

Here was a lady with a confusing identity, to herself and to others, a natural Choleric who had to suppress her desire to control and put on a Phlegmatic mask of obedience alternated with a Sanguine mask of almost boisterous cheerfulness. What happens to a "closet Choleric" when this person marries a Phlegmatic? She takes over with a vengeance and so Fred's mother did. Possibly, had she really been able to "leave and cleave," she might have "come into her own" and been able to establish her inborn personality, but because her parents stayed strongly influential and they all worked together, she remained a mixed bag of tricks, shifting roles readily while in the middle of a sentence.

Her repressed Choleric would surge out in her raising of five children, instructing the maids before going off to business, and in dealing with people on a level below her brilliant abilities.

Fred's Melancholy caused him to pull back from her power and when he dared put forth a Choleric thought of his own, it caused conflict. His Melancholy tendency toward depression caused him to don a Sanguine mask during teen years in his quest for popularity and later a Phlegmatic mask to get along with his mother.

Again, what happens to a "closet Choleric" when he gets married? He takes over with a vengeance, and so Fred did. I'd been steeped in Sanguine fun and games and my Choleric had been in high gear from shepherding my mother, to supporting my brothers, to stimulating my students. I gave no thought to the realities of marriage as I expected to live happily ever after, so I was in for a shock when Fred announced he was putting me on a training program. It was a simple "shape up or ship out" approach and I became instantly submissive on the surface while chafing underneath.

Fred took off his Phlegmatic mask at the wedding (although he kept it in a drawer for when his mother came for a visit), and his strong Choleric control came out to join his perfectionistic Melancholy. He became a temperamental duplicate of his grandpa and forced me into a "yes, Fred dear" approach. I put on a Phlegmatic mask for the first time in my life. My Sanguine sense of humor was no longer found funny and any sign of Choleric decision-making was considered bucking for control.

As our children were born, Fred took over the complete direction. Nothing was left to chance. Before our first arrived, Fred wrote pages of sample names, assessing their value as to how each one would look on a high school diploma. Lauren Luise Littauer won. By the time of her birth, Fred had become somewhat discouraged with his training of me. My Phlegmatic mask often slipped revealing a rebellious spirit that Fred found frustrating.

Lauren represented a blank page, a new life untainted by the past, his chance to create a perfect child. His dedication to her training made my contributions superfluous, and I often felt like the proverbial fifth wheel. As the two of them became increasingly devoted to each other, I sometimes felt in the way, and when Fred and I would go into our bedroom, Lauren would sit sadly at the door awaiting Fred's return. In retrospect, I was somewhat the "other woman."

Both Lauren and I played Phlegmatic for Fred. When I left the house I became myself and achieved the presidency of each organization I touched. When Lauren got with her peers she became bossy and tried to run the nursery school. When Cholerics are held down at home, they will, without even knowing what they're doing, find something or someone to control. They may wear a Phlegmatic mask at home, but there's a Choleric will lurking underneath waiting for any chance to take over.

When Marita was born, four-year-old Lauren, looking for a project, took her on. Lauren was a mature and competent child and always assumed responsibility beyond her years. Lauren had learned that conscientious "good works" impressed her father and freed me up to have fun, so she became a junior mother.

Marita was bubbling and happy right from the beginning and she became my toy, my baby "Bundle." Now we each had a child who served our needs even though neither one of us would have admitted this division had it been pointed out to us at that time.

The next few years threw us all into a most unnatural situation as I gave birth, one after another, to two sons who were both fatally brain-damaged.

Lauren dedicated her little self to being their mother-nurse, and she was broken-hearted when the first one died and the second went to a children's hospital never to return. In those days no one talked about depression, there were no books or seminars on handling grief, and we were of the school "the less said the better," added to my mother's favorite cliché, "Never air your dirty wash in public."

Fred's Melancholy could not allow him to think that he could be responsible for two imperfect sons. His Choleric said, "Put it behind you and get on with life," and his religion taught, "Deny any sin, disease, or death and smile, smile, smile."

As Fred expanded his business and came home less, Lauren was deprived of her father's attention and her brothers' presence. My response to depression was to run away from it to theatrical productions where I could create fairy tales on a stage where they all lived happily ever after.

Neither Fred nor I spent time in self-analysis, counseling was unheard of unless you were crazy, and we both tried to make the best of two excruciatingly painful losses. In our quest for activities to keep us from crying round the clock, we didn't realize that Lauren's heart was breaking. We neither discussed the babies' incurable problems or explained where each one had gone. "She's just a child. She'll get over it."

She never really "got over it" and she has written an impressive chapter, "The Forgotten Griever," in her helpful book *What You Can Say When You Don't Know What To Say.*

During that period of mourning we were all depressed in different ways. The Sanguine in me could see no hope for fun at home any more so I went to seek diversions. The Melancholy in Fred could see no hope in a family that would never be perfect so he stayed at business where he could direct the details. The Choleric in Lauren had learned that no matter how hard her young self tried, she had no control over her circumstances. She had nowhere to go, and she wore a dutiful Phlegmatic mask. Marita was too young to be involved in the tragic circumstances so she remained happily above it all and became our dose of much needed sunshine.

Lauren grew up seriously, obediently without rebellion. She was always mature beyond her years, stayed close to her father in business, and was the family's rock of dependability. What happens to a "closet Choleric" when she gets married? She chooses a Phlegmatic and takes over quickly.

Because Lauren and her delightfully easy-going husband Randy had studied the different personalities before marriage and knew what they could expect from each other in both strengths and weaknesses, they have been able to accept each other realistically as they are and not try to transform each other.

They now have two boys, Randy, Jr., a Melancholy/Choleric, and Jonathan, a Sanguine/Choleric personality duplicate of his Aunt Marita and perhaps a little like me! With a newly added Bryan Frederick, what a challenge Lauren and Randy have to raise these three as they were created to be and not try to mold them into the "perfect" children they might want. It's time to break the cycle of Cholerics being forced to wear Phlegmatic masks and to train up these children in the way each one should go.

Tracing My Roots

While I was writing this book, Fred and I went back to my home area in Massachusetts. Our first stop on our roots trip was the MacDougall home in Merrimac where my mother was brought when she was less than a year old. Even though some new rooms had been added on the back, the frame of the house was just as it was when I got married from it in 1953. As Fred took pictures, standing at the foot of the cracked cement front walk, I wandered around the side to the grape arbor where I had picked Blue Concords as a child. The present owners, the Lavelles, who had purchased the house from my mother in 1959, were at home and warmly invited us in.

Upstairs I stood in the front bedroom where Grandma Mac had given birth to her last four babies. I pictured each one in the handcarved cradle Grandpa Mac had created that sits in my living room today. As I descended the narrow stairs to the front hall, I saw the sparkle of the square window full of colored glass where I as a child had sat on the steps with my little brothers trying to catch rays of color in our hands.

A lump came into my throat as the setting sun danced rainbows of memories into my life.

We moved into the parlor where my mother had been married by the bay window and where I had played the wedding march on the piano while my mother accompanied on the violin when Aunt Sadie Beatrice MacDougall, in her fifties, had wed Charlie Porter the upholsterer.

Mrs. Lavalle reminded me that Grandma Mac had been "laid out" in front of that same bay window where the sisters had said their vows before the soft syllables of Reverend Loud.

As I looked around this room, where as children we could only enter if we were good, it seemed strangely empty without the huge portrait of Queen Victoria that had stared sternly down upon us.

The dining room was just the same except that Aunt Sadie's piano, where she'd taught me and many other little ones their scales, was missing. I could easily remember those Christmases around what could have been the same table, especially after Aunt Sadie married Charlie and he brought his sister Carrie Bacon for the holidays. She was both a foot doctor and hairdresser and I can still hear my father say, "She tries to make both ends meet."

As I looked at the table, I remembered how upset my mother got when Dad encouraged Carrie to do her infamous imitation of a sea gull during Christmas dinner, causing little brother Ron to laugh so hard he spit his milk out on the table.

Oh, what memories flood back when we stand in the traces of former times.

A visit to the Locust Grove Cemetery was a personal parade into the past. Grandma and Grandpa MacDougall, the founders of our clan, their names chiseled on the same stone with Aunt Sadie's. Behind them lay Aunt Annie with her husband Benjamin Franklin Sargent and their son James who'd been killed in the Battle of the Bulge when I was in high school. Across the way was Uncle Willie and his infant son William, Jr., and a marker for Uncle Donald's baby grandson. I told Fred what I could remember of each person, and he got to know those in my family he'd never met.

An added note of sadness struck both of us as we knelt by the stone of my father "Walter Chapman, 1878–1948," and the fresh markings of "Katie F. Chapman, 1898–1984."

That same day we went back to Mitchell's Department Store where I had my first job selling chocolates, to the defense factory where I worked one summer in a noble effort to help win the war, to Haverhill High School where I attended and taught so many years ago, and to the Riverside Variety Store, now turned into apartments. As we drove away from Haverhill Fred said, "This has been one of the most beautiful days we've ever spent together."

Littauer Family Personality Tree

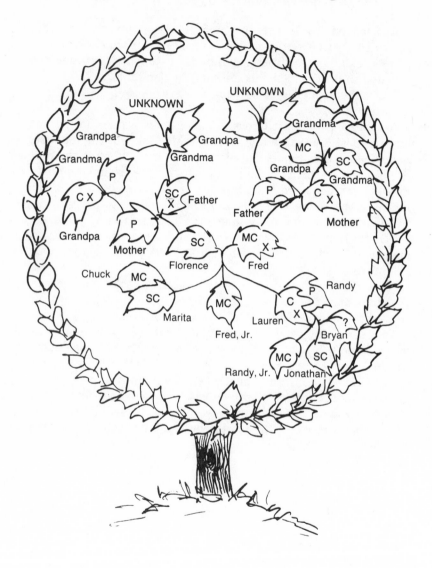

YOUR PERSONALITY TREE

So often as young couples marry, they assume that because they are in love and are Christians all will be well with their souls. They quote, "Love covers a multitude of sins," (1 Pet. 4:8 RSV) and "Perfect love casts out fear" (1 John 4:18, RSV).

The maiden marries a robust acorn and expects him to grow into a mighty oak. She'll fertilize him into strength and prune him into shape. She forgets that as the twig is bent so will it grow. She assumes that once she transplants him into her yard, the fresh air will do him good and he will leave behind the aroma of the little bushes he buddied up with on the old plantation.

She doesn't realize that when she pots up this one sapling to take him home to her garden, she's buying a whole forest of family—parents, siblings, aunts, uncles, grandparents. He may renounce them or refuse to see them, but he can't remove their influence for they all came out of the same package of seeds. Some may be bigger, better, or brighter, but they've got the same rootstock underneath.

Since you, at your best, cannot weed out the whole heritage, even though you can clearly see the crabgrass in the other family, you would do better to research their history, write down what you find, and recognize the repeated traits. You will then find the reasons for reactions your mate has that have nothing to do with your behavior.

I used to think that if Fred had married anyone but me, he could have been happy. But as I traced back his family, I found that before he even met me, he had a Melancholy personality that was predetermined to persist until he produced a perfect wife no matter who she started out to be. If Fred had married the Proverbs 31 woman, he would have made her get up earlier than dawn, polish the gates where he sat, and stop wearing purple. I used to encourage our children to rise up and call me blessed but only so we would present a unified front of insurrection as we mutinied against our master.

Now that I've spent time perusing Fred's predecessors and see him as a duplicate of his grandfather, I can accept that he came to me prepackaged as a pure progeny of his past and that I'm not his problem. What a relief!

As I've learned that "closet Cholerics," those made to play a

Phlegmatic role in the past, take over their mates with a passion for producing perfection, I can see why he put me on a training program. I can let him alphabetize the spices and not take it as a weakness in me that I had basil behind salt.

As Fred has examined my background of taking charge of everybody from the time I was a child, he now can accept a directive statement from me without expecting me to wrest control of his life away from him. Now that he understands how my mother unintentionally planted seeds of poverty in my mind, he can see why I seem to be preoccupied with ready cash.

There are two major reasons for taking the time to plot out your Personality Trees: You'll see where you've all come from and why you are the way you are; then you'll be aware of what you are passing on to your children when you have no understanding of their individual needs or personality profiles.

In the process of researching these forebears, you may get acquainted with some fascinating faces of the past who step into the reality of the present.

As you look at our completed tree do you see how Grandma and Grandpa Oelkers were the same personality pattern as Fred and me? How Fred's mother, Fred, and Lauren had the same traits and as Cholerics were forced into unnatural submissive roles? Do you see how the three of them before marriage, and me after marriage, had to wear Phlegmatic masks for survival? Do you see how easily we fall into raising our children as we want them to be, according to our personalities instead of helping them develop their own unique God-given abilities?

Fred's mother didn't have a chance to be herself. She was a natural Choleric with a touch of Melancholy depth, forced to wear a Phlegmatic mask for her father and a Sanguine one for her mother. I had personally felt there was little hope of ever understanding her, but that was before two things happened. Fred and I committed our lives to the Lord Jesus, and we plunged into a personality study of ourselves, trying to restore our lost years that the locusts had eaten.

We stopped attending the "Cult of the Perpetual Smile" where the whole church was a grand masquerade. We'd been so disillusioned when our sons had not been healed by their religious practices and I'd been told it was all my fault. "These babies are perfectly healthy and the error is in your mind. When you can see them as whole, they will be whole."

It had been hard to pretend that my convulsive babies were normal and to force a smile on Sundays, so I was relieved to attend a church where I didn't have to play charades and where God's Word was preached clearly.

One Sunday evening when Fred's mother was visiting, the pastor gave an altar call, and our family was stunned as Mother pushed past us in the pew, walked up the aisle and committed her life to the Lord Jesus. As the Lord began to work in her heart, she needed her masks less and less and she allowed herself to reveal the realities she'd hidden even from herself.

I found we had something sincere to talk about, and as we both changed for the better, we were drawn together in a mutual "open-heart operation."

What a blessed opportunity you have right now to examine your family background for a cushion of knowledge and then prayerfully seek God's wisdom. Open your eyes and view the vision that he has in mind for your children so that you won't be guilty of changing his plans.

What happens when we try to change other people? Even if we're successful and get a Choleric so under control, he appears Phlegmatic, or a Melancholy forcing big smiles to appear Sanguine, or a Phlegmatic exhausting himself trying to run up mountains, or a Sanguine following charts so closely he's no fun any more—what if we are successful? What do we have on our hands? A person who has no idea who he really is.

It's like crossing a Poodle with a Schnauzer. The puppy's cute, but what is it?

For Further Study, Thought, and Action

God created each one of us as individuals with different personalities, strengths, and weaknesses. If he'd wanted us to be alike, he could have created us that way. Since he didn't, our job is (1) to find out what our natural personality is and who we really are so we can function at our maximum ability and (2) to make sure we're not changing our children into confused mongrels.

Before reading further, stop and think about your family background. Join your two halves together and fill out Your Personality Tree. How I wish I'd done this years ago before my father and Fred's father were gone, taking with them the knowledge of their parents. You will be amazed as you question grandparents and older aunts and uncles at how much you can learn about family personalities and how much they will love you for caring enough to ask.

As you're filling in the different temperament combinations, your eyes may be opened as to why your mate is one way with you and a different personality with his mother; or one way at home and one way at work. You may see repetitions in succeeding generations and become aware of masks that some have worn based on parents' personalities or extraneous circumstances. Try to find your original God-given temperament pattern, for we can only function in our fullest capacity when we know who we really are.

Put your complete tree in your personality notebook.

In the process of digging up information for your Personality Tree, you may want to take a trip back to your hometowns, as Fred and I did while I was writing this book. Take pictures of significant landmarks and include these in your notebook for the enjoyment of your family. You may even want to organize a family reunion. Be creative. My sister-in-law Katie designed T-shirts for her Tharp Family Reunion. On the front of each shirt she put the individual's name, and on the back she put a silkscreen of the entire family tree. On the first night of the reunion she gave each member of the family his or her own personalized family tree T-shirt.

Each one of us has a fascinating background, a cast of characters that would defy fiction. How often we let it all slip by without sharing it with our partners or our progeny. How much we could learn about each other's personality if we'd take the time to find out where we've really come from.

I heard Alex Haley on a TV talk show and the host asked, "Where did you get your material and your storytelling ability for *Roots?*"

Alex replied, "From sitting around the cracker barrel with my father listening to all the men tell stories of how life used to be." He told of this rich tradition where the men passed down the family tales to the boys at the general store and the women did the same for their girls in rocking chairs on the front porch.

What a shame it is that so many of us today watch television versions of other people's lives instead of passing on our own heritage while rocking on the front porch.

Start today to make a Personality Tree of your background. Whenever you find an ancestor whom you don't know, ask some relative about him, settle down by the cracker barrel and be prepared to hear a story that may defy the "soaps."

Never be afraid when God brings back the past. Let memory have its way. It is a minister of God . . . who will turn the 'might have been' into a wonderful culture for the future.[2]

Your Family Personality Tree

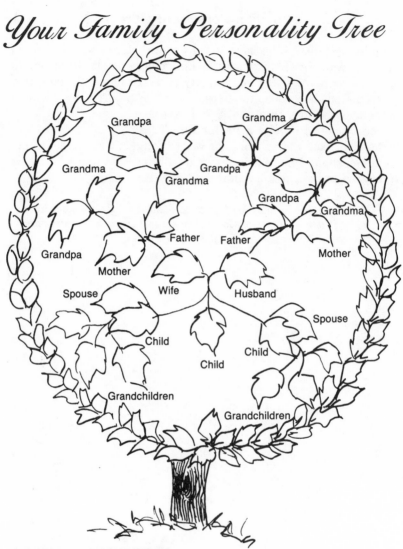

Grandpa · Grandma · Grandma · Grandpa · Grandma · Grandpa · Grandma · Grandpa · Grandma · Father · Father · Mother · Grandpa · Mother · Spouse · Wife · Husband · Spouse · Child · Child · Child · Grandchildren · Grandchildren

GENERAL INSTRUCTIONS

1. With help of spouse, complete your "Family Personality Tree" in pencil.
2. Starting with yourselves, mark in each leaf, the primary and secondary personality traits of each person. (i.e., "SC" = Sanguine/Choleric)
3. Put an "X" in the leaf of the <u>one</u> partner of each couple on the tree whom you perceive to be the dominant personality.
4. Now fill in the personality traits of all other persons as indicated.
5. Consider which ones may be wearing, or have worn a mask.

Fred and Florence Littauer • 1814-E Commercenter West • San Bernardino, CA 92408 • (714)888-8665
Tree designed by Gretchen Jackson

❧ 8 ❧

What Are Your Children's Personalities?

Tis education forms the common mind
Just as the twig is bent the tree's inclined[1]

As I have taught *Personality Plus* over the years, some of the most gratifying results have come when parents suddenly realize why they haven't been able to understand a certain child. One couple came up to me and said, "You have just saved our child's life." The father, a Choleric, then explained his problem with what was obviously a Phlegmatic boy. "I just can't get him moving. No matter how I bribe him or threaten him, he just won't jump! This morning on the way to the seminar I said to my wife, 'That kid has got to shape up or I'm going to kill him.' I've always had pep and ambition and this kid is never going to make it."

The Melancholy mother added, "He's really a sweet boy; he never gives us a moment's trouble and everyone loves him but us. Now that I see he is Phlegmatic and that we've been trying to make him Choleric like his father and that's not going to work, I feel so guilty."

The father added, "I really thought there was something wrong with him, but now I see he's just different from me and that's okay. You've saved the boy's life."

How many fathers are there like this man who assumed his son would be like him and when he didn't perform, let him know how disappointed he was. Without an understanding of the temperaments we assume everyone ought to function as we do, and

153

when they don't, we abandon them emotionally and give our attention to the one who fulfills our image of what a child should be.

Another couple came up to me to discuss their twelve-year-old twin sons. One was Melancholy and one Sanguine. They had shared the same bedroom since they were born and had been in the same school class each year. The Melancholy boy was serious, a good student, well-behaved, and kept his half of the room neat. His parents both complimented him in front of the brother, and then they would admonish the Sanguine by saying, "Why aren't you like your brother?" The boy got the same comments from the teachers as he seldom did his homework on time and talked when he was supposed to be quiet. His parents looked at his popularity as a negative since he tied up the phone, and the teachers didn't find his spontaneous humor to be funny but a class distraction. Because no one understood the boy's temperament, he was constantly the bad guy, and one day he came home from school and went berserk. He pulled the sheets off the brother's bed, emptied all the drawers onto the floor and pulled the drapes, fixtures, and all off the walls. When his mother yelled at him to stop wrecking the room, he lunged at her and pushed her to the floor. He ran wildly through the house as she called the police who came and strapped his hands behind his back and took him off to the mental ward.

As the mother told me this sad story, the boy was still in the hospital where he was being tranquilized and counseled by a Melancholy therapist who was trying to make him perfect like his brother. The mother cried as she realized what they had all done to this Sanguine child who just wanted to have fun and instead was laden with guilt that he was never going to be good enough for his parents' approval.

Unfortunately, this boy is not an isolated case. According to the data compiled by the House Select Committee on Children, Youth, and Families, admissions to inpatient psychiatric services of children under eighteen more than doubled between 1970 and 1980. Between 1980 and 1984 adolescent admissions to private psychiatric hospitals increased more than 350 percent.[2]

The use of drugs at a young age and early sexual promiscuity account for many of the teen problems and are situations which were not heard of twenty years ago, but the majority of the young patients are under treatment for general depression. Ralph Alsopp, an Atlanta psychologist reports that the teenagers he sees "feel helpless, not in control of their lives. Their support structures are falling away."[3]

As I have talked with depressed teens, some who have attempted suicide, they all indicate a vague feeling of not knowing really what's wrong with them, and they seem to have no sense of who they are.

While I am not so naive as to think a knowledge of the temperaments would solve the problems of troubled youth today, I do know from my own family experience and the hundreds of other families I've counseled over the years that when they will take the time to sit down as a family and check off the profile together there will be a positive result. Possibly if we sat down and played a national game of Monopoly, family life would also improve, but I know if we were able to discuss in a nonjudgmental manner the strengths and weaknesses of each family member and let them see their uniqueness, we would not have so many young people wandering around wondering who they are and trying to find themselves.

Why don't we Christian families make it a point to develop each child according to his talents and temperament? Doesn't Proverbs 22:6 tell us to "Train up a child in the way *he* should go" (italics mine) not in the way *we* dreamed up? What guidelines do we have available by which to measure their abilities? Do we have to take them to a psychiatrist?

Dr. Judith Wallerstein, speaking about adolescent insecurities on the "Good Morning America" television show said, "They are in so many changes, physically and emotionally, that they desperately need coherent rules and family stability."[4]

As Fred and I ask our children what was meaningful to them in our bringing them up, they mention the family meetings where we set the rules of operation for the family. They will admit they were a little apprehensive about what new standards would be set each time, but there was a feeling of security in knowing there were some accepted standards. Understanding their personal abilities and temperaments was the other major plus they remember.

I had always assumed that since education was such a high priority for Fred and me that my children would all go to college.

Since I worked literally night and day to get myself through college when there was no money available, I knew my children, without this struggle, would be excited to go. Lauren followed what I felt was a normal program. She got excellent grades in high school and majored in business and psychology at Cal State, San Bernardino. She married a brilliant numismatist and is raising three boys, the three little Briggs. Her Choleric nature with a secondary in Melancholy has made her both capable and sensitive to others. She helps her husband with his stamp and coin gallery, has been on the stage since I put her in a Christmas play at the age of four, and is both a speaker and author of a most helpful book, *What You Can Say When You Don't Know What To Say.*

Had I stopped with Lauren I might have been a little smug about my motherhood abilities; having Sanguine/Choleric Marita who was going to do things her way right from the beginning showed me differently. While Lauren wanted me to be room mother, Marita tried to keep me away from school. Mischievous would have been a mild term for Marita.

One night when I was prepared to go to PTA in her junior year of high school, she suggested I stay home as I looked so tired and needed rest. Since she was right, I almost fell for her ruse, but a flood of good sense came over me and I pulled myself together and went. When I arrived in Algebra, the teacher said she did all right when she came but somehow his class frequently interfered with her lunch at McDonalds. The typing teacher suggested she drop the course and the French teacher said she couldn't keep her quiet. Only in scuba diving where she was the only girl in a class of boys was the male teacher enthusiastic; however, I wasn't sure she was good enough to make a living scuba diving.

Had I not known her temperament pattern and been assured of her basic intelligence, I would have been a wreck trying to get her through school, but since I knew she could achieve anything she wanted to do and could charm her way through the rest, I didn't waste much time in worry. I was amazed when the guidance counselor phoned me in Marita's senior year of high school. I assumed Marita was going to be reprimanded for cutting too many classes, but instead the counselor said Marita was so far ahead of the others that they were going to graduate her early. Right then I knew the whole educational system was in trouble.

Instead of going to Vassar or Radcliffe or Westmont or Biola, Marita went to the local junior college, started her own business at eighteen, traveled with me learning to be a speaker and now is a full-time Christian speaker and on our CLASS staff. I am so grateful that I did not try to push her into a "perfect child" mold. Instead, I encouraged the talents she had in verbal skills and didn't worry about college degrees.

Young Fred never liked school and even though he went away to college for one year, he left to come back and take over his father's car business. He likes cars and cares little for books. He is a deeply sensitive Melancholy and has never moved as fast as Fred and I would have liked, but we have accepted his choices, encouraged his strengths, and praised his sweet spirit.

Two years ago when I went on a speaking tour through Europe I took young Fred along. There was a girl who followed me around taking my picture whenever I was in a somewhat ungainly position. One day she said to me, "Your son sure loves you a lot." She then told me that the day before on the bus I had fallen asleep with my head against the window. She had thought a picture in this position would be humorous so she had focused on me from across the aisle. As she was peering through the lens a dark shadow filled the square and she looked up to see young Fred leaning across in front of me. He asked, "What are you planning to do?"

She replied, "I'm going to take a picture of your mother asleep."

He stated, "No you're not. You will *never* take a picture of my mother without asking her permission first."

The girl had been stopped in her little tracks, and Fred didn't move until she had put the camera away. He never mentioned what he'd done, but she didn't take any more pictures of me without asking me first.

There may be some mothers with sons who have gone to Harvard or Stanford or Yale, but I doubt they have ever been touched so deeply by the loving protection of their young man as I was by Fred's.

We have learned in our family to train up our children in

the way each one of them should go according to their abilities and temperament even if it was not always what we originally had in our minds.

How many young people I talk to who have been pushed into schools or careers where they didn't want to be, have socialized with the right people at the right club, even married the catch of the town and yet have never had an independent thought of their own and are miserable.

In the other direction, how many parents have let their young men and women do their own thing with so little guidance or encouragement that they are still wandering aimlessly in life not having quite settled on anything?

We are to train them up—guide them, love them, discipline them—but in the way *they* should go, according to their own personality traits. We will never regret the time we spend with each child showing him his unique strengths that may be nothing like those of his brother and making him aware of his weaknesses so he will know what he needs to overcome to be his own brand of success in life.

Lana Bateman remembers the first time she heard Haddon Robinson, Dean of Homiletics at Dallas Theological Seminary, explain this verse.

> He said that the original Hebrew was more literally translated, "Train up a child according to his way. . . ." It wasn't until I understood the temperaments that I began to realize what this verse really meant. Did every child have a particular way to be raised? Did that mean that all children should not be treated the same way?
>
> Within the confines of my childhood family, there was a certain pride taken in the fact that all three children were treated and raised the same way. I'm afraid that most parents feel this attitude is the fair and correct one for raising more than one child. What a tragedy, for if the words of this proverb are true, then each child has a certain bend which makes him/her different from every other child in the family. This unique being would require a special understanding in order to draw each one to his/her greatest potential for living a wise and full life. We as parents have an obligation and duty before God to discern the way of each child and endeavor to maximize strengths and diminish weaknesses in the most loving way possible. With an understanding of the temperaments, we have tools readily available.

Cathye Stout of Austin, Texas, wrote me the following after hearing me teach about the temperaments.

> . . . each of my three teenagers and husband (only one of him!) evaluated themselves and then each other.
>
> This was used as a great tool for family discussion (the TV actually went off before 10:30) as we looked at our strengths *and* weaknesses.
>
> It led into our nightly family devotions and prayer. Out of our strengths, we were able to praise and thank the Lord for the gifts and abilities He created us with. We reaffirmed our commitment to give back to Him what He's given us, for *His* honor and glory and His use.
>
> And out of our weaknesses we could see where improvement was needed in each of us. . . .

Debby Laurie of El Toro, California, wrote me the results of her teaching her two children, eleven and fourteen, to understand the temperaments.

> They never cease to be a daily help. One day our kids figured out the 'First Family.' Eve was a definite Sanguine. She'd talk to anyone, even a snake. Adam was Phlegmatic. When it came time to make the important decision whether to eat or not to eat he let Eve influence him. She was much better at decisions anyway. Abel was Melancholy. He made the perfect sacrifices, and that garden was so tidy and precise. Cain, the Choleric, got so mad at his brother he decided to take matters into his own hands. He felt the end justified the means. And there we have it: the birth of the four personality types!

Who knows what kind of a discussion your family may have, but it will surely be better than TV!

YOUR CHILD'S TEMPERAMENT

Although you probably understand the basics of the temperaments by now, let's apply the principles as they relate to children and see what we can learn about training our children in the way they should go. We must realize first that young children grasp love in two ways. One is physical touching, hugging, kissing, and affirming; and the other is verbal communication given by parents who take the time to get to know their children and listen to what they're saying. I remember when Marita was first reading books and she would want to tell me the story. She would follow me all over the house and the book review was longer than it took to read the book. When I would stop, sit down and listen, the review would be much shorter, but as long as I kept moving the review kept going. She could make the *Cat in the Hat* sound like *Gone with the Wind!*

A child who does not have the warm physical touch of a loving parent and the open communication that child desires will grow up with a deep unfulfilled longing for love and may end up "looking for love in all the wrong places."

Beyond this universal need for love in each child, there is a personality need. Understanding the temperaments gives us a special grasp of the particular "way" or need of each child.

As the twig is bent, the tree will grow. Is it true? Let's take a look at some twig-benders and let you decide for yourself.

SANGUINE

Your lively, bright-eyed Sanguine child is full of curiosity and laughter. He may not always have an audience, but that never seems to stop the constant chatter which is the first step toward that center stage personality. This child is full of wonderful creative ideas but is often defeated in carrying them out by a short attention span which keeps this child from doing as well as others academically. He will, however, excitedly strive to be in any production the class has to offer, from singing to playing the bird-whistle in the rhythm band. Education takes a back seat to more important pursuits such as cheerleading, drama class, student . council, dancing lessons, or anything else that will provide an escape from the books.

Look for this child to come up with endless excuses when facing confrontation, not because of a need for peace which is the Phlegmatic's reason for avoiding conflict, but because of his deep need to be accepted. Your disappointment or anger spells rejection to this temperament and is to be avoided no matter how many excuses the child makes.

Popularity is an overwhelming need for this boy or girl. The lack of it can cause a great deal of pain and frustration for there is no other temperament that needs social acceptance as badly as this one. Because of this need, the Sanguine child is the most likely to "go along with the crowd" or be drawn into an unwise situation. If he is a Sanguine/Choleric he will be more bossy and organized; if he is Sanguine/Phlegmatic, he'll have fun but never get his act together and not even care.

Tools to Help[5]

1. Have the child tested at a children's learning center or with a child psychologist to determine the area of creativity and aptitude.

2. Encourage this child in the areas of performance singing, dancing, acting, speaking, art, design, sports, scouts, or group play. This child is very active and needs something exciting going on every minute. Because of a short attention span, this child will have some difficulty with those pursuits such as piano that require practice and will need an adult to sit with him on the bench in order to give constant encouragement and approval. Unfortunately he will only do well if the duty can be made into a game, for only with a prize ahead will the Sanguine child keep pressing toward the goal. In some cases, simple peer approval will suffice, but if the parent desires a final accomplishment, he will probably need to hang in there with the child to produce results.

3. The parent of a Sanguine child must carefully weigh the wisdom of allowing each activity, keeping in mind this child's deep need for acceptance and knowing they always want to do what "everybody" is doing. You can be encouraged by knowing if you don't let them go to some event, they will soon forget and not hold grudges or sulk long.

4. This child has a greater need for physical affection than any of the other temperaments so parents need to do a lot of hugging, holding, and touching.

5. Start early to teach this child the discipline of a clean room and the importance of handling money wisely. Understand that you will have to stay right with this offspring to guarantee any kind of results. Without such a commitment from parents, this child can easily slip into irresponsibility and never quite grow up.

6. Understand that when your Sanguine child tells a fib, it is out of a deep need for approval. Find other healthy ways to give that approval as you deal with this problem and praise them for telling the truth. Some of their colorful stories get such attention that they begin to believe what they're saying.

7. Find at least one thing your Sanguine child can do well and then encourage, encourage, encourage. Sanguines have the greatest potential, but often fall far short of the mark when parents don't understand their needs.

8. Remember that a Sanguine child will do more through one word of encouragement than he will ever accomplish through your yelling, criticizing, or constant spanking.

9. Don't foster negative behavior by telling everyone how cute she was when she did it. Marita used to take money from my purse and then go down the hill behind our house and buy me a plant from the florist. She was so adorable bringing me presents that I would praise her for thinking of me. Suddenly I realized I was promoting stealing as long as she spent the money on me.

Remember

Virtually every move this child makes is based upon a desire to have FUN and a driving need for APPROVAL with a deep sensitivity to even the slightest possibility of rejection. The Sanguine child must be a part of the gang, whoever the gang is today.

MELANCHOLY

Your Melancholy baby came into the world with intensity written all over his face. When we adopted Fred the case worker said, "He lies quietly in the crib analyzing everyone who goes by. This is that special infant of whom everyone says, 'Doesn't he look intelligent? Are you sure he's not a big person in a little person's body?' "

Intensity is a word that cannot be overworked for this little one feels, thinks, reacts, responds, and reflects everything deeply. In *Parade Magazine* there was an article "When Your Baby Seems Depressed." The author, Susan Lapinski, described a perfect Melancholy baby and pointed out how parents with what appears to be a depressed baby feel they must have done something wrong. They assume the baby doesn't like them, and they don't know what to do. "The goal of the therapists is to help parents avoid a build-up of problems that can send a whole family into worry and despair. These problems usually spring from an inability to understand and cope with a baby's puzzling temperament."[6]

Throughout the article health professionals describe the Melancholy baby, but without ever using the term or explaining why some children are so different. They suggest that parents not blame themselves but "concentrate on respecting the baby's individual personality and on reacting appropriately to the baby's responses."[7] Even though the depressed babies they describe are not compared with the Sanguine (bubbly), Choleric (demanding), or Phlegmatic (passive), Dr. T. Berry Brazelton of Children's Hospital, Boston, does conclude, "Babies are competent little numbers. They can tell you a lot. And when you can spot the differences in your baby and value them, being a parent becomes a lot more rewarding and a lot more fun."[8] He's right and that's why it's so important that we know all the types so we won't think we've got the only unusual baby in town.

Of all the temperaments, the Melancholy is the most deeply creative and genius-prone. Some parents may actually feel threatened by the innate mental capacities of such a child. Sadly, the Melancholy child cannot grasp why no one else seems to experience such depth of emotion and understanding, why no one else seems to care.

In early childhood, your Melancholy boy or girl will cling most closely to you and will have the greatest need to have parents physically present. This temperament can be damaged by neglect or abuse during childhood more than any other personality due to his deep sensitivity and propensity to withdraw when he really wants to reach out.

Through Lana Bateman's counseling in Philippian Ministries, she notes that many alcoholics, drug addicts, and homosexuals appear to be of the Melancholy temperament. It isn't difficult to understand why when we think of how easy it is to wound or scar such gentle, sensitive children and how their insecurities make them vulnerable to outside substances which offer to give them confidence or relieve their depression.

The intelligent Melancholy offspring will seldom need prodding, for he will be a good student with very high standards. If your child is heavily Melancholy, you will find he has a deep need for perfection in many areas of his life. If he is Melancholy with Choleric he will be meticulous about his desk and paper work and be more outgoing and bold than a straight Melancholy. One four-year-old Melancholy/Choleric girl was driving her mother crazy, and the mother said in exasperation, "Don't be such a perfectionist!"

The child responded quickly, "I'm not a perfectionist. I just want things done right."

If he is Melancholy/Phlegmatic he will not care quite so much whether things are in order and will be less compulsive about getting life pulled together perfectly.

One of the great struggles for this child will come in the area of negative thought patterns and refusal to communicate needs before his feelings are hurt. This lack of communication causes the Melancholy child to internalize his deep need for approval rather than openly seeking that approval in the manner of the Sanguine child. He feels if you really loved him, you would be sensitive to his needs and he wouldn't have to tell you.

Tools to Help

1. Check your child's school to see if testing is available to determine your son's or daughter's educational and creative bent. If it is not available, go through a local children's hospital or psychologist. Look for ways to affirm and encourage your child in those areas of his/her own personal expertise, knowing that he probably has some special talent waiting to be discovered. Some children may be gifted in the area of music, the arts, design, or may show an intense interest in a chosen hobby such as photography or model building.

2. Protect your child from too much involvement in sad books, music, or television programs. Because this child has such a vivid visual memory and tendancy toward intense reaction, keep him away from disturbing entertainment such as horror movies or films depicting violence or macabre behavior. They're not good for any child, but the Melancholy may be seriously affected by trauma dramas.

3. Starting early in childhood, focus the Melancholy minds on what they have to be thankful for. Spend some time at least once or twice a week having these boys or girls list all the good things God has done for them or given them. It is important to constantly direct their thoughts to the positive rather than the negative. One mother actually has her Melancholy son verbalize a praise list every morning with her before she takes him to school, and she has been very pleased with the results.

4. One of the most important things you can do for this tempera-ment is to teach him to communicate his needs and feelings with-out your having to play twenty questions each time he gets moody. Use every tool you can muster to draw out the thoughts and emotions of this child. Remember, he will be quick to withdraw without ever verbalizing what caused the pain, so be quick to help this child find words to express what he is feeling.

Example: "Honey, I know there are times when others do or say things that really hurt your feelings. Try to help me under-stand when I do that to you. If you will stop the moment you feel that pain and just say, 'Mom, you probably didn't mean to, but you hurt my feelings when you said or did that.' It is so much better when we can talk about hurt feelings. Then we don't have to hold that pain inside because we can love away the hurt with a special, 'I'm sorry,' and a big hug. I want to understand when you are hurt because I love you and I know that talking about these things can keep them from taking away your happiness."

6. It is important to begin early to teach the Melancholy child that both success and failure are a part of what our Lord allows in each life in order to make us ready for heaven. This child is terrified of failure and has a difficult time trying anything unless success is guaranteed. He will often spend excess time on prepara-tion to perform a doubtful project. Explain to him that each setback in life gives us compassion for others who are hurting. How could we ever know how *they* feel if we have never known failure ourselves.

Remember

This Melancholy child is driven not only by a need for perfec-tion but also by a desire for you to sense and respond to his needs and feelings without their ever having been verbalized. Teaching this child to communicate needs and feelings is a powerful key to short-circuiting chronic unhappiness and may be the salvation of a future marriage.

CHOLERIC

Your Choleric child is the original strong-willed child, full of energy, adventure, and impatience. This toothless wonder is born to lead. Hard to believe, isn't it? Leadership begins with demanding to eat and to sleep only when he chooses and moves on to exercising control through temper tantrums. One lady told me her Choleric child's first sentence was a loud, "Eat now!"

These anger displays seem to express themselves in one of two ways, depending on the temperament combination. The Choleric/Sanguines tend to have both verbal and physical temper tantrums, the Choleric anger and the Sanguine performance which may include kicking, screaming, and pounding the floor, wall, or whatever is near. Breaking a dish or two is a dramatic addition.

The Choleric/Melancholy, however, tends toward a more dignified tantrum. Not wanting to call undue attention to himself, the Choleric/Melancholy child is more likely to hold his breath until turning blue and then quietly passing out on the floor. This apparent swoon is a quiet attention-getter and tells mother not to let this happen again.

Control is the key Choleric word here, and it follows this child to the grave. Whether it is through leadership or anger, the Choleric must be in control. A tantrum gives this child just that!

How excited I was when I opened a December *USA Today* and saw a full-page headline "Temperament, Not Poor Training, Ignites Tantrums." It told about little Jillian who cried all night, threw tantrums daily, and wouldn't eat. Her father, a child psychiatrist, couldn't believe he was involved in a power struggle with a two-year-old. The more he fought the worse it got, but Dr. Stanley Turecki did what any psychiatrist in his position would do; he wrote a book about Jillian and others like her. The book is called *The Difficult Child.* In it he says, "These children aren't spoiled brates. They have difficult traits, but their behavior is a result of their temperament which they can't help. These children aren't out to get their parents."[9]

Dr. Saul Brown of Cedars-Sinai in Los Angeles warns parents not to make a scapegoat out of this child; doing so could lead to possible child abuse. He also tells them to only fight battles that they need to win, not to make a scene out of everything, and not to look for a source to blame for the difficult child's behavior. "Some people are just born with different personalities."[10]

This little Choleric powerhouse is very productive, is able to make quick and competent decisions, and often can outsmart his parents. He is full of confidence and pride and is often bossy and tactless.

Tools to Help

1. You have on your hands the greatest potential for future leadership positive or negative. Marita's teacher once said, "I hope Marita never goes wrong because she would lead the whole school over the cliff with her." Remember that this adventuresome child needs challenge and change. Because of an innate logic, this child will thrive on educational toys, puzzles and play times that allow for expression of leadership.

2. It is important to stand "toe to toe" with this strong-willed child in order to break the will and not the spirit. Phlegmatic Lana Bateman says, "When my Choleric son reached eighteen months, we squared off for control of the home. For three months, we battled. I never let him win, not even the battle over bedtime. Because I hung in there, the victory was won, and we never contended over leadership again. Be willing to stand against the will of this child no matter what the cost. You won't be sorry. The rewards are great!" If you don't persist and if you aren't consistent with your discipline and follow through, he will soon be in charge of you.

3. Keep this child busy and give him responsibilities, for this temperament has a deep need to be productive. If he is not in control of something, his room, the dog, the back yard, he will take it out on his friends at school. Cholerics often have poor peer relationships.

4. Be sure to reason sensibly with your Choleric child for he will tend to rebel when discipline or demands lack a logical explanation. He will want to know why before doing what he's told.

5. Respect this child's innate need for fairness and justice and be open and honest with him or he will catch you up on your inconsistencies.

6. Use those situations when your Choleric child is hurt or disappointed to point out that our Lord will sometimes allow us to experience these struggles in order to give us a compassionate heart toward hurting people who may come into our lives. Since the Choleric child is short on mercy and tenderness, it is important to utilize each of their struggles as a teaching tool for these very areas. Don't let them develop the "look down on the dummies" attitude. Show them that while goals are good, occasional failure is part of life and doesn't mean the person who didn't make it is stupid.

Remember

The Choleric child's greatest need is to be in control. With that need comes impatience-based anger when things are not going his way. Because the Choleric is thinking way ahead of his parents, plotting for control, he will sense when you are most vulnerable and attack. When you have ladies in the living room, he will feel free to eat a dozen cookies, a chance he would not take if you were alone. A young woman came up to me after I spoke on children. "I think my three-year-old is in control of me." She then told me how the child kept taking cookies while she was visiting a friend. She told the child quietly not to take another one, but she did. After several gentle warnings to no avail she said sternly, "If you take one more cookie, I'll spank you when we get home." The child looked her in the eye and took one.

I asked, "What did you do?"

She replied, "Well, I couldn't do anything there in front of my friends."

"What did you do when you got home? Did you spank her?"

"I forgot."

This little imp has got her mother under firm control. She

knows the first rule of battle. Attack when the enemy is weak. Don't let this happen to you. On the first disobedience drag the child off to the bathroom and explain you mean business. If she reaches for one more cookie, remove her again and spank her. Do not worry about your friends' reaction. They are probably delighted to see that you're as strong as the child and that you may have a fighting chance at keeping her from being the child that no one wants to come to their house.

It is most important that a Choleric's parent provide healthy areas where the child can exercise control while at the same time standing firm and immovable when that need for control supersedes the limits of balance for that child's life and relationships. For instance, the Choleric child might be allowed to construct a circus in the back yard and invite friends to come be involved in the performance. He could be encouraged to direct the activities and delegate jobs to the children who want to participate. This would be an opportunity to monitor such things as bossiness or a domineering attitude and at the same time teach your child to be a wise leader. A Choleric child may want to start a children's neighborhood newsletter with tidbits of information about each child living nearby. These are constructive activities that allow the child some healthy control and expression of leadership; however, when that need for control extends itself to defiance, such as refusing to come home when told or refusing to adhere to an appointed bedtime, then the parent must consistently stand firm. Inconsistency can be fatal with this particular temperament as he's out to win and will take great pride in outsmarting you.

Years ago when Lauren was in high school, a church friend of mine came to visit and brought her four-year-old son. When it was time to leave she called Bobby out of the pool. He pretended not to hear her and continued splashing around. She sighed and said, "He never does a thing I tell him."

After a few more feeble attempts that failed, she settled down and stated, "I'll just have to sit here until he decides to get out of the pool."

That comment was all Lauren had to hear. She marched over to the edge of the pool and yelled, "Bobby, get out of this pool and do it now!" Instantly Bobby swam to the steps and climbed out. As Lauren wrapped a towel around him, his mother said, "I just can't believe it. He'd never do that for me."

He would if he knew she meant business, but this Choleric child already had his mother under firm control. Imagine what this undisciplined boy will be like by the time he's fourteen!

PHLEGMATIC

Your easy-going Phlegmatic child with simple goals of sleeping and eating is seldom a problem. Phlegmatics seem to entertain themselves so easily, it takes little to make them happy and they seem to require minimal care and attention. They are permanent press children. Of all infants, this one is the most calm, agreeable, and undemanding.

As your Phlegmatic child begins to grow, you may notice that he seems to be watching the world go by. That's because watching requires far less energy than getting involved. Because virtually every Phlegmatic action is subconsciously evaluated in terms of how much energy it will require, this child finds few activities worth the effort. Television was no doubt invented by a Phlegmatic who remembered his childhood longing for a movie he wouldn't have to walk down the street to view. What greater gift could mankind provide than a box which would be entertaining and would allow one to lie down and do nothing but watch! That is Phlegmatic heaven but also a breeding ground for laziness.

The Phlegmatic child is not an openly rebellious one but is known to possess a quiet will of iron. This child may smile and agree to do whatever you ask while inside he knows he has no intention of complying with your request. He may even lie to avoid any form of conflict or contention. He doesn't set out to be dishonest, but if shifting blame will eliminate responsibility, he's willing to take a chance.

While your Phlegmatic child is a good listener and peacemaker, his indecisiveness and lack of motivation can paralyze him with procrastination and inactivity. A Choleric parent cannot understand why this child has no ambition and doesn't want to get on with life.

Tools to Help

1. This temperament has the greatest need to be tested in order to discern areas of interest, creativity, or motivation. This is by far the most difficult child to direct toward a lifetime work for there is little the Phlegmatic can get excited about enough to persist to a positive conclusion. Check for a local child learning center or children's hospital for a testing referral and don't give up until you have a clear picture of your child's special strengths both educationally and creatively.

2. This child, of all the temperaments, has the least natural imagination so begin early in childhood to read to him and to stimulate creativity through games of make-believe and mental challenge.

3. Seek to involve this child in sports, tumbling, or dancing in order to encourage physical activity. He may not do well in team sports as he doesn't have much drive, and he may upset the other children when he's dreaming in left field.

4. When the parents of a Phlegmatic child seek to eliminate the problem of lying, they must deal first with the root problem which is not the lie itself but the fear of conflict. Because of this paralyzing fear, the child will say anything the parent wants to hear to avoid anger or punishment and that isn't always the truth. Conflict robs the Phlegmatic of peace, so the parent should first control his own anger and then face the child with quiet reason. Once the Phlegmatic is taught to deal with conflict in a healthy way, and he is assured you won't yell at him, the need for lying disappears. You need a heavy hand to control the Choleric and sometimes the Sanguine, but the same strong language will depress the Melancholy and overwhelm the Phlegmatic.

5. Begin at a very early age to present simple choices to the Phlegmatic child. Help him to make decisions on his own and praise him warmly for each one even if it wouldn't have been your selection. Remember that the Phlegmatic's problem with procrastination is based not just on inactivity but indecisiveness as well. He literally does not know which way to turn. The decision-making process is in very low gear in this temperament and must be taught simply, lovingly, and patiently with much

affirmation along the way. Let him choose the dinner menu once a week or select the cookies before his Choleric sister has grabbed the Oreos.

6. Your Phlegmatic child is the most underdeveloped in the area of expressing anger. Because anger must find some form of expression, it bubbles up as sarcasm in this personality. Sarcasm always hurts some vulnerable victim. The Phlegmatic child may exercise a twisted type of control over others through his use of sarcastic humor and has the ability to make another seem very foolish in the process. Begin at a very early age to explain the link between sarcasm and anger and how this type of humor can destroy friendships and alienate others. Help this child to find a creative outlet for his repressed anger through "talking out" his responses to conflict in an unthreatening environment. Never tell him, "Don't cry; that's for sissies; grow up and be a man!" This repression of his inner feelings will accentuate the negative, and if stored up, these hurts will later lash out on to others.

Remember

Your Phlegmatic child is driven by a need for peace and can become physically ill in the face of conflict or contention. When forced to deal with another's anger, the Phlegmatic actually loses all thought processes and goes mentally blank. This child has a deep need to feel special to someone so don't ignore him just because he's not demanding. Value your Phlegmatic child and say so!

We've talked about the most basic love needs of each child and we've looked at the temperaments as they relate to childhood personalities. We've even discussed the need to understand each one of our children and the particular strengths and weaknesses that cause him or her to require unique care and nurturing. Scripture has shown us that child-rearing using the group technique of treating everyone the same will not meet our children's needs if we are to raise a child up in the way he should go.

For Further Study, Thought, and Action

Spend some family time in teaching your children about the different personalities. Help them find who they really are and don't tell them they are wrong. Any negatives will cut off communications and turn what should be fun into a parental lecture, the dread of all children.

Add your children's personality types to your family tree and show them what relatives they resemble temperamentwise. Let them choose a picture of themselves to add to your personality notebook.

Restudy this chapter and mark any suggestions that fit a certain child with his initials. Check back often to see how you are doing in training up each child in the way he should go.

In a group study share what you have done with this information in your home. Take a quick survey of the personality types for the group's collective children. Those who find they have children that are alike will be able to share helpful tools with each other in the future.

The time you spend in thoughtful and prayerful training of your children today may well keep them from being rebellious teens. The understanding of who they really are based on the temperament tools will give them something to share with their friends who are floundering for some sense of identity.

In this day when permissiveness often leads to confusion, don't be afraid to teach, train, and discipline your children.

The rod of correction imparts wisdom, but a child left to itself disgraces his mother.
                                                —Proverbs 29:15, NIV

❧ 9 ❧

How Can You
Bend the Twigs
As They Should Go?

No one sets out to be a bad parent; no one desires to fail. In that case, how do so many of us end up feeling that we've blown it—that there's no hope?

As we grew up we could so easily see where our parents went wrong. One was too easy, one too hard. One was fun; one was serious. In our childish wisdom we vowed we would never be like them; we would never make their mistakes. And yet, here we are doing exactly what they did. Even though we didn't mean to, we subconsciously picked up their method of reacting in stressful situations. I was in one home where the young father grabbed the noisy Sanguine child by the ear and pulled him screaming from the room. When I dared ask about this off-beat manner of discipline, he replied, "Well, that's what my father did to me."

"Did you like it?" I ventured.

"No, I hated it, but you're not supposed to like discipline."

This young man had not given any rational thought or fervent prayer over proper methods of discipline. He reacted out of his past and did just what his father had done.

Dr. Harold Bloomfield, author of *Making Peace with Your Parents* writes, "The relationship of our parents, because it is so fundamental, affects virtually all relationships, including those with our children. Parents often repeat the same objectionable behavior they resented as children."[1]

Statistics prove that a large majority of those who were beaten as children, much as they hated it, do the same thing to their children. Marilyn Murray, CLASS staff and abuse therapist, says of the young rapists she works with in the prisons, "Almost all of them were abused in some physical way as children, and they are subconsciously lashing back at their parents by molesting or attacking others."

Dr. Bloomfield also says that 90 percent of the people he counsels have an "incomplete relationship with at least one of their parents."[2]

Considering that the odds aren't with us that we will be inspired parents properly blending love and discipline, shouldn't we grasp for any help we can find? There are no simple answers or Paul would have written more specifics than "Fathers, do not exasperate your children; instead, bring them up in the training and instruction of the Lord" (Eph. 6:4, NIV). While these are surely words of wisdom you may need more specific advice.

As we look at the different personalities relating them to parenting, you will have to fit together the blend you and your mate have as they are probably not the same. Since the Bible aim is for unity of spirit, you can easily grasp that with two parents who see things from a totally different point of view, harmony is far from automatic. A child does not need to have studied the temperaments to know how to play one parent against the other. He has an inbred sense that says:

"Go to Sanguine Mother when you want fun, but don't be surprised when she forgets to pick you up at school."

"Melancholy Father will be on time, but he'll make you feel guilty for needing a ride."

"Don't try to pull anything on Choleric Mother or she'll let you have it. Test out her mood before you ask for anything."

"Try to ask Phlegmatic Dad first as he'll let you do anything as long as it's quiet and out of sight."

Are these not similar to thoughts your children may have? In order to be "of one mind" the parents must first understand who they are separately and then discuss their blending as to how it affects the training of children. The thought of making a job out of raising children sounds "too much like work" to most parents. It's much easier to deal with each emergency as it comes along. That may be true, but think of the confusing signals you are sending your children. There's no consistency and you encourage them to pit you both against each other, turning family life into a sporting event with opposing teams.

Please take the time to examine your temperaments as they relate to parenting for if you make major mistakes of neglect, indulgence, or abuse, you are affecting other lives and not just your own.

SANGUINE PARENTS

Sanguine parents are obviously the most fun. The Sanguine loves the storytelling, wrestling-on-the-floor years of a child's life and of all parents is the most free to play with the children. Sanguine parents elicit laughter and squeals of delight as they read or tell childhood stories and often act them out. I memorized *Green Eggs and Ham,* then taught it to the children so we could perform it in choral speaking at the drop of a "Cat in the Hat." It is no surprise that this parent is best liked by the children's peers. What other parent can turn a house into a circus and a disaster into a hilarious story?

Paula Lively of Dallas is the most perfect Sanguine I have ever met. She is adorable, has huge expressive eyes, and captures that youthful innocent look that is ageless in Sanguines. Her husband Fred is a classic Choleric/Melancholy who by living with her has developed a reflective sense of humor. She wrote to tell me how understanding the temperaments had helped her as both wife and mother:

By the time Monday afternoon had come I was so tired of washing 16 loads of clothes (not really—only 4). Fred had a meeting and wouldn't be home for dinner so I didn't want to cook. Carrie and Jim were begging me to make pizza so I decided the quickest way to get out of this work was to make them do it. (My children even at age 10 are totally self-sufficient; do their own beds, can wash their own clothes, prepare recipes, on and on). Realizing they would be much more willing to make pizza themselves if it were fun, I decided to have a pizza-making contest!!! The winner (most creative AND best clean-up [who cares what it tasted like]) wins a $2.50 shopping spree at the 5 and 10 store. (There still are some bargains at M. E. Moses!) Jim, my precious and thoughtful Melancholy/Choleric son made a pepperoni with perfect rows, I mean PERFECT, of mushrooms, carefully arranged with all the stems turned in towards the center so as to achieve that sun-burst effect!!! Are you ready for this one? Our Sanguine/Choleric daughter, Carrie, topped the pepperoni pizza by making a sausage pizza with the head of a mallard duck in the center. We collect mallards so she knew that would sway the judge! She chopped up a green pepper and somehow very creatively filled in the sausage-duck with bell pepper for color. The beak was made of crushed Doritos and the breast feathers were strips of bacon. When I came into the kitchen for the judging I immediately became hysterical at my own textbook case of a Sanguine turning work into fun and my children's textbook cases of being so classic, practically right off the pages of *Personality Plus*. We invited the Japanese neighbors from across the street and the Orthodox Jewish neighbors from next door (they didn't eat but enjoyed the company). Fred came home and was so upset 'cause he'd missed the party that he went into a depression! Not really. Oh, what fun!

Don't you wish Paula had been your mother?

There are, however, problem areas of parenting even for the "Santa Claus" personality.

Because it isn't fun to be consistent, the Sanguine is often a permissive parent. Setting standards for behavior and enforcing them is not something the Sanguine mom or dad does easily, and equally painful is the prospect of facing rejection from the offspring. Yes, the Sanguines even need to be accepted by their children, and let's face it, structuring healthy behavior and discipline in one's children doesn't put a parent in a popular position.

When the children become teens, the Sanguine parent may look for ways to escape the increased demands and responsibility. Sports, social functions, the country club, even a fun job can become excuses for not spending time at home. When the fun-loving, disorganized Sanguine can't be bothered by the details of keeping up with appointments or getting the children where they need to be on time, the more responsible parent, usually a Melancholy, has to be the family manager, sighing with martyrdom while doing it, "Your mother would lose her head if it weren't attached" or "Your father never knows which end is up!" This struggle may not be quite so radical if the Sanguine's secondary temperament is Choleric, bringing a more responsible and organized balance to the personality.

It is truly amazing how quickly the Sanguine parent disappears when the children become demanding or aren't fun anymore.

This retreat can cause a spouse to feel like he or she is raising a single-parent family with the questionable help of a drop-in playmate now and then to provide entertainment.

One area that is troublesome for the child of a Sanguine is that of competition where friends are involved. Often there is some jealousy when the child's friends seem drawn to the Sanguine parent more than they enjoy spending time with the child they came to visit. This type of personality competition can become more severe as the years pass and dates arrive at the front door to be charmed away by a Sanguine mother.

The combination Choleric/Sanguine seems to be the parent most enjoyed and accepted by children growing up for they have the Sanguine magnetism and yet know how to lead effectively and accomplish something when properly motivated by potential praise.

Often the Sanguine/Choleric mother who has trouble getting a simple dinner on the table at a consistent time can produce instant banquets for crowds of cheering teen-agers. While this excited mother is accepting the accolades of the youth, her Melancholy husband comes home to find a circus with his wife as the cooking ringmaster. Instead of joining in the fun with her, he tends to take her talents as a personal affront wondering why she can't get this enthusiastic over cooking for him, not understanding that if he gave her a standing ovation for each steak, she might grill one more often. He can't tolerate the noise of the crowd, so he withdraws to his room waiting for her to come and soothe his hurt feelings. Since she's insensitive to his needs and wouldn't leave the party anyway, she shrugs and asks, "I wonder what's wrong with your father tonight?" Waiting alone for sympathy that doesn't arrive shows the husband that his evaluation was right. "She doesn't really love me—in fact, she cares more for that bunch of strangers than for her own husband." He sinks into a deep depression, doesn't speak to her for two weeks, and she has no idea why.

What a lot of hassle we can be spared when we understand why we behave as we do. The father in this case can save himself heartbreak if he knows her cooking for the crowd has no bearing on her love for him. Even if he told her how hurt he was, she would not have the sensitivity to understand and would call the whole idea ridiculous. He should join in with the gang and force himself to have a good time or greet everyone and retreat with a positive attitude.

If the Melancholy does not have the authority to handle this situation, we could hope the Sanguine wife could develop an awareness of his needs and lovingly take a tray of food to his room. An improvement on either side would make a difference in the harmony of the home.

Because Sanguine/Cholerics are able to combine goals with fun, they make excellent youth leaders and can influence questioning teens in a positive and godly direction.

I was in one church where the youth pastor was a straight Sanguine, charm without discipline. He had taken fifty youth for a hike in the mountains to return at 5:30 P.M. at the church. Parents were sitting in cars waiting and no one came. The pastor was called and two hours later the police. At 8:00 P.M. the group arrived happy and singing. They'd had a great time, and no one, including the youth pastor, had any idea what time it was!

MELANCHOLY PARENTS

The Melancholy is a dutiful, responsible parent who will often try to expose the children to piano, trumpet, dancing, art, or other cultural pursuits. Because Melancholies set such high standards, they usually press for intellectual achievement as well and long for a child to appreciate the deeper things of life. They read them poetry, listen to classical music, and get them to their lessons on time.

Fred and I were recently the guests of Dr. and Mrs. Hans Diehl. Mrs. Diehl holds a doctorate in musical arts and is an accomplished concert pianist who performs all over the country, and Hans is both a doctor and lecturer on nutrition. The grand piano filled a large section of their living room and next to it under a spotlight were two chairs each with a violin leaning against them. Mrs. Diehl explained that the instruments were left out at all times to encourage their two children Byron (age ten) and Carmen (age eight) to play their violins whenever they wanted to. "Their violins should be their friends."

After dinner we found out these two precocious, talented children were dear friends with the violins as they gave us an astonishing concert. Byron also played duets with his mother on the piano, not little plodding numbers like "Row, Row, Row Your Boat," but sonatas by Schubert and Mozart.

I was so overwhelmed with the depth of talent and the obvious loving care that the parents had given these two brilliant children that suddenly I felt like a laggard. My mother had been a violin and cello teacher. Where had I gone wrong? I remember my mother trying to teach ten-year-old Marita the violin. Somehow just seeing her hold the instrument in her hand was hilarious. Each time she picked it up to practice we all laughed so hard we cried. She was somewhat a child's version of Jack Benny.

As I listened to Byron and Carmen performing so effortlessly, I wondered would Marita have been a violinist today if I'd been a Melancholy mother?

Unfortunately, the Melancholy's child may be overwhelmed and discouraged if the parent sets the standards too high and consistently puts those goals beyond the child's reach. Such a child would feel as if he could never do enough to please the Melancholy parent, for indeed, nothing is quite good enough. It is of paramount importance that the Melancholy parent learn to set those standards at a reachable level for the child to experience feelings of accomplishment and to realize that unless the child is also a Melancholy, he may not be able to achieve what the parent desires. This understanding alone can be such a healing instrument in those parent-child relationships.

Some parents with this Melancholy temperament will subconsciously choose an opposite sex child to be a special companion. Generally, the Melancholy has become badly disenchanted by inability to conform his spouse to the image he has of a perfect wife and will then move on to the more flexible material of a child. This parent will tend to draw that little one out of a child's world and into an early adult one by sharing everything from emotional struggles or discouragements to business problems or failures. Without realizing what is happening, the parent robs the child of a childhood and draws him into an adult world of problems, pressures, and emotions. The parent feels he's giving this child special attention and can't possibly see that what he's doing is causing future emotional problems.

Eventually the child reaches adulthood but not without an illusive root of bitterness and anger due to that lost childhood.

Eventually those feelings will surface in a negative or resentful way, and the parent will place the blame on the child. "I can't imagine why she turned against me after all the love I've given her." Lana Bateman tells of one such situation that was presented to her for prayer counseling.

A lovely Choleric/Melancholy lady named Terry came to see me complaining of marriage problems. She didn't believe that her husband loved her, but when I asked her to explain his actions toward her, she told a different story. He sounded like a gentle, caring husband who longed for his wife to be herself and not to put unhealthy worth in him.

As we talked, I found that this young woman grew up with a Melancholy father, who made her his companion from her first breath. He told her of his hopes, dreams, inventions, disappointments, and struggles. He drew her into his world of business and emotions. She lost her real identity and became the extension of a great man. She also lost her childhood as he opened his world with all of its stresses to her.

Because this father didn't know how to give healthy love, Terry had to redefine love in terms of what he *was* able to give. Love became an aspiration to carry on his greatness. Love became being that extension of a man who would constantly push you on to bigger and better achievements.

It is no surprise that this young woman couldn't accept healthy love from her husband. He just wanted her to be herself and not an extension of her father. She had never experienced such a strange attitude. He must not love her! Her idea of what love really was had been so distorted by the Melancholy parent who made her a substitute wife, that she couldn't perceive genuine love when it was presented to her. This distortion almost destroyed her marriage and took several years to successfully grow beyond.

While this relationship problem certainly doesn't exist for all Melancholies, it does occur with some frequency among those who may have experienced painful childhoods. This is an area for preventative prayer if a parent with this temperament finds himself seriously favoring and spending time with one particular child.

The Melancholy mother with Sanguine children has difficulty realizing the value of laughter for these little ones. They will work to "make mother happy" and if mother responds they will be overjoyed. I can remember how my father, two brothers, and

I would do everything we could to amuse my Phelgmatic/Melancholy mother who would just sigh and say to my father, "If you don't stop teaching them all these tom-fool things they will never amount to a row of pins." Every once in a while we'd get to Mother and she'd really laugh. These were high points in our childhood. So Melancholy mothers realize, life may be difficult but a laugh here and there may help.

A woman from Texas wrote me this following letter.

I have just finished reading your book, *Personality Plus,* and wanted to tell you how very much I enjoyed it and how helpful I found it to be. It met the *true* test of "enjoyable," as my mainly Melancholy temperament (with much Phlegmatic) rarely is moved to LAUGH OUT LOUD! Your delightful illustrations were so *true* to life . . . that I repeatedly found myself laughing with deep "ha, ha, ha's." My precious, Sanguine four-year-old daughter had no idea what I was laughing at, but, delighted for the chance to laugh and have some fun, would laugh in high-volume unison. And once she even brought me the book, saying, "Here Mommy . . . let's read your book and laugh together."

But the laughter was a "fringe" benefit . . . the main thing I thank you for is the understanding this book has given me. My husband has always believed . . . that "everything would be all right if she'd just loosen up," while I, on the other hand, have had trouble even *believing* that someone would hang a picture without "measuring the wall."

Reading to my daughter yesterday, P. D. Eastman's *The Best Nest,* a delightful children's book, I found myself chuckling to discover why Mr. and Mrs. Bird kept relocating their nest . . . poor Mr. Bird—Phlegmatic, contented—prodded on by his Choleric Mrs. Bird. Even the illustrations prove the theory: she *looks* bossy!
Linda Klatt

Some Melancholies are hampered during the parenting years by constant bouts with depression while others battle the syndrome of martyrdom. While it is true that any temperament could fall prey to the beast of martyrdom, the Melancholy is by far the most susceptible. This forces us to take a closer look at the most self-sacrificing temperament for an understanding of its vulnerability. The Melancholy may suffer from one of two different types of "martyrmania."

The first is called *the overt martyr.* This type of martyr is constantly verbalizing all he has done for the children. The overt martyr might sound something like this, "Don't you care how hard I have to work to give you what you have?" or "I never get any time to myself. All I ever do is work my fingers to the bone, and this is the thanks I get." Obviously this type of emotional unloading produces a burden of guilt in the child.

The second type of Melancholy martyr is called *the subtle martyr*. The subtle martyr seldom if ever verbalizes his or her self-sacrifice, but simply pours out a life on the altar of the children's needs. The subtle martyr's children may spend a lifetime watching the parent pick up after them, clean their rooms, and in some extreme cases even do their homework.

This type of martyr will give all to the child even when it is extremely unwise to do so. Such a parent will often sacrifice his own needs to buy for the child without ever verbalizing the personal cost.

The child of the subtle martyr will feel tremendous guilt but the guilt will be on a subconscious level. Just as the martyrdom of the parent is subtle or hidden from open understanding, so is the guilt of the child hidden away in the subconscious mind. The only touch such a child might have with that illusive pressure might be a sense of needing to spend a lifetime repaying the parent for that which no one can explain. The child might verbalize it this way, "I'll never be able to do enough to pay my mom or dad back for all they've done. I try so hard and it never seems to be enough. Why do I always feel guilty?"

We're beginning to see that while the Melancholy is a dependable, concerned parent, there are definitely trouble areas in the parent-child relationship.

The Melancholy is one of two controlling personalities, second only to the Choleric. Perhaps in a quiet way the Melancholy is the most controlling of all. This temperament can do more damage with eye-rolling, looks of disappointment, and deep sighs than all of the other temperaments can do with a thousand words. This is a powerful and subtle control and makes the child feel guilty, inadequate, and smothered all at the same time.

When the Melancholy lets these tendencies get out of hand, a child will pull hard and fast to get away from home and in adulthood many will effectively distance themselves from Melancholy parents who will weep to their friends in self pity.

CHOLERIC PARENTS

The Choleric parent is dutiful and responsible and will virtually never forget where the child needs to be or when he needs to be there. A Choleric exerts sound leadership in the home and invariably has the right answer for every question a child might ask.

Not only does the Choleric establish goals for his children but has no trouble moving the whole family to action. The Choleric can be counted on to organize and perform what is necessary to meet the needs of his children in almost every area except that of emotions. Since the Choleric looks upon people who cry as weak, he transmits to his children that they should not let their feelings show.

Like the Melancholy, the Choleric must maintain absolute control of his children. While the Melancholy controls emotionally, the Choleric controls openly and is known as the aggressive temperament. His children learn there is only one way to behave and many put on Phlegmatic masks of submission hiding their real personality even from themselves.

Another area of struggle for the Choleric parent-child relationship is that of quality time spent together. The Choleric is often a workaholic and assumes if he makes a good living that's all that should be expected of him. When the Choleric *is* home, he demands constant productivity from children and gives them little time to relax. One lady told me she had been raised on a farm and once a week they all went to town to a drive-in movie. Her Choleric mother could not let them waste time, and so the children would all sit in the back of the pick-up truck and husk corn, string beans, or shell peas while watching *Snow White*. The Choleric's motto is "Never let them rest." Productivity is next to godliness. Sadly, the Choleric would rather do a task himself than put up with what is conceived as a poor performance by a child. Unfortunately, there is no other way but the Choleric's way and this can wipe out a child who needs so badly to learn from an open and patient teacher and be allowed to make mistakes.

Often the Choleric parent will grab the project out of the child's hand and say, "I knew I should have done this myself." A comment such as this devastates the child and signals to him he is incompetent. Later when this parent says, "What's the matter with you stupid?" the child confirms in his mind that he is worthless.

This type of parental behavior is so frequent with Cholerics that I often see very successful men whose children have all turned out to be failures. They can't understand how this happened when they gave them every opportunity in the world to succeed.

A millionaire who came to a *Personality Plus* seminar took me afterwards to see his new private airplane. When we were alone he told me a typical story of his son. The young man had been given every advantage imaginable and had doors opened to him that the average person could never hope to enter. He'd done poorly in school and seemed inept in the family business. "Have you sent him out on his own?" I asked.

"Oh yes and that was a fiasco. He ruined both a family and a business while he was gone, and I had no choice but to bring him back home and support him. He wants to be rich, but he has no idea of how to work." Then the man dropped his head and calmed his anger. "After listening to you today, I can see I'm a Choleric, and I guess I did all the wrong things as a parent."

It is so hard, close to impossible, for a Choleric to see that his drive and supposed inspiration make a child feel worthless. "What's the use? I'll never make it anyhow." Sometimes a Choleric child will determine to show his father up, but in his angry pursuit, he overshoots the mark and fails. He may come home subdued like the prodigal son or sink into a way of life that brings shame onto his parents. This negative life-style seems to be the only way he can exert control and win. He's no longer in competition and he's caused his father to have a heart attack.

Teens who have lived under a strong Choleric parent and who know they can never be what Superdad or Supermom want them to be tend to become depressed. Parents are always stunned when smart children from good homes suddenly commit suicide "for no good reason."

If you are a Choleric parent be brave enough to sit down with your children and ask them if you are somewhat like these parents I've described. Watch their body language as well as their words as they may be too afraid to tell the truth.

The Choleric parent quickly becomes impatient with a child's immature decision-making abilities so he makes all the child's decisions. This problem area coupled with a demanding, unemotional, domineering personality can crush and wound a young child's sensitive spirit and produce rebellion in an older youth making them unable to decide on anything in life.

Lana Bateman tells of an experience with her son.

> Our Phlegmatic son, Rob, was in from college. He had done something that was thoughtless, and his dad responded out of Choleric impatience with volatile anger. This resulted in Rob's being embarrassed in front of a friend who was present. After the natural instincts of that Choleric had been communicated, God began to press Marc's heart and show him that while he had stated a valuable principle to his son, the message would be lost amidst the embarrassment of calling him down in anger before his friend. God showed Marc that while his words were wisdom, his manner of expressing them destroyed their influence.
>
> Marc got up out of bed that night, got dressed and went upstairs to apologize to Rob in the presence of his friend. What a beautiful illustration of what God can do to overcome our natural temperament weaknesses if we will just be open to him and desire to please him in our parenting. God longs to deal with the destructive parts of our personalities, and for the Choleric, rash anger is often at the top of the list.

One memory a child has difficulty releasing is the sensation of a parent's anger which seems to have a profound and lasting effect on a young mind.

If you are a Choleric parent do not give up in disgust and brand yourself a failure. You have probably not done many of these things yourself, but the tendency is surely there, and you must take caution not to wipe out the needed ego-strength of your child. You have a strength other parents covet—you can get more accomplished in a shorter time than anyone else, but relax, take the pressure off the home front, and let them see the charm you exhibit when out in the world. If your son never wins a game pitching for Little League, it won't matter if you let him know you love him as he is—with or without winning games. But if he wins nine out of ten and you ask why he didn't win the tenth, his whole season will become a wipe-out.

Motivate, encourage, and inspire, but don't dominate and put the family on an endless treadmill experience.

PHLEGMATIC PARENT

The Phlegmatic's peaceful personality has a way of stabilizing children. Little ones have a need for routine in their lives, and the Phlegmatic is a person who will thrive on that very thing, for they don't like change and don't feel a need to be unnecessarily creative. That easy-going quality of this temperament makes them calm, accepting parents who don't get upset easily and always seem to have time for the children. The Phlegmatic mother will put playing with the children ahead of cleaning the house. There are, however, certain drawbacks for the Phlegmatic parent just as there are with the other three temperaments we've already discussed.

The Phlegmatic tends to be a permissive parent in order to avoid conflict. Duty and responsibility are not words in the Phlegmatic vocabulary, and he or she often takes the easy road. Since the Phlegmatic does not like to be told what to do because of the underlying stubborn streak, the pressures of responsibility are most easily left to the Choleric whom the Phlegmatic usually marries.

Children of a Phlegmatic often see this parent as lazy and weak and feel he or she is unwilling to defend himself in time of conflict. It is important that this attitude be faced if the Phlegmatic is confronted by a child approaching adulthood.

One Choleric young man went to his mother and complained bitterly that she was weak and let "Dad" run over her. It was obvious that this boy was taking up the offense for his mother, but, unfortunately for him, he had not properly perceived the relationship between his parents. This was his mother's response.

> You don't seem to understand, son. When an issue truly matters to me, I will work it through with your dad. Most things just don't matter that much. Why should I have it my way when the outcome means so little to me—and why shouldn't we do it his way, when it means so much to him?

This young man finally began to realize a temperament truth where his mother was concerned. She really *didn't care!* He was wasting his frustration on a situation that didn't really exist. He was able, at last, to lay down the emotional responsibility of protecting his mom. She may have appeared to be vulnerable, but she wasn't quite as helpless as he had thought.

Another type of family struggle may occur because of the Phlegmatic parent's tendency toward being somewhat slow or lazy. Children may witness parental conflict over lack of organization in caring for both home and children. A Phlegmatic father might neglect to get the bills paid or necessary house repairs accomplished. A Phlegmatic mother may not get the Christmas decorations put away until Easter looms on the horizon. Although the Phlegmatic has the ability to accomplish these tasks, we must remember that this personality evaluates almost everything in subconscious terms of how much energy it will take, up to and including the raising of children. Unfortunately this parent can often be found in front of the television set doing what comes most naturally, watching!

While the Phlegmatic parent is the most easy-going and unpressured, he must make the major effort to get what needs to be done finished on time and to get out of the chair and discipline the children.

For Further Study, Thought, and Action

Because parenting is such a serious subject, you should take time to sit down with your mate and list your individual strengths and weaknesses as parents. Look at the different approaches you have to discipline because of your temperaments. See where your conflicts are. Do your children pit one of you against the other? Does one of you always give in? Is one of you the easy mark?

As Fred and I were raising our children, we had a simple rule: Whichever one of us was asked first gave the answer and that was it. There was no running to the other parent for a second opinion. This eliminated bartering and established unity.

As you list your differences as parents in your personality notebook, discuss each one and begin to make some basic rules for each one of you to follow. To win as parents you both must be on the same team, not on opposing sides. You must be playing the same game with the same set of instructions. Even young children know when there is no unity between the parents, and they begin early to work the moods of their mother and avoid the anger of their father.

In your group study, bring in articles and case histories about teen depression and suicide. Notice what characteristics these disheartened teens have in common. Read my chapters on teen depression, one in *Lives on the Mend* and one in *Blow Away the Black Clouds* (revised edition). Discuss the causes of teen depression listed in these sources and consider those which might apply to any of your children. Has there been divorce or death in the family giving them a feeling of rejection? Have there been frequent moves causing instability? Have there been illnesses, deprivation, or traumas leading to fears?

Have your children watched frightening or explicit TV? Do they play Dungeons and Dragons? Do they have friends who take drugs? As you go over these and other questions in your study group, make some basic policies of parenting that you all agree on. Make this a beginning for your whole church to take a new interest in raising up their children under godly and practical principles.

Parents are desperate for help today. Why not be the catalyst for a unified approach to childraising in your church and community? If you are a single parent, it is even more important that you initiate a group with similar problems that may work together for positive solutions.

Fathers, do not exasperate your children; instead, bring them up in the training and instruction of the Lord.
—Ephesians 6:4, NIV

PART III

RECOVER
THE PAST
WITH
A FUTURE
THAT WILL LAST

RECOVER:

To restore to its original form

Now that you have looked deeply into your life, taken off the masks that had hidden the real you, and begun to understand those other people in a new light, it is time to recover the original spirit that God had in mind for you and to restore your emotional health and inner peace. If in examining your roots you find some repeated negative traits or actions, determine to halt them now before you pass on to your children what may have been transmitted to you. Be an encourager to others and help them become what God has in mind for them. He created each one for such a time as this.

For the Lord is always good. He is always loving and kind, and
his faithfulness goes on and on to each succeeding generation.
—Psalm 100:5, TLB

❧ 10 ❧

What about
the Bruised Fruit?

As we aim to RECOVER from the mistakes or maskings of the past, we want to restore ourselves and our children to our "original form." What were we intended to be like?

The birth of each new child brings with it an exciting opportunity for creative growth. Grandparents instantly spot physical features like someone on their side of the family. Mothers hope she'll be pretty and fathers wonder what he'll be like when he grows up. The range of potential for each new life is limitless, and yet not all of us achieve the abundant life God offers.

In the parable of the Sower in Luke 8, Jesus tells of four types of growth. Using the seed as the word of God, he shows how seed develops differently according to where it is planted and how it is nurtured. Let's apply these same truths to our seed, our children, or to ourselves.

"Some fell along the path. It was trampled on, and the birds of the air ate it up" (Luke 8:5, NIV).

Some of us grew up as seed scattered on the path. We had life in us, but somehow it got trampled down; people walked over us and some kicked us. Birds flew over head and some pecked at us and made fun of us. After a while on the dry road of life, we withdrew, built a wall of protection around us and said, "I'm not going to let anyone hurt me ever again."

"Some fell on rock, and when it came up, the plants withered because they had no moisture" (Luke 8:6, NIV).

Some of us grew up on the rocks with no moisture to maintain us, no nurturing to let us know we were of value. We didn't have the encouragement we needed; we wondered who we really were. When we cried out for attention, we were told to be quiet like our sister or sit still like our brother. We were trained up to be good, but not to be anyone in particular. We tried shifting our personalities to be what others wanted us to be, and we grew up confused with roots that never quite took hold. We thirsted for love from parents who had hardened hearts and who had lived on the rocks themselves. They did the best they knew how, but it wasn't enough for us, and we withered and dried up emotionally.

"Other seed fell among thorns, which grew up with it and choked the plants" (Luke 8:7, NIV).

Some of us grew up among the thorns, choked by the worries of the world; we had parents who were fearful or who always thought the worst of us. Some told us what was wrong with us, but seldom what was right. Some of them sought riches and some the pursuits of pleasure, and we seemed somehow to be in the way. Some left us completely and our little hearts were broken as we wandered in the weeds of the world hiding our feelings and smiling at grief. We felt we must be to blame for each one of their failures, and we tried to free them from their briar patch without getting caught up ourselves.

Some of us had siblings who were our thorns, who mocked us, who were considered better than us, who may have even abused us—thorns who grew up with us and choked out our emotional growth.

"Still other seed fell on good soil. It came up and yielded a crop, a hundred times more than was sown" (Luke 8:8, NIV).

Some fortunate ones of us grew up in good soil with parents who were emotionally mature and stable themselves, who gave us healthy unselfish love, and who treated each one of us as a precious gift from God. These parents knew Proverbs 22:6 not only as a verse but as a clear directive. They sought to understand each child's individual temperament, creative talents, and spiritual gifts and to train us up as we should go so that when we grew up, we would know who we were and wouldn't have to be on an endless search to find ourselves.

How rewarding it is to a parent to look at his crop and see it has matured beyond expectation. Each child has grown to his own potential. The rose hasn't been painted to look like a zinnia;

the smile hasn't been wiped off the daisy's face; the bluebell hasn't been told not to ring.

In God's Garden there are many people who are blossoming for his glory, but what about the bruised fruit: those who have grown up in soil that was far from ideal, those who have had to struggle to stay alive, those whose roots aren't deep enough to keep their tree upright, those who have fallen off and been hurt when hit by winds of adversity? What about the bruised fruit?

If you have read through each chapter in this book, have thought introspectively about your life and still have some unanswered questions about your identity, perhaps you have grown from seed that was trampled on, that had no watering or fertilizing, that was choked out by the demands of others. Think back on your childhood and ask the Lord to reveal any traumas you may have stuffed away in the cracks of your life, any hurts or bitter weeds that you have not pulled up and dealt with realistically and spiritually. We first have to see the wound before we can repair the damages. Counselors usually agree that it is difficult to help a person with a problem who is in firm denial of its existence.

As I have been teaching seminars based on my book, *Lives on the Mend,* I have increasingly encountered women who have suppressed the hurts of the past and who have denied that childhood deprivations or abuse have anything to do with their chronic headaches or eating disorders.

Often after listening to me review the symptoms of a victim, a woman will come and say quietly, "I've never told this to anyone in my life before." I then take the person aside and listen to the hurts and heartaches of a lifetime. We know today that abuse of all types—physical, sexual, and emotional—is rampant in the world, but few of us realize that there are victims with repressed pains of the past sitting in our congregations, victims who have never dared to tell the pastor or the other apparently perfect parishoners of their problems.

Some who do confess their hurts are told by well-meaning Christians to pray about it, think positive thoughts, or forgive the perpetrator—all good ideas; however, some have sincerely followed all these suggestions and are still in emotional pain.

Much as we would wish to ignore the facts, incest and abuse

are alive in our churches, and we are just becoming aware of the devastating and long-range effects. Aside from the abuse itself, the great tragedy is that these children grow up emotionally crippled. As adults they are still suffering from the pains of their past, and often they have submerged their bruised feelings so deeply that they have gaps in their memories, often an indicator of severe childhood trauma.

Do all victims respond the same way to childhood trauma? Obviously not, as there are so many variables, such as intensity and frequency of the attack, the relationship of the victim to the perpetrator, and the basic temperament pattern before the fruit was bruised. Although this chapter is not intended to be a psychological treatise, I have found that when I show a generalized picture of the responses according to personality types, it helps people examine themselves, their hurting friends, and even their own children.

When a child is abused—physically, sexually, or emotionally— he or she is initially in a state of shock. Even though the attack or the emotional abuse is not the child's fault, the victim feels guilty and somehow to blame. Way inside, the child feels dirty and of little value. Whatever the child's basic temperament, the inner child accepts the verdict, "I'm guilty." However, the reaction to the abuse varies according to the innate personality.

To give us a tool, a simple set of guidelines, let's divide ourselves into two categories: the combination of (1) Melancholy/ Phlegmatic—introverted, guilt-absorbing, easily depressed, and passive—and (2) Sanguine/Choleric—outgoing, optimistic, achieving, and resilient. How would each set probably respond to trauma?

The symptoms of the Melancholy/Phlegmatic start with an acceptance of themselves as unworthy of love and unable to amount to much in life. From normal children they become pessimistic, unenthusiastic, guilt-ridden, and often withdrawn after being abused or emotionally deprived. They often have early depression, seldom seem truly happy, and may suffer from phobias. Some develop a dependency on other people, and later on alcohol or drugs to keep them going or to make them feel of worth. As they grow up, some develop eating or digestive disorders and signs of emotional problems. Because of the guilt they assume from their past victimization, some may develop deep inferiority complexes or associate with people of a lower class to lift their self-image.

Sending them for assertiveness training or even to seminary may do nothing more than pull them up a few notches, unless the underlying root cause is exposed and dealt with.

They see others succeeding while everything they touch seems to turn to ashes. Even their achievements appear to them as failures. As women, they often seek counsel from each visiting speaker or evangelist but never seem to profit from logical advice. They keep hoping the next counselor will give them a formula for success, but all too frequently the counselors never even asked about the possibility of childhood molestation or deprivation. Until the abuse victim with this type of personality gets loving counsel that deals with her deep-seated guilt, she will continue to be depressed and not really understand why.

The Sanguine/Choleric victim who is of a stronger personality feels the guilt but refuses to give in to it. She determines not to let this trauma or series of events ruin her life. She wants to achieve, no matter what; she has a compulsive need to prove to herself, God, and others that she is all right. She covers up her abuse, puts a big Band-Aid over her hurts, and gets on with life. In school she is hard-driving, active, and often over-achieving. She becomes a caretaker for those with problems, is usually an aggressive leader, and often dates older and successful men. As an adult she may become a perfectionistic workaholic. Often these victims go into full-time Christian service or become social workers where they seem to live sacrificial lives. They may exhibit obsessive, even neutrotic, drives which cover the deep hurts hidden inside and the physical problems which they don't let anyone know about, such as allergies, migraines, ulcers, colitis, and unexplained aches and pains.

While the symptoms of the passive victims show as emotional problems to those who are at all observant, the aggressive victim fools most people and even is praised in church for her all-consuming dedication to God and charitable works.

The Sanguine/Choleric victim-achiever many times feels proud of how she has handled past abuses and, without realizing the differences in personalities, looks down on those who can't hold it all together. They are usually the ones who speak out against counseling or any outside help because they've been able to control themselves in spite of problems. "If I can make it, what's the matter with you?" They often have little compassion for the "weak links" and add guilt to them by saying, "If you were really a Christian you would have gotten over this by now." While I'm sure they mean well and may help some hypochondriacs, their confidence and authority may be the proverbial straw that broke the camel's back, the word that says, "I'm okay but you are pitiful and surely not spiritual." We must all be so very careful to avoid heaping guilt on people who can't cope with life as we are able to do. How helpful it is when we realize the different personalities and their reactions to adverse circumstances so we can handle others with wisdom and not ignorance.

In CLASS we find many Sanguine/Choleric victims who have stayed on top of their emotions appearing to be confidently in control until they hit forty. Why that is the turning point we don't know, but suddenly this over-achiever begins to fall apart. She apologizes for crying and hates herself for being weak. Some have been taking medication for pain that suddenly does no good, and they are driven into a depression they have always been able to control in the past. Pain is a great leveler of all personalities and often forces the strongest of us to seek help.

No matter which personality combination a person is, the first step in overcoming the pains of the past is to admit there is a problem and be willing to deal with it. Denial only deepens the depression.

For Further Study, Thought and Action

Read the parable of the Sower in Luke 8 about the different types of seeds and soils. Does any one of these situations ring any familiar bells from your past? As a child did you feel pushed around? stepped on? walked over? Were you ever abused? Was your childhood spent on the rocks with no attention or nuturing? Did you seldom receive selfless love? Were you fighting your way through the weeds feeling rejected, lonely, or guilty?

Or were you the child of loving, emotionally stable parents who treated you with respect and trained you according to your own personality and talents?

Start by asking a friend to listen to your life story and see if he or she discerns any inconsistencies. If you are doing this study in a group, don't turn it into a mass confession time which will embarrass some of the members. Instead, pair up for this part of the analysis and have each person sensitively share with one other person what he or she remembers of childhood pains. Often the verbal expression of past hurts will initiate a healing process. Encourage the individual who has never shared this with anyone before and insure confidentiality. Some will be helped by talking with the pastor, although often women tell me they are afraid if the pastor "knew all" he wouldn't like them. Victims of sexual abuse frequently cannot relate to a counselor of the same sex as the perpetrator.

Read the "Incest" chapter (10) in *Lives on the Mend,* and review the ten steps to recovery plus the chapter on "Emotional Pains of the Past" (15) which includes the process for inner healing. Many have also found that writing down their thoughts and feelings in a journal can be very helpful.

Do a study on the available counselors and support groups in your area. Find out what assistance your church has and then inquire about others. Sometimes one church in an area will have a staff person who specializes in incest cases while another church may deny they have any victims. It takes people who care for others to spend the time necessary to provide a list of sources for those in need.

Trees whose fruit withereth, without fruit, twice dead, plucked up by the roots.

—Jude 12, KJV

❧ 11 ❧

How Can You Dig Up
the Old Roots?

Because they had no root, they withered away.
—Matthew 13:6, KJV

As you have thought over your past and researched your ancestors, you may have found more than positive personality traits;
you may have unearthed some patterns of abuse or some repeated
diseases. Statistics prove that those who were abused often become abusers, that those who had parents who were fearful often
become phobic, that over half of those who had an alcoholic parent marry or become alcoholics.[1]

A girl we shall call Jan did a study to see the effects of alcohol-
ism on her family. She researched her own background and with
her brother and husband interviewed many relatives, all of whom
were delighted to add their opinions and anecdotes. As I recount
what she wrote to me, perhaps these summaries will encourage
you to ferret out some of your family stories and trace repetitive
problems.

Jan's grandfather on her father's side was an extremely abusive alcoholic who deserted his family, refused to support them,
yet dropped by often enough to get his wife pregnant and produce
nine children whom he beat up whenever he came home. With
this background of a pathetically poor childhood and a loathing
for their father, nine out of nine became alcoholics, one of them
Jan's father. He had nine auto accidents in ten years, ran over
a child while drunk, and was once pronounced dead and on his
way to the morgue before he revived.

Jan's mother came from a family full of emotional, physical, and sexual abuse. She was one of six children, two of whom died in infancy and one in a hunting accident. In her anguish Jan's grandmother made a commitment not to love any of her other children so she wouldn't be hurt when God took them away. Jan's mother, one of the remaining three children, felt rejected and eventually married to get away from home and find some one who would really love her.

Wed to an alcoholic, she became a foodaholic and together they produced five children who grew up in this sick setting. Jan describes and labels each one as the cast in an alcoholic drama.

Oldest brother—SUPER HERO—Choleric.

He is both a workaholic and an alcoholic, is verbally abusive to his wife and neglects his children who feel unloved. He totally denies he has a problem, he is filled with hidden hostilities and repressed rage, and he feels because he keeps a job that he is not an alcoholic.

Oldest sister—BORN LOSER—Phlegmatic.

At thirty-nine this sister cannot function without the help of her mother who cooks for her and stuffs the four children who range from fourteen to newborn. She has been married twice to "losers" and is both physically and verbally abusive to her children. There is little hope for any of them as she is emotionally incapable of any healthy relationships.

Me—GOOD GIRL—Choleric

By God's grace I could see early in life that I didn't want to be like the others. I determined not to marry a loser or jump into a marriage to get away from the home problems. I was the good girl who went to church and did her homework. God's love helped me deal with the family neglect and abuse on a level I could bear. I married a pastor whose unconditional love has given me a feeling of worth and his fathering of our children has given me a model of God's love for us.

Younger brother—SCAPEGOAT—Melancholy.

He was the black sheep of a dark family, a whiney sensitive little boy raised by women (mother, grandmother, and sisters). He had a dependency personality and went into drugs and sex in high school. By a miracle of the Lord he has been redeemed and is in training to be a pastor.

Younger sister—PET—Sanguine
She was the last, became the family pet, and is both spoiled and dependent. She is divorced and is emotionally, verbally, and physically abusive to her children often kicking and slapping them. She is still seeking someone to take care of her and is pursuing a lifestyle which will lead to no good end.

From Jan's summary of her family history, we can see how amazing it is that she extricated herself from the repeat patterns and became proof that with God all things are possible.

On a trip from Cleveland to Chicago I was placed next to an off-duty male flight attendant. As he poured out his life story to me, he told how his father was an alcoholic and never came to any of his school functions. "All I wanted was a normal father who would show up sober." By questioning I found that the grandfather was also an alcoholic. When I explained to him how important it was that he break this chain of addictive weaknesses, he told me, "My friends tease me because I'm too straight and won't do the things they do, but I'm not taking any chances."

Alcoholic problems are not the only ones passed down from generation to generation.

One woman who came to CLASS later wrote me that she had done a study on her family and found that in five generations the first child born was conceived out of wedlock. Another person told of how she couldn't understand why she felt a strong compulsion to beat up her child. As she controlled her urges and prayed fervently for deliverance, she remembered how her mother had beaten her. By asking an uncle, she learned that her mother had been abused by both of her parents.

A friend's father after watching *The Burning Bed* on TV became irate at the abusing husband and later disclosed how his father had beaten up his mother. He had never told anyone in the family how he as a six-year-old had grabbed a broom and hit his father with it in an attempt to protect his mother. The father had kicked him across the room, and the son had kept a burning anger within him since that time. This revelation explained why he had seldom wanted to spend time with his father and the discussion brought out hidden feelings he had never disclosed. As the family talked with him, he remembered his father's hatred of his own father and began to wonder if he had been abused also.

A counselor told me how frequently she finds divorce repeats itself in succeeding generations, often with the same excuses given as to why they could no longer stay together.

Migraine headaches, allergies, and other stress-related problems seem to wind a repetitive thread through families.

Even the manipulation of the Cholerics—the remaking of succeeding generations into submissive children no matter what the original temperament—forms a pattern that needs to be broken. People with high IQs who never seem to reach their potential are often similar to a parent and have an underlying fear of their inability to handle success.

Physical problems repeat themselves. In my family, diabetes and hypoglycemia have appeared many times in each generation as far back as we can trace. The reason doctors take down family histories is to help them spot potential problems and hopefully halt them in early stages.

As you look through your family's background, be alert to signs of negative patterns that need to be changed so that the REAL YOU can stand up.

One of the comments we get about our CLASS staff is that we are so real, so open, so honest. As people observe us for three full days, they can see that it is possible for people to be genuine. How sad that this Christian reality is also considered a novelty. What they see in us is not a lack of problems or stress, but the fact that we have dealt with the pains of our past. We have searched our backgrounds for repeated sins, and we have consciously brought these before the Lord. Each one of us has been through a day or two of counseling and prayer with Lana Bateman, and we have forgiven those who have wronged us. Some of us have spent time with Marilyn Murray at her Restoration Therapy Center and have received grace for a healing journey.

A girl from Ohio wrote on her CLASS evaluation:

> I praise God for calling me here (which he very clearly did). I have been so longing to share Jesus with my world yet not feeling confident. I discovered I had many pains passed down in my family that I hadn't dealt with, and I now realize I don't have a message of healing for the world until I first am healed myself.

During these three days God released me of masks I didn't know
I had because of the genuineness of the staff and the open acceptance
of the women in my small group. I know I will be healed by the
great physician so one day I too will have a message to share.

In an article, "Eliminate Your Pain by Knowing Its Cause,"
Dr. Katherine La Guardia challenges women to take responsibility for learning about their bodies and how they function.

Pain, especially chronic pain, is a combination not only of the
physical symptoms but also of historical biases, social factors, and
the environment.[2]

Do you have some pain that needs to be healed? Do you have
some heavy chains that need to be broken? Do you have some
roots that need to be dug up?

John said, "Produce fruit in keeping with repentance. . . .
The axe is already at the root of the trees, and every tree that
does not produce good fruit will be cut down and thrown into
the fire" (Matt. 3:8,10, NIV).

Throughout the Bible God blesses those who obey and punishes
those who are rebellious. He warns the people over and over.

You shall walk in all the way which the Lord your God has com-
manded you, that you may live, and that it may be well with you,
and that you may prolong your days in the land which you shall
possess (Deut. 5:33, NASB).

God not only wants life "to be well with you" but also with
your children.

So you shall keep His statutes and His commandments which I
am giving you today, that it may go well with you and with your
children after you, and that you may live long on the land which
the Lord your God is giving you for all time (Deut. 4:40, NASB).

Know therefore that the Lord your God, He is God, the faithful
God, who keeps His covenant and His lovingkindness to a thou-
sandth generation with those who love Him and keep His commandments (Deut. 7:9, NASB).

Because God loves his children, he grieves when we disobey and must be punished just as we are saddened when we must discipline our children.

If only you had paid attention to My commandments then your well-being would have been like a river, and your righteousness like the waves of the sea. Your descendants would have been like the sand, and your offspring like its grains; their name would never be cut off or destroyed from My presence (Isa. 48:18, NASB).

As we have thought over our families and analyzed their personalities, we may have come up with some distorted roots that need the axe. God is patient, he has great mercy, and he forgives our transgressions; but his Word tells us that the sins of the fathers are visited upon the third and fourth generation.[3]

For Further Study, Thought, and Action

Follow these steps individually and share the scripture and the lessons learned with your group. If you have gone through this book alone, start a support group for people who want to understand themselves and learn to get along better with others.

Trace your roots: Spend some time with the group in tracing any repeated traits rooted in your family tree. List these in your personality notebook and write a paragraph on each member of the cast as Jan did with her family. What sins have been visited upon your succeeding generations? Could you perhaps write a book? Copy each prayer into your notebook adding your personalized lists and petitions.

Dear Jesus, here are some of the problems and sins of our past generations. I repent for them and ask your forgiveness and cleansing power to break the hold these sins have on our family.

Pull up the weeds: As you observe the sins of the past, you may find some weeds in the present. What do you see in your life that needs to be uprooted now? Jesus says, "Every plant which My heavenly Father did not plant shall be rooted up"

(Matt. 15:13, NASB). He wants us to pull up anything that is not pleasing to him, any weeds sprouting up in his garden.

In Hebrews we read, "See to it that no one misses the grace of God and that no bitter root grows up to cause trouble" (Heb. 12:15, NIV). As you jot down the list of weeds that are tripping you up, remember what you are to do with them. "Throw off everything that hinders and the sin that so easily entangles, and let us run with perseverance the race marked out for us" (Heb. 12:1, NIV).

> Lord Jesus, I have found this list of weeds that are entangling my progress and keeping me from that harvest of righteousness you have prepared for me. I confess these failures in my life and ask you to forgive me and make clear my path before me.

Burn the dead branches: The Lord Jesus tells us that he is the vine and we are his branches. "If anyone does not remain in me, he is like a branch that is thrown away and withers; such branches are picked up, thrown into the fire and burned" (John 15:6, NIV). What dead branches have you been saving from the fire? What temperament weaknesses have you held on to and pretended that they were strengths?

List five behavioral weaknesses that the Lord has shown you while reading this book. Lay these on the altar of God's grace and burn the dead branches of your life. "The Lord called thy name, A green olive tree, fair, and of goodly fruit: with the noise of a great tumult he hath kindled fire upon it, and the branches of it are broken" (Jer. 11:16, KJV).

> Dear Jesus, I want to be a branch that bears fruit, but here is a list of weaknesses that I've been saving even though they are withered and dried up. I place them on your altar that you might kindle fire upon them and remove them from my sight.

Repair the wastelands: As you review your life and that of the preceding generations you may see some deserts without living water, some relatives who never knew the Lord. You may become aware of some years in your life that were wastelands that need to be repaired. "And they shall build the old wastes, they shall raise up the former desolations, and they shall repair the waste cities, the desolations of many generations" (Isa. 61:4, KJV).

God wants to rebuild your life and repair the desolations of many generations. Write down the periods of waste, the days in the desert. Remember that God often gets our attention by sending us to a desert. What did you learn from your wilderness experience?

> Dear Jesus, I reminisce with you about those days in the desert with no living water. Please restore unto me "the years that the locusts hath eaten" (Joel 2:25, KJV).
>
> Show me how to rebuild my wastelands, how to repair the damages I've done to my family. Refresh me with your living water and remind me again of the lessons you've wanted me to learn. Bring me out of my darkness into your light that I might praise your name forever. For we are "a chosen generation, a royal priesthood, an holy nation, a peculiar people; that ye should show forth the praises of him who hath called you out of darkness into his marvelous light" (1 Pet. 2:9, KJV).

Produce fruit that endures: In this day of teen depression and suicide, of child abuse and incest, of physical and emotional deprivation we must be aware of the special needs of our children. We must remember that money never makes up for mother; television and video games when watched alone don't equal a Big Mac with father. In an era when *things* have replaced *time,* we must stem the tide. We don't want to lose our children before their maturity; we want to produce fruit that endures. Write down some changes you must make as a parent.

> Dear Jesus, I have not been the parent I know you want me to be. I've tried to bend the twigs my way without any thought of what you had in mind. I've trained them up in the way I wanted them to go and sometimes not trained them at all. Please forgive me for bruising the fruit, forgive me for what I've done to _____,
> _____, and _____. Break the chains of defeat that my family has been tethered by and release my offspring to be free. "All who see them will recognize them Because they are the offspring whom the Lord has blessed" (Isa. 61:9, NASB).

Love and obey your God: Even though the Bible tells us that the sins of the father are visited upon the children to the third and fourth generation and that we do in fact reproduce after our own kind, God gives us a way out. As he carries on the results of sin to four generations, he shows mercy and love to a thousand generations of those who love him and keep his commandments. (See Exod. 20:6).

> Oh that they had such a heart in them, that they would fear Me and keep all My commandments always, that it may be well with them and with their sons forever! (Deut. 5:29, NASB).

How gracious of our God to show mercy to those who love and obey him for thousands of generations, in fact forever. When we consider the influence our present actions and attitudes can have upon our succeeding generations, can we do less than love and obey our God? Write down whatever "commandments" of God that you have had trouble keeping. Why have you disobeyed? Is it rebellion toward your parents? Some church rules with which you disagree? A lack of belief that God either knows or cares? A determination not to give in to God?

After David had disobeyed three of the Ten Commandments he taught to others, coveting his neighbor's wife, committing adultery, and instigating murder, he cried out to God in Psalm 51. "I know my transgressions and my sin is always before me" (v. 3, NIV).

Dear Jesus, here are my transgressions:

_____,
_____,
_____.

You desire truth in the inner parts.

Jesus, I've hid these thoughts and actions from others, from myself, and I thought from you, but you know the truth. Grant me a willing spirit to sustain me.

Until now I've not been willing to change, but I see what the past generations have done to me and what I may be doing to my children. Grant me Lord, a willing spirit that I may want to change. Open my lips and my mouth will declare your praise.

Yes Lord, let me sing a new song of praise to your power and glory. Let me love you with all my heart.

David had so much money, so many possessions, so many animals to sacrifice, but that's not what you want, dear Lord. You want a broken and a contrite heart. Lord, I give up my rebellious spirit, my wanting to do things my way, my lack of real concern for others. I pray to the God who saves me and loves me that I may be willing to obey what is your good will for my life.

Lord Jesus, I call upon your sacrificial blood to cleanse me from my secret and open faults. I call upon your Holy Spirit to empower me to necessary change and I call upon you to bind Satan and any dominion he may have on me and upon my children to the third and fourth generations. Get thee behind me, Satan, and away from each member of my family. I call upon you, Jesus, the name that is above all names, knowing that "Everyone who calls on the name of the Lord will be saved." (Rom. 10:13, NIV). Jesus save me and my family—forever.

In your precious name I pray, Amen.

❦ 12 ❦

Have You
a Song to Sing
in the Spring?

Come before his presence with singing.—Psalm 100:2, KJV

What lessons have you learned from tracing your personality tree? Have you found out who you really are? Have you accepted God's direction? Do you know you are created for such a time as this? Have you seen how parents, siblings, or mates may have warped your original personality to make you what was acceptable for them? Have you viewed, perhaps for the first time, what influence you have over your own children in training them up in the way you want them to go?

God created each one of us, and each one of our children, to be unique creations, special blendings of the four basic humors—Sanguine, Choleric, Melancholy, and Phlegmatic. As we have used these terms from Hippocrates as tools in following God's command that we examine ourselves and as we've seen how people have tampered with God's original plan for our life, each of us should now have a better understanding of our personality and the traits of those other members of our family tree.

In this closing chapter let me share two stories from our two families—the first about my father and the second about Fred's mother.

When I was a senior in college, I came home for Christmas vacation and anticipated a fun-filled fortnight with my two brothers. We were so excited to be together we volunteered to watch the store so that my mother and father could take their first day off in years. The day before my parents went to Boston, my father took me quietly aside to the little den behind the store. The room was so small that it held only a piano and a hide-a-bed couch. In fact, when you pulled the bed out it filled the room and you could sit on the foot of it and play the piano. Father reached behind the old upright and pulled out a cigar box. He opened it and showed me a little pile of newspaper articles. I had read so many Nancy Drew detective stories that I was excited and wide-eyed over the hidden box of clippings.

"What are they?" I asked.

Father replied seriously, "These are articles I've written and some letters to the editor that have been published."

As I began to read, I saw at the bottom of each neatly clipped article the name Walter Chapman, Esq. "Why didn't you tell me you'd done this?" I asked.

"Because I didn't want your mother to know. She's always told me that since I didn't have much education I shouldn't try to write. I wanted to run for some political office also, but she told me I shouldn't try. I guess she was afraid she'd be embarrassed if I lost. I just wanted to try for the fun of it. I figured I could write without her knowing it, and so I did. When each item would be printed, I'd cut it out and hide it in this box. I knew someday I'd show the box to someone, and it's you."

He watched me as I read over a few of the articles and when I looked up, his big blue eyes were moist. "I guess I tried for something too big this last time," he added.

"Did you write something else?"

"Yes, I sent into our denominational magazine to give some suggestions on how the national nominating committee could be selected more fairly. It's been three months since I sent it in. I guess I tried for something too big."

This was such a new side to my fun-loving father that I didn't quite know what to say, so I tried, "Maybe it'll still come."

"Maybe, but don't hold your breath." Father gave me a little smile and a wink and then closed the cigar box and tucked it into the space behind the piano.

The next morning our parents left on the bus to the Haverhill Depot where they took a train to Boston. Jim, Ron, and I ran the store, and I thought about the box. I'd never known my father liked to write. I didn't tell my brothers; it was a secret between Father and me. The Mystery of the Hidden Box.

Early that evening I looked out the store window and saw my mother get off the bus—alone. She crossed the Square and walked briskly through the store.

"Where's Dad?" we asked together.

"Your father's dead," she said without a tear.

In disbelief we followed her to the kitchen where she told us they had been walking through the Park Street Subway Station in the midst of crowds of people when Father had fallen to the floor. A nurse bent over him, looked up at Mother and said simply, "He's dead."

Mother had stood by him stunned, not knowing what to do as people tripped over him in their rush in the subway. A priest said, "I'll call the police," and disappeared. Mother straddled Dad's body for about an hour. Finally an ambulance came and took them both to the city morgue where Mother had to go through his pockets and remove his watch. She'd come back on the train alone and then home on the local bus. Mother told us the shocking tale without shedding a tear. Not showing emotion had always been a matter of discipline and pride for her. We didn't cry either and we took turns waiting on the customers.

One steady patron asked, "Where's the old man tonight?"

"He's dead," I replied.

"Oh, too bad," and he left.

I'd not thought of him as the old man, and I was hurt at the question, but he was seventy-three and Mother was only fifty-three. He'd always been healthy and happy and he'd cared for frail mother without complaint, but now he was gone. No more whistling, no more singing hymns while stocking shelves; the Old Man was gone.

On the morning of the funeral, I sat at the table in the store opening sympathy cards and pasting them in a scrapbook when I noticed the church magazine in the pile. Normally I would never have opened what I viewed as a dull religious publication, but just maybe that secret article might be there—and it was.

I took the magazine to the little den, shut the door, and burst into tears. I'd been brave, but seeing Dad's bold recommendations to the national convention in print was more than I could bear. I read and cried and then I read again. I pulled out the box from behind the piano and under the clippings I found a two-page letter to my father from Henry Cabot Lodge, Sr., thanking him for his campaign suggestions.

I didn't tell anyone about my box; it remained a secret until we closed the store two years later and moved in with Grandma leaving the piano behind. I gave my last look to the empty kitchen with the old black stove standing staunchly alone while the bottle of kerosene gurgled loudly in the corner. I went quietly to the den, and as if in some religious rite, I reached behind the old piano where I'd practiced lessons and played hymns on Sunday evenings and pulled out *the box*.

Father left me no money, but he left me the box. He had little education and no degrees, but he gave me and my brothers a love for the English language, a thirst for politics, and an ability to write. Who knows what Father could have done with just a little encouragement?

Today as I stand in my study and look at Dad's article there on the wall matted in blue next to his picture smiling down at me and reread the letter from Lodge framed with his picture just below Father's, I realize how close I came to knowing none of this. How grateful I am that Father chose that day to reach behind the piano and pull out the box.

I'll never know what Walter Chapman, Esquire, could have been. Was there a great American novel inside him or at least a weekly column for the *Haverhill Gazette?* Could his charm and sense of humor have brought him political acclaim?—or could he at least have been the mayor of Haverhill?

How many of us as wives hold down our husband's aspirations, stifle a little bud of genius that's longing to burst forth? Why? Because we're afraid if he fails, we'll be embarrassed. How many are daunted by lack of degrees and don't dare to have their reach exceed their grasp?

Oh God, let us encourage one another unto good works (Heb. 10:24–25).

In one rare evening of genuine disclosure Fred's mother told me of her disappointments. "I never could please my father no matter how hard I tried, and I did my best to make my mother the queen she really wanted to be." I encouraged her to tell me how she really felt, and she shared one heart-breaking story.

She was in love with a young man while at Cornell and they had talked of marriage. Her mother disapproved because she felt he did not come from an important or wealthy enough family. After college they went in separate directions for the summer, and he was to call her in the fall. She never heard from him again.

At the mention of this fact, this beautiful woman burst into tears, and I thought the sad story was over. I'd never seen her let down her guard before, and I felt so sorry for how this rejection still bothered her. As I sat quietly, wondering what I should say, she looked up and continued. "That's not the end of it. I went to a party just a few years ago and there he was. I found out he was a successful lawyer, and then I asked that question, 'Why didn't you ever call me?' 'Oh, I called all right,' he replied. 'I talked to your mother on the telephone, and she told me that you were engaged to another man, that you didn't love me, and that you'd asked her to tell me never to call again.' "

Mother's ample frame shook as she sobbed out these last words. I knelt beside her and felt a warmth and compassion for her I'd never known before. How seldom we sense what's stored up inside a person just waiting for a quiet moment, a nonthreatening situation to be set free. My heart was broken with hers as she confessed, "I never felt right about Mother, but I didn't know why. I felt guilty because I couldn't love her enough, so I waited on her like a slave to ease my conscience. I tried to become what she wanted me to be, and I'll never know what I might have been."

"Was there anything you really wanted to be?" I asked.

"An opera singer," she answered quickly. "I wanted to study music, but my parents felt that was a waste of time, that I'd make more money in the millinery business. But I was in one show in college, and I had the lead."

She got up quickly, went to a closet and pulled out a box of old pictures. She showed me a large photo of a stage setting with the cast posed for review. "There I am." She pointed proudly to a confident and beautiful young girl seated on an ornate chair, center stage, the obvious star of the show.

I'd not known of her operatic ambitions before, and I shared how I loved the theatre and had wanted to be an actress until my drama teacher told me I was much better at directing others. At the end of this memorable and meaningful evening, Mother gave me the picture of her on stage in her one starring role, and I treasure this memory of what might have been.

We'll never know what this talented, creative woman could have become had she been allowed to pursue her natural aims and abilities instead of being brought up to play the role of "perfect daughter." Suppressed ambitions never die; they wait inside for some moment of possible expression in the future.

Mother Littauer is now eighty-five years old, and her conscious mind is no longer functioning correctly. When Fred and I visited recently she had a peaceful expression on her face although she didn't seem to know who we were. When I talked with the nurse who cares for her, she said, "It's the strangest thing. She can't talk at all, but she sings opera each day and practices her scales."

As I told this story of Mother's broken dreams to an informal group of only twenty people, several responded with similar experiences. One pretty girl with sad eyes said, "I always wanted to be a dancer. My parents let me take lessons, but when I wanted to make dancing a career, they scoffed at the thought. 'You're not *that* good, and you'll never make it.'" Tears came to her eyes as she continued. "They may have been right, but I wanted to give it a try while I was young. Now I'll never know what I might have been."

A middle-aged lady stated clearly, "You've made me realize I gave up too quickly. I'm going to start back with my violin and get a chamber music quartet together again."

An elderly lady surprised me with, "I wanted to be an explorer, but my father wouldn't let me leave town. Every time I wanted to go out and seek adventure, he'd tell me about those 'other kinds of people' lurking out there ready to pounce on me. All my life I've had an adventurous spirit, but because of the few of those 'other kinds of people' I've never had an adventure."

This fascinating response to the operatic hopes of my mother-in-law led me to wonder how many others have had their dreams thwarted by well-meaning parents who, by insisting their off-spring play it safe, destroyed a dream of the future.

How many of us have a suppressed opera, an imagined painting, a possible poem, the plot for a novel, the potential for a political career, or a thwarted adventure locked inside of us waiting for that magic key to set us free. Are you ready to sing a song in the spring? Perhaps like the Song of Solomon?

> *Arise, my darling,*
> *my beautiful one, and come with me.*
> *See! The winter is past;*
> *the rains are over and gone.*
> *Flowers appear on the earth;*
> *the season of singing has come.*
> —Song of Songs 2:10–12, NIV

You were made for such a time as this.

NOTES

Chapter 1.   WERE YOU BORN LIKE THIS?

1. Dr. William R. Bright, "Have You Heard of the Four Spiritual Laws?" Campus Crusade for Christ, Arrowhead Springs, CA.
2. Winston Churchill, tape purchased in London, recorded live.
3. William Manchester, *The Last Lion*, Little Brown, 1983, p. 7.
4. Alice Vollmar, "Together Again," *Friendly Exchange*, 1985, p. 28.
5. Ibid.
6. Oscar Wilde, *The Importance of Being Earnest*, Act I.

Chapter 2.   WHAT IS YOUR PERSONALITY?
1. Michael Gartner, "About Words," *Austin American-Statesman*, January 7, 1985.
2. William Shakespeare, *Julius Caesar*, Act V, Scene 5.
3. Bishop Ernest A. Fitzgerald, "It's All Right to Worry," *Piedmont Airlines*, July 1985.
4. Oswald Chambers, *My Utmost for His Highest* (New York: Dodd, Mead & Company, 1963), p. 347.

Chapter 3.   WHAT ARE YOUR DESIRES AND UNDERLYING NEEDS?
1. M. I. Blackwell, *The Dallas Morning News*, May 4, 1986.
2. Robert William Service, *The Law of the Yukon*.

217

3. Ludwig van Beethoven, as cited in *Forbes*, January 30, 1984.
4. *Time*, July 7, 1986, pp. 12, 16.
5. William Shakespeare, *Hamlet*, Act I, Scene 3.
6. Norman Vincent Peale, "Today," NBC Television program, February 14, 1985.

Chapter 5.   WHAT GETS YOU DEPRESSED?
1. William Shakespeare, *Macbeth*, Act V, Scene 5.
2. *USA Today*, "The Lure of the Store: It's OK If Shopping Buys You a Thrill," Nanci Hellmich, February 4, 1986.
3. Norman M. Lobsenz, "How to Make a Second Marriage Work," *Parade Magazine*, September 1, 1985.

Chapter 6.   ARE YOU WEARING A MASK?
1. Guillaume de Salluste Seigneur du Bartas, *Dialogue between Heraclitus and Democritus*.
2. "Illusions of Competency," *Piedmont Airlines*, July 1985.
3. Ibid.
4. William Shakespeare, *The Twelfth Night*, Act II, Scene 5.
5. William Makepeace Thackeray, *The English Humorists*.
6. William Shakespeare, *Merchant of Venice*, Act I, Scene 1, line 77.
7. William Henry Davies, *Hunting Joy*.
8. Lucan, *The Civil War*, Book IV.
9. Sir Walter Scott, *Marmion*.

Chapter 7.   WHAT IS A PERSONALITY TREE?
1. Stephen Vincent Benét, *John Brown's Body*.
2. Oswald Chambers, *My Utmost for His Highest* (New York: Dodd, Mead & Company, 1963), p. 94.

Chapter 8.   WHAT ARE YOUR CHILDREN'S
              PERSONALITIES?
1. Alexander Pope, *Moral Essays*, Epistle 1.
2. "Treating Teens in Trouble," *Newsweek*, January 20, 1986.
3. Ibid.
4. Dr. Judith Wallerstein, "Good Morning America," ABC Television program, January 16, 1986.
5. The sections in this chapter labeled "Tools to Help" are

based on material from Lana Bateman, *Personality Patterns,* Philippian Ministries, Dallas, Texas, copyright, 1985.

6. Susan Lapinski, "When Your Baby Seems Depressed," *Parade Magazine,* February 14, 1985.

7. Ibid.

8. Ibid.

9. Sally Ann Stewart, "Temperament, Not Poor Training, Ignites Tantrums," *USA Today*, December 11, 1985.

10. Ibid.

Chapter 9. HOW CAN YOU BEND THE TWIGS AS THEY SHOULD GO?

1. Harold Bloomfield, *Making Peace with Your Parents,* (New York: Random House, 1983), as cited in *U.S. News and World Report* (Book Review), May 21, 1984.

2. Ibid.

Chapter 11. HOW CAN YOU DIG UP THE OLD ROOTS?

1. Dr. Ron Daugherty, lecture at Pennsylvania Medical Society, April 30, 1986.

2. Carol Towarnicky, "Eliminate Your Aches and Pains by Learning about Their Causes," *The Dallas Morning News,* April 7, 1986.

3. Exodus 20:5, 34:7, Numbers 14:18.

Name _____

Directions— In *each* of the following rows of *four words across*, place an X in front of the *one* word that most often applies to you. Continue through all forty lines. Be sure each number is marked. If you are not sure of which word "most applies," ask a spouse or a friend, and think of what your answer would have been *when you were a child*.

Strengths

1 ___	Adventurous	___	Adaptable	___	Animated	___	Analytical
2 ___	Persistent	___	Playful	___	Persuasive	___	Peaceful
3 ___	Submissive	___	Self-sacrificing	___	Sociable	___	Strong-willed
4 ___	Considerate	___	Controlled	___	Competitive	___	Convincing
5 ___	Refreshing	___	Respectful	___	Reserved	___	Resourceful
6 ___	Satisfied	___	Sensitive	___	Self-reliant	___	Spirited
7 ___	Planner	___	Patient	___	Positive	___	Promoter
8 ___	Sure	___	Spontaneous	___	Scheduled	___	Shy
9 ___	Orderly	___	Obligingly	___	Outspoken	___	Optimistic
10 ___	Friendly	___	Faithful	___	Funny	___	Forceful
11 ___	Daring	___	Delightful	___	Diplomatic	___	Detailed
12 ___	Cheerful	___	Considerate	___	Cultured	___	Confident
13 ___	Idealistic	___	Independent	___	Inoffensive	___	Inspiring
14 ___	Demonstrative	___	Decisive	___	Dry Humor	___	Deep
15 ___	Mediator	___	Musical	___	Mover	___	Mixes easily
16 ___	Thoughtful	___	Tenacious	___	Talker	___	Tolerant
17 ___	Listener	___	Loyal	___	Leader	___	Lively
18 ___	Contented	___	Chief	___	Chartmaker	___	Cute
19 ___	Perfectionist	___	Pleasant	___	Productive	___	Popular
20 ___	Bouncy	___	Bold	___	Behaved	___	Balanced

Weaknesses

21 ___	Blank	___	Bashful	___	Brassy	___	Bossy
22 ___	Undisciplined	___	Unsympathetic	___	Unenthusiatic	___	Unforgiving
23 ___	Reticent	___	Resentful	___	Resistant	___	Repetitious
24 ___	Fussy	___	Fearful	___	Forgetful	___	Frank
25 ___	Impatient	___	Insecure	___	Indecisive	___	Interrupts
26 ___	Unpopular	___	Uninvolved	___	Unpredictable	___	Unaffectionate
27 ___	Headstrong	___	Haphazard	___	Hard to please	___	Hesitant
28 ___	Plain	___	Pessimistic	___	Proud	___	Permissive
29 ___	Angered easily	___	Aimless	___	Argumentative	___	Alienated
30 ___	Naive	___	Negative attitude	___	Nervy	___	Nonchalant
31 ___	Worrier	___	Withdrawn	___	Workaholic	___	Wants credit
32 ___	Too sensitive	___	Tactless	___	Timid	___	Talkative
33 ___	Doubtful	___	Disorganized	___	Domineering	___	Depressed
34 ___	Inconsistent	___	Introvert	___	Intolerant	___	Indifferent
35 ___	Messy	___	Moody	___	Mumbles	___	Manipulative
36 ___	Slow	___	Stubborn	___	Show-off	___	Skeptical
37 ___	Loner	___	Lord over	___	Lazy	___	Loud
38 ___	Sluggish	___	Suspicious	___	Short-tempered	___	Scatterbrained
39 ___	Revengeful	___	Restless	___	Reluctant	___	Rash
40 ___	Compromising	___	Critical	___	Crafty	___	Changeable

Now transfer all of your "Xs" to the corresponding words on the personality scoring sheet and add up your totals.

Created by Fred Littauer

PERSONALITY TEST
WORD DEFINITIONS

Reprinted with permission from
Personality Patterns
by Lana Bateman

STRENGTHS

1.

ANIMATED —Full of life, lively use of hand, arm, and face gestures.

ADVENTUROUS —One who will take on new and daring enterprises with a need to master them.

ANALYTICAL —One who is constantly in the process of analyzing people, places, or things.

ADAPTABLE —One who easily adapts to any situation.

2.

PERSISTENT —Refusing to let go, insistently repetitive or continuous, can't drop it.

PLAYFUL —Full of fun and good humor.

PERSUASIVE —One who persuades through logic and fact rather than charm.

PEACEFUL —One who seems undisturbed and tranquil and who retreats from any form of strife.

3.

SUBMISSIVE —One who easily submits to any other's point of view or desire. This person has little need to assert his own view or opinion.

SELF-
  SACRIFICING —One who constantly sacrifices his/her own personal well being for the sake of or to meet the needs of others.

SOCIABLE —This sociable refers to one who sees being with others as an opportunity to be cute and entertaining. If you are one who enjoys social gatherings as a challenge or business opportunity then do not check this word.

STRONG-
   WILLED — One who is determined to have his/her own way.

4.
CONSIDERATE — Having regard for the needs and feelings of others.

CONTROLLED — One who has emotional feelings but doesn't display them.

COMPETITIVE — One who turns every situation, happening, or game into an arena for competition. This person always plays to win!

CONVINCING — This person can convince you of anything through the sheer charm of his/her personality. Facts are unimportant.

5.
REFRESHING — One who renews and stimulates or pleasantly lifts spirits.

RESPECTFUL — One who treats others with deference, honor, and esteem.

RESERVED — Self restraint in expression of emotion or enthusiasm.

RESOURCEFUL — One who is able to act quickly and effectively in virtually all situations.

6.
SATISFIED — A person who easily accepts any circumstance or situation.

SENSITIVE — This person is intensively sensitive to self and others.
SELF-RELIANT — An independent person who can fully rely on his/her own capabilities, judgment, and resources.

SPIRITED — One who is full of life and excitement.

7.
PLANNER — One who prefers to work out a detailed arrangement beforehand, for the accomplishment of project or goal. This person much prefers involvement with the planning stages and the finished product rather than the carrying out of the task.

PATIENT — One who is unmoved by delay—calm and tolerant.
POSITIVE — Characterized by certainty and assurance.
PROMOTER — One who can compel others to go along, join, or invest through the sheer charm of his/her own personality.

8.

SURE — One who is confident, not hesitating or wavering.

SPONTANEOUS — One who prefers all of life to be impulsive, unpremeditated activity. This person feels restricted by plans.

SCHEDULED — This person is controlled by his/her schedule and gets very upset if that schedule is interrupted. There is another type of person who uses a schedule to stay organized, but is not controlled by the schedule. If the second description is you, do not check this word.

SHY — Quiet, doesn't easily instigate a conversation.

9.

ORDERLY — A person who has a methodical, systematic arrangement of things. Can be obsessively tidy.

OBLIGING — Accommodating. One who is quick to do it another's way.

OUTSPOKEN — One who speaks frankly and without reserve.

OPTIMISTIC — This optimist is an almost childlike, dreamer type of optimist.

10.

FRIENDLY — This person is a responder to friendliness rather than an initiator. While he/she seldom starts a conversation, he/she responds with great warmth and enjoys the exchange.

FAITHFUL — Consistently reliable. Steadfast, loyal, and devoted sometimes beyond reason.

FUNNY — This person has an innate humor that can make virtually any story a funny one and is a remarkable joke-teller. If you have a dry humor, do not check this word.

FORCEFUL — A commanding personality. One would hesitate to take a stand against this person.

11.

DARING — One who is willing to take risks; fearless, bold.

DELIGHTFUL — A person who is greatly pleasing, fun to be with.

DIPLOMATIC — One who deals with people both tactfully and sensitively.

DETAILED — A person who prefers working with the minute or fields that require detail work such as math, research, accounting, carving, art, graphics, etc.

12.

CHEERFUL — Consistently being in good spirits and promoting cheer.

CONSISTENT — A person who is agreeable, compatible, not contradictory.

CULTURED
—One whose interests involve both intellectual and artistic pursuits, such as theatre, symphony, ballet, etc.

CONFIDENT
—One who is self-assured and/or certain of success.

13.

IDEALISTIC
—One who visualizes things in an ideal or perfect form, and has a need to measure up to that standard.

INDEPENDENT
—One who is self-sufficient, self-supporting, self-confident and seems to have little need of help.

INOFFENSIVE
—A person who never causes offense, pleasant, unobjectionable, harmless.

INSPIRING
—One who encourages others to work, join, or be involved. There is another personality that is deeply inspirational and has a need to bring life-changing inspiration. If you are the latter, do not check this word.

14.

DEMONSTRATIVE
—One who openly expresses emotion, especially affection. This person doesn't hesitate to touch others while speaking to them.

DECISIVE
—A person with quick, conclusive, decision-making ability.

DRY HUMOR
—One who exhibits dry wit, usually one-liners which can be sarcastic in nature, but very humorous.

DEEP
—A person who is intense and often introspective with a distaste for surface conversation and pursuits.

15.

MEDIATOR
—A person who consistantly finds him/herself in the role of reconciling differences in order to avoid conflict.

MUSICAL
—One who either participates in or has an intense appreciation for music. This type of musical would not include those who find it fun to sing or play. The latter would be a different personality that enjoys being an entertainer rather than one who is deeply committed to music as an artform.

MOVER
—One who is so driven by a need to be productive, that he/she finds it difficult to sit still.

MIXES EASILY
—One who loves a party and can't wait to meet everyone in the room, never meets a stranger.

16.

THOUGHTFUL
—A considerate person who remembers special occasions and is quick to make a kind gesture.

TENACIOUS
—One who holds on firmly, stubbornly, and won't let go till the goal is accomplished.

TALKER —A person who is constantly talking, generally telling funny stories and entertaining everyone around him/her. There is another compulsive talker who is a nervous talker and feels the need to fill the silence in order to make others comfortable. This is not the entertaining talker we are describing here.

TOLERANT —One who easily accepts the thoughts and ways of others without the need to disagree with or change them.

17.
LISTENER —One who always seems willing to listen.

LOYAL —Faithful to a person, ideal, or job. This person is sometimes loyal beyond reason and to his/her own detriment.

LEADER —A person who is a born leader. This is not one who rises to the occasion because they *can* lead, but one who is driven to lead and finds it very difficult to believe anyone else can do the job.

LIVELY —Full of life, vigorous, energetic.

18.
CONTENTED —One who is easily satisfied with what he/she has.

CHIEF —A person who commands leadership.

CHARTMAKER —One who enjoys either graphs, charts, or lists.

CUTE —Bubbly-beauty, cutie, precious, diminutive.

19.
PERFECTIONIST —One who desires perfection but not necessarily in every area of life.

PERMISSIVE —This person is permissive with employees, friends, and children in order to avoid conflict.

PRODUCTIVE —One who must constantly be working and/or producing. This person finds it very difficult to rest.

POPULAR —One who is the life of the party and therefore is much desired as a party guest.

20.
BOUNCY —A bubbly, lively personality.

BOLD —Fearless, daring, forward.

BEHAVED —One who consistently desires to conduct him/herself within the realm of what is proper.

BALANCED —Stable, middle of the road personality, without extremes.

WEAKNESSES

21.

BRASSY
—One who is showy, flashy, comes on strong.

BOSSY
—Commanding, domineering, overbearing. (Do not relate this to the raising of children. All mothers seem bossy and domineering.) Think only of adult relationships.

BASHFUL
—One who shrinks from notice, resulting from self-consciousness.

BLANK
—A person who shows little facial expression or emotion.

22.

UNDISCIPLINED
—A person whose lack of discipline permeates virtually every area of his/her life.

UNSYMPATHETIC
—One who finds it difficult to relate to the problems or hurts of others.

UN-
ENTHUSIASTIC
—A person who finds it hard to get excited or feel enthusiasm.

UNFORGIVING
—One who has difficulty forgiving or forgetting a hurt or injustice done to them. This individual may find it hard to release a grudge.

23.

RETICENT
—One who is unwilling or struggles against getting involved.

RESENTFUL
—This person easily feels resentment as a result of real or imagined offenses.

RESISTANT
—One who strives, works against, or resists accepting any other way but his/her own.

REPETITIOUS
—This person retells stories and incidents to entertain you without realizing he/she has already told the story several times before. This is not a question so much of forgetfulness, as it is of constantly needing something to say.

24.

FUSSY
—One who is insistent over petty matters or details, calling for great attention to trivial details.

FEARFUL
—One who often experiences feelings of fear, apprehension or anxiousness.

FORGETFUL
—This person is forgetful because it isn't fun to remember. His/her forgetfulness is tied to a lack of discipline. There is another personality that is more like the absent-

minded professor. This person tends to be off in another world and only remembers what he/she chooses to remember. If you are the latter, do not check this word.

FRANK   —One who is straightforward, outspoken, and doesn't mind telling you exactly what he/she thinks.

25.
IMPATIENT   —A person who finds it difficult to endure irritation or wait patiently.

INSECURE   —One who is apprehensive or lacks confidence.

INDECISIVE   —This person finds it difficult to make a decision at all. There is another personality that labors long over each decision in order to make the perfect one. If you are the latter, do not check this word.

INTERRUPTS   —This person interrupts because he/she is afraid of forgetting the wonderful thing they have to say if another is allowed to finish. This person is more of a talker than a listener.

26.
UNPOPULAR   —A person whose intensity and demand for perfection can push others away.

UNINVOLVED   —One who has no desire to become involved in clubs, groups, or people activities.

UN-
  PREDICTABLE   —This person may be ecstatic one moment and blue the next, willing to help and then disappear, promising to come and then forgetting to show up.

UN-
  AFFECTIONATE   —One who finds it difficult to verbally or physically demonstrate affection openly.

27.
HEADSTRONG   —One who insists on having his/her own way.
HAPHAZARD   —One who has no consistent way of doing things.
HARD TO
  PLEASE   —A person whose standards are set so high that it is difficult to ever please them.

HESITANT   —This person is slow to get moving and hard to get involved.

28.
PLAIN   —A middle-of-the-road personality without highs or lows and showing little if any emotion.

PESSIMISTIC   —This person, while hoping for the best, generally sees the down side of a situation first.

PROUD —One with great self-esteem who sees him/herself as always right and the best person for the job.

PERMISSIVE —This personality allows others (including children) to do as they please in order to keep from being disliked.

29.

ANGERED
   EASILY —One who has a childlike flash-in-the-pan temper that expresses itself in a child's tantrum style. It is over and forgotten almost instantly.

AIMLESS —A person who is not a goal-setter and has little desire to be one.

ARGUMENTATIVE —One who incites arguments generally because he/she is determined to be right no matter what the situation may be.

ALIENATED —A person who easily feels estranged from others often because of insecurity or fear that others don't really enjoy his/her company.

30.

NAIVE —A simple and childlike perspective, lacking sophistication or worldliness. This is not to be confused with uninformed. There is another personality that is so consumed with his/her own particular field of interest that he/she simply could not care less what is going on outside of that sphere. If you are the latter, do not check this word.

NEGATIVE —One whose attitude is seldom positive and is often able to see only the down or dark side of each situation.

NERVY —Full of confidence, fortitude, and sheer guts.

NONCHALANT —Easy-going, unconcerned, indifferent.

31.

WORRIER —One who consistently feels uncertain or troubled.

WITHDRAWN —A person who pulls back to him/herself and needs a great deal of alone or isolation time.

WORKAHOLIC —This is one of two workaholic personalities. This particular one is an aggressive goal-setter who must be constantly productive and feels very guilty when resting. This workaholic is not driven by a need for perfection or completion but by a need for accomplishment and reward.

WANTS
   CREDIT —One who is almost dysfunctional without the credit or approval of others. As an entertainer this person feeds on the applause, laughter, and/or acceptance of an audience.

32.
TOO

SENSITIVE	—One who is overly sensitive and introspective.
TACTLESS	—A person who can sometimes express him/herself in a somewhat offensive and inconsiderate way.
TIMID	—One who shrinks from difficult situations.
TALKATIVE	—A compulsive talker who finds it difficult to listen. Again, this is an entertaining talker and not a nervous talker.

33.

DOUBTFUL	—A person who is full of doubts, uncertain.
DISORGANIZED	—One whose lack of organizational ability touches virtually every area of life.
DOMINEERING	—One who compulsively takes control of situations and/or people. Do not consider the mothering role. All mothers are somewhat domineering.
DEPRESSED	—A person who struggles with bouts of depression on a fairly consistent basis.

34.

INCONSISTENT	—Erratic, contradictory, illogical.
INTROVERT	—A person whose thoughts and interest are directed inward. One who lives within him/herself.
INTOLERANT	—One who appears unable to withstand or accept another's attitudes, point of view or way of doing things.
INDIFFERENT	—A person to whom most things don't matter one way or the other.

35.

MESSY	—This person is messy because it isn't fun to discipline him/herself to clean. The mess is hardly noticed. There is another personality that gets messy when depressed, and yet another that is messy because it takes too much energy to do the cleaning. Be sure you are the first one mentioned if you check this word.
MOODY	—One who easily slips into moods. This person doesn't get very high emotionally, but does experience very low lows.
MUMBLES	—This person may mumble quietly under the breath when pushed. This is a passive display of anger.
MANIPULATIVE	—One who influences or manages shrewdly or deviously for one's own advantage. One who *will* find a way to get his/her own way.

36.
SLOW — One who is slow-moving, easy-going.
STUBBORN — A person who is determined to exert his/her own will. Not easily persuaded; obstinate.
SHOW-OFF — One who needs to be the center of attention.
SKEPTICAL — Disbelieving, questioning the motive behind the words.

37.
LONER — One who requires a lot of alone time and tends to avoid other people.
LORD OVER — A person who doesn't hestitate to let you know that he/she is right or has won.
LAZY — One who evaluates work or activity in terms of how much energy it will take.
LOUD — A person whose laugh or voice can be heard above others in the room.

38.
SLUGGISH — Slow to get started.
SUSPICIOUS — One who tends to suspect or distrust.
SHORT-
   TEMPERED — One who has a demanding impatience-based anger and a very short fuse. This type of anger is expressed when others are not moving fast enough or have not completed what they have been asked to do.

SCATTER-
   BRAINED — A person lacking the power of concentration, or attention. Flighty.

39.
REVENGEFUL — One who knowingly or otherwise holds a grudge and punishes the offender, often by subtly withholding friendship or affection.
RESTLESS — A person who likes constant new activity because it isn't fun to do the same things all the time.
RELUCTANT — One who is unwilling or struggles against getting involved.
RASH — One who may act hastily, without thinking things through, generally because of impatience.

40.
COMPROMISING — A person who will often compromise, even when he/she is right, in order to avoid conflict.
CRITICAL — One who constantly evaluates and makes judgments. Example: One who is critical might see someone coming down the street and within seconds might try to evaluate

their cleanliness, look of intelligence or lack of it, style of clothing or lack of it, physical attractiveness or lack of it, and the list goes on. This person constantly analyzes and critiques, sometimes without realizing he/she is doing so.

CRAFTY   —Shrewd, one who can always find a way to get to the desired end.

CHANGEABLE   —A person with a childlike short attention span that needs a lot of change and variety to keep from getting bored.

Personality Scoring Sheet

Name _____

Strengths

	SANGUINE		CHOLERIC		MELANCHOLY		PHLEGMATIC
1	Animated		Adventurous		Analytical		Adaptable
2	Playful		Persuasive		Persistent		Peaceful
3	Sociable		Strong-willed		Self-sacrificing		Submissive
4	Convincing		Competitive		Considerate		Controlled
5	Refreshing		Resourceful		Respectful		Reserved
6	Spirited		Self-reliant		Sensitive		Satisfied
7	Promoter		Positive		Planner		Patient
8	Spontaneous		Sure		Scheduled		Shy
9	Optimistic		Outspoken		Orderly		Obliging
10	Funny		Forceful		Faithful		Friendly
11	Delightful		Daring		Detailed		Diplomatic
12	Cheerful		Confident		Cultured		Consistent
13	Inspiring		Independent		Idealistic		Inoffensive
14	Demonstrative		Decisive		Deep		Dry humor
15	Mixes easily		Mover		Musical		Mediator
16	Talker		Tenacious		Thoughtful		Tolerant
17	Lively		Leader		Loyal		Listener
18	Cute		Chief		Chartmaker		Contented
19	Popular		Productive		Perfectionist		Pleasant
20	Bouncy		Bold		Behaved		Balanced

Weaknesses

	SANGUINE		CHOLERIC		MELANCHOLY		PHLEGMATIC
21	Brassy		Bossy		Bashful		Blank
22	Undisciplined		Unsympathetic		Unforgiving		Unenthusiastic
23	Repetitious		Resistant		Resentful		Reticent
24	Forgetful		Frank		Fussy		Fearful
25	Interrupts		Impatient		Insecure		Indecisive
26	Unpredictable		Unaffectionate		Unpopular		Uninvolved
27	Haphazard		Headstrong		Hard-to-please		Hesitant
28	Permissive		Proud		Pessimistic		Plain
29	Angered Easily		Argumentative		Alienated		Aimless
30	Naive		Nervy		Negative attitude		Nonchalant
31	Wants credit		Workaholic		Withdrawn		Worrier
32	Talkative		Tactless		Too sensitive		Timid
33	Disorganized		Domineering		Depressed		Doubtful
34	Inconsistent		Introlerant		Introvert		Indifferent
35	Messy		Manipulative		Moody		Mumbles
36	Show-off		Stubborn		Skeptical		Slow
37	Loud		Lord -over-others		Loner		Lazy
38	Scatterbrained		Short-tempered		Suspicious		Sluggish
39	Restless		Rash		Revengeful		Reluctant
40	Changeable		Crafty		Critical		Compromising

Totals ____   ____   ____   ____

PERSONALITY STRENGTHS AND WEAKNESSES

STRENGTHS

	THE TALKER SANGUINE	THE WORKER CHOLERIC	THE THINKER MELANCHOLY	THE WATCHER PHLEGMATIC
EMOTIONS	Appealing personality Talkative, storyteller Life-of-the-party Good sense of humor Memory for color Physically holds onto listener Emotional and demonstrative Enthusiastic and expressive Cheerful and bubbling over Curious Good on stage Wide-eyed and innocent Lives in the present Changeable disposition Sincere at heart Always a child	Born leader Dynamic and active Compulsive need for change Must correct wrongs Strong-willed and decisive Unemotional Not easily discouraged Independent and self-sufficient Excludes confidence Can run anything	Deep and thoughtful Analytical Serious and purposeful Talented and creative Artistic or musical Philosophical and poetic Appreciative of beauty Sensitive to others Self-sacrificing Conscientious Idealistic	Low-key personality Easygoing and relaxed Calm, cool, and collected Patient, well-balanced Consistent life Quiet, but witty Sympathetic and kind Keeps emotions hidden Happily reconciled to life All-purpose person
WORK	Volunteers for jobs Thinks up new activities Looks great on the surface Creative and colorful Has energy and enthusiasm Starts in a flashy way Inspires others to join Charms others to work	Goal-oriented Sees the whole picture Organizes well Seeks practical solutions Moves quickly to action Delegates work Insists on production Makes the goal Stimulates activity Thrives on opposition	Schedule-oriented Perfectionist, high standards Detail-conscious Persistent and thorough Orderly and organized Neat and tidy Economical Sees the problems Finds creative solutions Needs to finish what he starts Likes charts, graphs, figures, lists	Competent and steady Peaceful and agreeable Has administrative ability Mediates problems Avoids conflicts Good under pressure Finds the easy way
FRIENDS	Makes friends easily Loves people Thrives on compliments Seems exciting Envied by others Doesn't hold grudges Apologizes quickly Prevents dull moments Likes spontaneous activities	Has little need for friends Will work for group activity Will lead and organize Is usually right Excels in emergencies	Makes friends cautiously Content to stay in background Avoids causing attention Faithful and devoted Will listen to complaints Can solve others' problems Deep concern for other people Moved to tears with compassion Seeks ideal mate	Easy to get along with Pleasant and enjoyable Inoffensive Good listener Dry sense of humor Enjoys watching people Has many friends Has compassion and concern

PERSONALITY STRENGTHS AND WEAKNESSES (Cont.)

WEAKNESSES

	SANGUINE	CHOLERIC	MELANCHOLY	PHLEGMATIC
EMOTIONS	Compulsive talker Exaggerates and elaborates Dwells on trivia Can't remember names Scares others off Too happy for some Has restless energy Egotistical Blusters and complains Naive, gets taken in Has loud voice and laugh Controlled by circumstances Gets angry easily Seems phony to some Never grows up	Bossy Impatient Quick-tempered Can't relax Too impetuous Enjoys controversy & arguments Won't give up when losing Comes on too strong Inflexible Is not complimentary Dislikes tears and emotions Is unsympathetic	Remembers the negatives Moody and depressed Enjoys being hurt Has false humility Off in another world Low self-image Has selective hearing Self-centered Too introspective Guilt feelings Persecution complex Tends to hypochondria	Unenthusiastic Fearful and worried Indecisive Avoids responsibility Quiet will of iron Selfish Too shy and reticent Too compromising Self-righteous
WORK	Would rather talk Forgets obligations Doesn't follow through Confidence fades fast Undisciplined Priorities out of order Decides by feelings Easily distracted Wastes time talking	Little tolerance for mistakes Doesn't analyze details Bored by trivia May make rash decisions May be rude or tactless Manipulates people Demanding of others End justifies the means Work may become his god Demands loyalty in the ranks	Not people-oriented Depressed over imperfections Chooses difficult work Hesitant to start projects Spends too much time planning Prefers analysis to work Self-deprecating Hard to please Standards often too high Deep need for approval	Not goal-oriented Lacks self-motivation Hard to get moving Resents being pushed Lazy and careless Discourages others Would rather watch
FRIENDS	Hates to be alone Needs to be center stage Wants to be popular Looks for credit Dominates conversations Interrupts and doesn't listen Answers for others Fickle and forgetful Makes excuses Repeats stories	Tends to use people Dominates others Decides for others Knows everything Can do everything better Is too independent Possessive of friends and mate Can't say, "I'm sorry" May be right, but unpopular	Lives through others Insecure socially Withdrawn and remote Critical of others Holds back affection Dislikes those in opposition Suspicious of people Antagonistic and vengeful Unforgiving Full of contradictions Skeptical of compliments	Dampens enthusiasm Stays uninvolved Is not exciting Indifferent to plans Judges others Sarcastic and teasing Resists change

PERSONALITY COMPARISON CHART

These comparisons are made for your enjoyment and are based on my personal study of these various systems.

Hippocrates	Sanguine	Choleric	Melancholy	Phlegmatic
[1] Merrill-Reid Social Styles	Expressive	Driving	Analytical	Amiable
[2] Fr. Werling	Butterfly	Elephant	Frog	Turtle
[3] Jack Williams Car Customers	Talkative	Impulsive	Deliberative	Timid
[4] Herbo-Psychiatrists	Pepper	Garlic	Ginger	Parsley
[5] Senn-Delaney	Promoters	Controllers	Analyzers	Supporters
[6] Leigh-Newcomb Business Personalities	Fast Track	People Catalyst	Hard Changer	Power Broker
[7] Friedman-Rosenman Cardiologists		Type A		Type B
[8] Furukawa Blood-types	Type B	Type A	Type O	Type A-B
[9] Peter Kostis Golf Personalities	Fuzzy Zoeller	Tom Kite	David Graham	Ben Crenshaw
[10] Dr. James Carr	Professional Good Guy	Fire-Eater	Resident Genius	Supreme Democrat
[11] Dr. Dennis Hensley Seminar Attenders	Late Arriver	Big Mouth	Would-Be Expert	Whisperer
[12] Billie Frazier Givers	Impromptu Givers	Strings Attached	Record Keeper	Hesitant Givers
[13] DISC Systems Performax	I = Influence	D = Dominance	C = Compliance	S = Supportive
[14] Activity Vector Analysis	Friendly	Aggressive	Prudent	Reserved
[15] Robert Bramson	Exploders	Sherman Tanks	Snipers	Indecisive Stallers
[16] Robert Lefton Effective Motivation	Dominant-Warm	Dominant-Hostile	Submissive-Hostile	Submissive-Warm
[17] Bernice McCarthy 4-Mat System	Colleague	Manager	Analyzer	Watcher
[18] Personal Dynamics	Expressive	Self-Reliant	Factual	Loyal
[19] Alessandra & Cathcart	Socializer	Director	Thinker	Relater
[20] Roger Hargreaves	Miss Sunshine	Miss Helpful	Miss Neat	Miss Shy
[21] Merrill Douglass	Talkers	Achievers	Thinkers	Affiliators
[22] Lawrence Crabb	Emotional	Volitional	Rational	Personal

235

PERSONALITY COMPARISON CHART

SOURCES

1. Susan Fletcher, "How Do They Manage?" *American Way,* October 1982, pp. 192–194.

2. Father Norman Werling, Ph.D., Master Graphoanalyst, Grapho Dynamics, Bergen Hall, Paramus, NJ 07652.

3. Jack Williams, "Selling to Customers' Dominant Characteristics," Jack Williams Chevrolet, Fort Worth, TX, 1976.

4. Jackie Richard, "Are You a Pepper, a Garlic, or a Parsley?" *The Sun,* San Bernardino, CA.

5. Beth Ann Krier, "Engineers Work on Developing the 'Fun Sides' of Their Brains," *The Los Angeles Times,* Los Angeles, CA.

6. Jason Leigh, "Executives & the Personality Factor," *Sky,* May 1985, pp. 34–38.

7. Jane E. Brody, "Slowing Down 'Type A' People," *The Dallas Morning News,* January 7, 1985, Section C, pp. 1–2.

8. "Japanese Resurrect Behavioral Theory Connected to Blood Types," *Austin American-Statesman,* May 24, 1984, p. D3.

9. Peter Kostis, "Analytical . . . Driver . . . Amiable . . . Expressive . . . Which One Is the Real YOU?" *Golf Digest,* September 1983, pp. 53–57.

10. Dr. James G. Carr, "Illusions of Competency," *Piedmont Airlines,* July 1985, pp. 20–2116.

11. Dr. Dennis E. Hensley, "Holding Successful Seminars," *Piedmont Airlines,* July 1985, pp. 66–68.

12. Dan Sperling, "The Presents We Give Unwrap Our Hidden Personality Traits," *USA TODAY,* December 18, 1984.

13. Judith D. Schwartz, "The Psychology of a Winning Team," *SUCCESS,* December 1985.

14. Kevin Shyne, "Personality Tests Get Down to Business," *SUCCESS,* August 1984.

15. Robert M. Bramson, Ph.D., *Coping with Difficult People,* (New York: Anchor Press/Doubleday, 1981.).

16. Robert Lefton, Effective Motivation.

17. Bernice McCarthy, 4-Mat System, 1980.

18. Personal Dynamics, 1983.

19. Alessandro and Cathcart, *Relationship Strategies and Personal Profile System.*

20. Roger Hargreaves, 2 series of children's books, Little Miss Books and Mr. Men Books, Price/Stern/Sloan, Los Angeles, 1981.

21. Merrill E. Douglass, The Douglass Companies, P.O. Box 5, Grandville, MI, 1984.

22. Lawrence J. Crabb, Jr., Ph.D., *The Training Manual,* Institute of Biblical Counseling, 1978.

FLORENCE LITTAUER is an internationally known speaker and author who exhorts, excites, and entertains all at the same time. Two of her twelve books—*Personality Plus* and *Your Personality Tree*—have been recognized by Religion in Media with *Your Personality Tree* winning the Silver Angel Award. For years her Bible teaching has delighted audiences across the country at women's retreats and church services. At present she is the founder-president of CLASS—Christian Leaders and Speakers Seminars. She has earned the Certified Speaking Professional designation and received the CPAE (the Hall of Fame award) from the National Speakers Association, and she is a member of the Council of Churchmen at Azusa-Pacific School of Theology.